Sea Fever

The Making of a Sailor

Also by Emery N. Cleaves
Plenty of Sea Room: A Yankee Boyhood

Sea Fever

The Making of a Sailor

by Emery N. Cleaves

Houghton Mifflin Company *Boston*

1972

The stanzas From "Christmas Eve at Sea"
appearing on pages 272–273 are reprinted with
permission of the Macmillan Company from *Poems* by
John Masefield. Copyright 1916 by
John Masefield, renewed 1944
by John Masefield.

First Printing w

ISBN: 0–395–13643–1
Library of Congress Catalog Card Number: 74-177538
Printed in the United States of America

To the Old Men

Who spent all, or nearly all, of their working
lives at sea in commercial shipping or in the
navy and who will find in these pages some of
the reasons why they did it

Foreword

AT SOME PERIOD in their lives most people think they are in love with the sea and want to live on it or near it. It is clearly the most romantic natural element in the universe — sometimes it seems too quiet to be trusted or too savagely powerful to be conquered and always so beautiful that it brings great peace to the soul.

This is a story of some early experiences that came about from a sentimental fascination for ships and the sea; I wanted to grow into robust manhood by working up as a sailor from the bottom rung on the ladder — "up through the hawse pipes" is the seagoing expression for it. I had to test my own strengths against those of the sea and the seafaring life.

Life at sea is the same today as it was yesterday, although more civilized, and always will be the same because the ever-

changing world of waters really never changes. Even a long
voyage divided between two ships in the early 1920s could
only be an introduction to the great satisfactions and miseries
of living through calm and storm.

The sea is so vast and the life so broad that little can be
said in one book of all the things that should be said. The
seafaring life is the making of some men — the ruin of others.
Growth, even survival, depends upon the strength of the moral
and physical fiber of those who follow the sea and successfully
achieve their ambition. But some people abhor the very idea
of such an existence, like old Dr. Samuel Johnson who suffered
severely from seasickness and wrote, "No man will be a sailor
who has contrivance enough to get himself into a jail; for
being in a ship is being in jail with the chance of being
drowned."

                                        Emery N. Cleaves

Contents

Sea Fever

The Making of a Sailor

1. All Aboard — No Matter How

I, Emery Cleaves, disdainful of the pallid faces in the class-room and having listened too long to some of my forefathers' eloquent portraits in our hallway, was going to sea. To sea! Blue water! My imagination showed me the streaming manes of the seahorses galloping by in a flurry of spume! I dreamed of thunderstorms in the tropics and a murky sky crackling with chain fire around a lone ship becalmed and dipping on liquid obsidian while awaiting the onslaught of a gale. I could see broken wreckage rolling in turquoise depths with green sea moss hanging crepelike from the timbers, a sightless horror of a memorial to those like my great-uncle Philip who had disap-peared without a trace at sea. To sea! To a tough, granite-hard, masculine sea! To the sea of my people!

Romantic though I was, I knew I would not hear the slap of

heavy canvas high above as the ship shook herself free from a harbor. But I was very curious about what I would actually experience. I knew that the American merchant ships built during and after the First World War were generally efficient and handsome, as such things go, and that they were officered by capable seamen and manned by mixed crews of Americans and foreigners. Beyond that I was really quite ignorant.

In mid-June 1922, I had just turned twenty, had completed the requirements for a bachelor's degree at Harvard College, and was free to spend a year as I might choose.

"Father," I began, "I've decided I should spend this next year at sea. I can get back in time to take my degree with my class next June. At the very least I'll acquire some useful experience and it ought to be a good thing for me. I hope you'll agree."

My father nodded his head at me sorrowfully. "I think this is a waste of time, but I suppose you might as well get it out of your system," he said, frowning. "Steam is as different from sail as day is from night. I don't think you'll like it a bit, but you seem determined to grow into wisdom the hard way, Mr. Emery Cleaves." When my father wanted to emphasize his convictions as they might refer to me, he called me mister.

"Well, I suppose I sound foolish," I replied, "but you know that all my life I've wanted to go to sea in a deepwater vessel. I want to see the world. And if I don't do it now, when I've got the time, I probably never will, and I'll always feel that I cheated myself out of a great experience. Moreover, I might be able to get into the shipping business and to do that I should climb up through the hawse pipes and learn the business from the ground up. I've just got to go."

What my father knew, and what I couldn't understand, more the pity, was that I was so pigheaded and incurably romantic that the immediate future would be filled with little else but discouragement, frustration, and heartbreak.

The reluctant approval of my father had been given with the warning: "Either sign up on deck or not at all. Don't get into any department except the deck; you won't learn anything as a messboy or a coal passer. So use your common sense and go only as an ordinary seaman."

"Yes," I replied, not having any intention of taking any advice from anybody unless it coincided with my own ideas.

Four days after my conversation with my understanding father I was on my way to join my first deepwater steamer and filled more with a sense of high adventure than any real misgivings. For four days I lingered in a hiring hall operated by the United States Shipping Board down by the old wharves on Atlantic Avenue in Boston. Several times a day a clerk would chalk up on a very large blackboard the name of a vessel, the exact ratings for which there were vacancies in her crew, her location, and the range of her destination, such as "Coastwise," "South America," "Far East," "Mediterranean," or "North Europe." I was still limited to the rating "ordinary seaman," and all the ships seemed to want A.B.s (able-bodied seamen), or firemen, or messboys. As I lounged on the hard wooden settees day after day I became acquainted with many seafaring men, most of whom eventually shipped out, and long before I did. There were several like myself who didn't seem to find a place.

On the morning of the fourth day, I arrived at eight o'clock to discover that a freighter lying in Montreal was signing on eight men. "There's only one job left," an acquaintance told me. "Third cook. Why don't you take it?"

"I'm not a cook," I expostulated.

"Why not? I'm not a coal passer either, but they'll be glad to have a strong back and a weak mind."

I was impatient. I thought I could handle the job, for I knew that a third cook in a freighter was little more than a pot washer in the galley. I stepped up to the counter and the clerk soon erased the last of the openings available in the American freighter *Amphitrite*, now loading grain in bulk in Montreal and bound to Gibraltar for orders.

That same evening seven other new members of the *Amphitrite*'s crew met at the train gate at North Station and were checked in by a Shipping Board official, who handed us our railroad tickets, Pullman reservations, and seaman's identification cards in lieu of passports. We were a motley-looking lot. Rather shabby in general appearance, we were encumbered with paper bundles, canvas sea bags, and cheap cardboard suitcases lashed up with belts, white string, and light manila line. We shifted uneasily from one foot to the other with shy and embarrassed glances.

"What d'ye know, the government's given us sleepin' car berths so we don't have to set up all night," someone said.

"Must be somethin' wrong with the ship if they want us this bad," another added.

"You might as well get aboard now," the agent said. "You'll be pullin' out in twenty minutes."

Sorting ourselves out in the Pullman sleeper, I thought it expedient to sit with the chief cook and the baker, with whom I would be spending all my time. The prospect was not reassuring. The chief cook, a small Scotsman who was naturally called Scotty, was very noisy and belligerent. He scowled and leered upon his fellow creatures from two red-rimmed pale eyes beneath a matted shock of the reddest hair I had ever seen. He was a wiry little man, still emaciated from a recent illness in a marine hospital, and he talked unceasingly, snarling at everyone from a drooping corner of his mouth in a curious mixture of Scottish and Cockney dialects. Under his baleful and cynical influence my hopes and spirits began to droop.

The baker and second cook was even noisier and more bellicose. He was a barrel-shaped Canadian with sharp, piglike eyes, a very broad nose, and an enormous mouth. Large ears stuck out sideways from under a battered derby hat, and when he walked it was with a side-to-side, lumbering motion. Rough as he was, there was something comical about him, and it soon became apparent that he enjoyed clowning to attract attention. This was Choucette. He, at least, tried to be funny — and was funny, regaling us all with his allegedly amorous adventures in Boston during the last few days while awaiting a ship.

So I enjoyed the night ride on the train, although I didn't sleep much. In the morning I got up and dressed very early so I could watch the lush green Quebec countryside before we rolled into the Montreal station. Everything was a new and romantic adventure.

After a local Shipping Board agent had got us processed through the immigration and customs officials he finally squeezed us all into a sort of horse-drawn van, the canvas cover of which had been removed from the frame. To the trepidation of the carter, we ultimately crammed ourselves and all our trappings into the wagon, the agent climbed up to sit beside the driver, and with the decrepit vehicle resting flat upon its axles, after a considerable effort of pawing and grunting, the bony horse slowly induced it into motion and drew it after him, at the speed of his aged walk, creaking and bumping heavily down the street.

In this manner the seamen recruited in Boston to join the crew of the American tramp steamer *Amphitrite* approached their ship.

Here was the sea! Well, not quite. At least it was a part of the sea, for here were three deepwater freighters in their dock-side disorder, dirty, their decks cluttered with scantling and rubbish and their hatches yawning wide for the streams of grain that poured down from the spouts. The very sight of that brown dirty water sent a shiver of excitement coursing through my veins. Here, I thought, was the source of high adventure, of black nights and salt wind, of strange new lands and people!

"Here we are," called Choucette. "Old Windmill Point!"

"Which ship is our'n?" someone asked as we began to disentangle ourselves and climb out of the cart.

"The one forward. Good-lookin', ain't she?"

The *Amphitrite* really was a good-looking ship; it was befitting that she had been named after a sea goddess. Nearly four hundred feet long and about 7600 tons displacement in size, she was the "three island" type — high fo'c's'le head and fantail, separated by well decks from her raised midship section. Her white forward house was surmounted by a mahogany-colored wheelhouse and flying bridge, much like a small castle atop a snowy white hillside. Her silver-colored funnel with its black top smoked serenely. She was even attractively painted — hull a dark green separated from the red underbody by a

clean white line, masts and deck fittings buff, and her cabins
and rails white- and aluminum-colored. Squatting there in the
filthy cove with her cargo booms lashed flat over the open
hatches while heavy clouds of dust from the pouring grain ed-
died up and begrimed everything, her very dirt and clutter became a romantic halo to me. I thought she was a thing of
exquisite beauty.

The eight new seamen at the gangplank attracted considerable curiosity from members of the *Amphitrite*'s crew amidships. Two of the newcomers were ordinary seamen, one a
tall, fair youth who had just completed his junior year at a
New England engineering college. The other was a youngster
who had been sailing in coastwise steamers between Norfolk
and New England ports in the coal trade. The two ordinaries
looked much alike — sturdy, quick, and restless. The A.B.
was a baldheaded and taciturn Norwegian. Impeccably
dressed in a good black suit with a white necktie that accentu-
ated the bronze of his smooth-shaven wrinkled cheeks, the fo-
cal point of his face was a very large and pink pug nose that
turned up sufficiently to cause a cluster of long hairs on the tip
to point straight ahead of him. These three sailors were Bob,
Pete, and Gus respectively.

Of the two coal passers, one was a dark, wrinkled little man
well past fifty years of age, a ne'er-do-well from the waterfront
of many cities. This was Mike Lang. The other coal passer
was a large and powerful youth who had been to sea before,
had decided to become a marine engineer, and was now working out his time to qualify for fireman's papers. His name was
Bill Sullivan.

And here was I, Emery Cleaves, equipped with what I con-
ceitedly regarded as the finest credentials possible, including

coastwise trips in sail, signed on as third cook — as a seagoing scullery maid in a tramp steamer under the influence of the chief cook's malignant frowns and the raucous whimsy of the baker.

The ship's galley was located in the forward end of the afterhouse, just forward of the fiddley. Out of this and over the top of the pile of ashes, upon which for several days they had dumped quantities of garbage that gave off a strong stench and swarmed with flies, peered the white eyeballs of the three cooks who were being replaced. They were trying to identify the new cooks. But Scotty, Choucette, and I mingled noncommittally with the other new seamen in the general traffic of stevedores scrambling over the debris. A group of mechanics from a local machine shop hammered and scraped at a pile of boiler tubing on the other side of the deck. The place was a filthy bedlam.

Into this confusion of bustle, noise, and dirt we entered the routine of a maritime day of toil. After half an hour of waiting for our predecessors to change their clothes and leave the ship, we three cooks were shown to a clean but disordered room in the afterhouse amidships. It had four berths, four steel lockers, an enamel lavatory, and an electric fan. Choucette and Scotty promptly appropriated the two lower bunks for themselves, but I was glad to have an upper beside the porthole. We changed at once into dungarees to go to work.

"Now, lad," said Scotty, "we've got to have a drink. I never go to sea without me bein' soused as a goat. Now, the baker and me will get to work on the dinner and you'll go ashore and get supplies. What d'you say to chippin' in on a wee bottle?"

"I have two dollar," volunteered Choucette, throwing down two wrinkled American bills.

"Well, I can put up two also," I added.

"An' I've got the same," Scotty concluded. "Now that ought to get us three bottles, hey?"

"Tha's right," the grizzled Choucette assented.

"Well, see if you can get Black an' White. An' if you can't, why get what you can."

Following a visit to the back room of a small saloon near the waterfront, I soon returned with three bottles rather awkwardly bulging under my blue shirt. It had been more of a feat to obtain this supply than I had anticipated because bottled liquor was legally sold only at government stores and the two dollars I paid for each bottle included a charge of fifty cents to compensate the saloon for its risk. When I entered the galley, Scotty and Choucette, who were in bread dough up to their elbows, hastily bolted the steel doors and pushed the dough pans aside.

"Ah, Black an' White!" crooned Scotty as I unloaded my shirt. "Ye're all right, lad! And how much did you pay for it?"

"Where is damn corkscrew?" growled Choucette.

"Here, break it — 'tis quicker!" And Scotty smashed the neck of the bottle against the galley range, presently pouring for himself a full tumbler of whiskey.

Together they quickly drank up one of the bottles. Then they started on the next while supervising me in the preparation of a beef stew and baking several loaves of bread. The dinner was served up with some pies the former cooks had left, and it didn't excite more than normal adverse comment from the crew. So far so good. The liquor actually mellowed the two cooks, and while I spent most of the afternoon scouring the large pots and kettles, Choucette prepared a rather good

chocolate cake and Scotty broke out some pork chops and cabbage for supper. When I had finished peeling two buckets of
potatoes, Scotty slyly said, "Now, lad, go up to the old man
and invite him down to have a drink with us."

Suspecting that he was trying to discover just how stupid I
might be, I went into the ship's saloon and talked briefly with
the pantryman, then returned and reliably reported that the
captain was ashore.

"Well, you don't seem to be in no hurry to drink your liquor, lad," Scotty observed. "Are you goin' to offer a drop to
me and the baker?"

"It's sitting up there looking at you," I replied. "I got it for
you fellows anyhow."

This generosity firmly established my acceptance. I hoped
that from now on I could expect decent treatment from the
cooks.

After supper I took a short walk along the waterfront with
Pete, returning about nine o'clock to find Scotty and Choucette very drunk and brawling in our cabin.

"This is hell of a ship," Choucette was roaring as I entered.
"Flour is for pastry; no damn good — dough no rise if she
blew him up with gun powder. Hell, she'll spoil the reputation! No, mister, me no sail in this old hack."

"Well, for the love o' God, man, we're all in it together. Ye
won't leave me like this, will ye?" Scotty pleaded thickly with
tears in his bloodshot eyes.

"Wot is stop you from get off, too?"

With that, Choucette dragged from his bunk a yellow
wicker suitcase into which he flung his carving knives, his
shoes, toilet articles, and underwear, all in a heap, tying the

two halves of the suitcase together so tightly with a heavy piece of line that it cut into the brittle straw. Clapping his faded derby down over his ears he cried, "Well, so long, mates! I'm bound! Toronto, it is!" and lurched through the door and away, with the arm of a shirt hanging from his suitcase. Scotty stared indolently into space until his red eyes began to blink and he fell fast asleep on the deck.

In the morning we found one of Choucette's shoes, his only necktie, and his razor. This fortune appeased Scotty considerably, almost reconciling him to the extra burden resulting from the baker's desertion. In the morning we also learned that during the night the pantryman had scurried ashore with some of the saloon plate and several articles of the steward's clothing.

" 'Tis a bad beginnin', lad," the chief cook confided to me after we had sent the breakfast out of the galley. "I don't like the way the wind is haulin'. Now, if the old man would only wait 'til we got a new baker I'd feel better. But no, damn his heart, here we are, all ready to sail, steam up and the tugs alongside, an' no baker nor nothin'."

Soon the *Amphitrite* started upon her long voyage, towed into the river beyond the cove stern foremost by two little red tugs that chuffed ferociously and spat showers of soot and sparks upon her fantail. Casting off from the tugs, she swung slowly about in the St. Lawrence, thrashed the water into a boiling froth, growled a long hoarse farewell to Montreal, and slowly gained headway in the current. My adventure was now on the ebb of the tide carrying me downriver into the unknown of a world still mysterious to me. All I knew was that I had shipped onto a slow, coal-burning ship that was already obsolete although only two years old, that she had too large a crew to be sailed economically, and that we didn't even know precisely where we were going except that it was toward Gibraltar for orders. And I knew it would be a long time before I would ever admit to my father that I had sailed off soundings in the cook's department.

2. A First Smell of the Sea

HAD *Amphitrite* not been designed in 1917 she would never have been built. Only the great need for wartime shipping and the possible limited supply of bunker fuel oil led to the design and construction of a few classes of coal-burning ships. They required much larger crews than oil burners and they were usually much slower. *Amphitrite* steamed at a standard speed of only ten knots.

Her large crew of forty-eight men required two fo'c's'les, one for the "black gang," the firemen and coal passers, forward in the bow of the ship, and one for the sailors, the men on deck, in the stern under the fantail. Each fo'c's'le had a separate messroom and complete toilet and bath facilities. Everybody else was berthed amidships. In general, she was typical of her class of freighter and could transport nearly any kind of dry or packaged cargo.

For three days the ship churned downriver over a sparkling avenue of water between bosky forests with the sound of wind soughing in the trees, through great expanses of green meadowland, dotted here and there with lonely little white farm buildings and tiny hamlets. At Quebec, the *Amphitrite* swung at her anchor several hours until a new pantryman gingerly climbed the unsteady gangway.

Again came an endless vista of meadows and forests, the meadows less frequent now and smaller, and the forests almost eternal, dark and beautiful beyond belief, until one sunrise when the *Amphitrite* found herself in a river mouth so broad that no land could be seen, and it was as if she were at sea. Now the ship was steering into the profound emptiness of a sea-rimmed horizon. Far to starboard we could descry the rusty hull of a large freighter standing on her bows over the ledge on which she had struck, her stern pointing straight to the sky in a dumb appeal to a power higher than that of the old Gods of the Sea who had tricked and murdered her. A little later there appeared on the horizon ahead a smudge of smoke; rapidly a ship approached, and in an hour a shining liner rushed by the *Amphitrite*, a billow of white froth dancing at her forefoot, people leaning upon her rails, and a long streak of foam stretching out far astern whence she had come. Although there was no wind, a heavy ground swell lifted the ship in a gentle, teetering motion. Now we knew we were at sea; we smelled the strong raw air and we felt the pulsation of that mighty spirit beneath. To me it was the beginning of life, of primitive life that is ages old and empty with the fullness of its mystery!

The following afternoon, just after eight bells, something

happened that made my existence much easier in the ship. I was paring a bucket of potatoes for breakfast when the second mate, a large, athletic-looking young man named Leighton, seated himself on the edge of the midships hatch beside me. He had just come off watch.

"What sports did you take up in college, Emery?" he asked.

"Well," I replied, "in the fall I played football with the scrubs on the second squad, and in the spring I used to row in a single shell on the river, and in the winter I used to box to fulfill the compulsory year-round exercise requirements. I was slow in developing, I guess," I added.

He turned toward me quickly and said, "You like to box? Well, that's good news to me. I do, too, and I got some twelve-ounce gloves with me but nobody'll box with me. I need the exercise, too. Say, how about a round or two after you finish these potatoes?"

"Fine," I replied. "I'll have a few minutes after this. But you're probably a pro and'll beat me up —"

"I said box," he interjected, "not fight. And if I beat you up I won't have *anyone* to practice with. Here, get another knife and I'll help you with those potatoes."

The second mate was in a hurry to start our boxing match, and we soon repaired to the broad foredeck beside number two hatch. Of course, we attracted a considerable audience instantly. Nearly everyone who wasn't on watch or asleep gathered on the hatch or along the bulwarks. The captain and the other mates hung out over the rail of the bridge. It soon developed that we were putting on a fairly skillful contest, not a slugging match. As it turned out, we were quite well matched — both by weight and skill. I was relieved and he was delighted. So was the crew.

During one of our rest periods, he said, "That's a good left you've got. Now let me show you how to improve it. Feint like this."

He would frequently stop to rehearse a parry or show me a blow and from the remarks of the audience, the spectators thought they profited as much as I did from the instruction. We put on a fairly good exhibition over a period of twenty minutes, at the end of which he put his arm around my shoulders and said, "Mister, you don't know how pleased I am. You're good enough to keep me in good shape, and you're going to be as good as I can take before this trip's over."

Thereafter we exercised almost daily during periods of good weather, and we never lacked a crowd. As a result of these performances I won tolerance from Scotty and possibly a little respect from the crew and nobody ever challenged me to a fight or tried to pick on me. Some even went out of their way to befriend me, and I was beginning to desire friendship rather desperately.

In North Sydney a new second cook joined us. He was an elderly man, over fifty, with iron-gray hair and a wrinkled skin, brown as parchment. Little gleams of light flickered in his pale blue eyes. A great breadth of shoulder, with enormous hands and arms quite disproportionate to his medium height, established an impression of nascent power under the austere calm of Bill Nadeau's expressionless face.

"Welcome, mister," cried Scotty to Bill, "I've had a bloody tough time alone here with the lad. And it's a hard wagon you're on, too."

"How many's she carry?" Bill asked huskily.

"Too damn many — forty-eight all told." There was a silence. "Cheerio, we'll make a go of it, I guess."

"Flour any good?" drawled Bill between puffs. "Many weevils?"

"Not yet. Steward's green though."

"Humph! He'll let us alone then." Neither spoke for a minute. Then Bill said, "Well, mister, if ye'll show me the room I'll change me gear and mix up some bread for ye."

Thus did that strong character, Bill Nadeau, one of the few survivors of his Canadian regiment at Vimy Ridge, come into our lives.

For the remainder of the day I scrubbed in a greasy sink and pared potatoes into a bucket, while coal dust rained about my head. Cinders and small particles rattled down steadily from above. Occasional blasts of wind caught up sheets of dust and lashed it, spinning in a cloud, into all open ports and crannies. It sifted into one's hair, down the open front of shirts, and everything became black and sooty. The carefully scrubbed white work of the cabins was ruined. Food crunched between the teeth. The mate stalked the decks gloomily, casting his eyes woefully up to the coaling shoots. But next morning, when the dust began to fly at break of day, I was sufficiently accustomed to a dry throat and sooty ears to go about my onerous tasks with greater cheer.

"Ah, lad," Scotty would say to me, "this'll break your heart! No, lad, you'll never get over it — it'll break your blasted heart, just the same as it did mine."

"Was your first trip a hard one?" I asked.

"Nineteen months square-riggin' — at first they let me lie

in the scuppers three days, I was that sick. And then they said — I was small, you know, they said I was useless and set me to work with the cook — and he died and I was cook — everybody cursing me and going to knock me bloody block off — and me trying me hardest." The cook paused and spat on the deck. "Ah, they broke my bloody heart all right, lad."

Although he may not have been aware of it, Scotty was rapidly breaking mine. I had never before known such long hours of toil. In the morning I was called at three forty-five to make coffee and start cooking oatmeal. After breakfast I washed pots and pans, washed the galley, peeled potatoes, and started cooking vegetables for dinner, which was eaten at twelve o'clock. After dinner, I had about twenty minutes to lie down before I started the work of washing pots and the galley and peeling vegetables all over again. By eight o'clock in the evening I was usually finished for the day and too tired to do anything but collapse in my bunk and fall fast asleep in the full glare of the overhead electric light.

Under the full burden of two men's work, Scotty had grown tired and nervous and abused me from morning until night. I did my best but simply could not satisfy the irascible Scot. I would have to find some sort of solution. I had even begun to wonder whether I had enough inner strength to overcome the challenge of this environment. This experience in the galley of a deepwater freight steamer was the first real test of character I had ever known and I knew I would have to survive it. After all, most of my shipmates — the seasoned men — had all surmounted equally tough demands and had learned to live under any conditions of strain and despair. My previous life had been too easy and soft, making my first real exposure to reality all the more difficult.

This was not the sea I had dreamed of, nor the seafaring life I had hoped to live. The adventure of stinging sunlit wind humming through the guy ropes of a ship off a strange coast, the mellow romance of pretty maids and sailormen ashore — all that must have been a part of some old liar's imagination long after he had forgotten the real sea — a beautiful metamorphosis of the merciless toil and the hourless days that he had forgotten. I was only beginning to learn the nature of the life into which I had hurried so blithely, and, like seawater, the taste was fearfully unpleasant.

Forgetting my schoolboyish pride, I sought out the ship's steward during our second evening in North Sydney. He was a large, florid-faced man and kindly, for many years an army commissary officer and now enjoying himself as chief steward in a ship. I told him I guessed I wasn't much of a success as a cook and thought I ought to leave the ship before I made a lot of trouble for everybody.

"Well, sonny, it isn't that bad," he laughed. "Or is it? I don't think anybody can please Scotty unless he came up through the hawse pipes the way he did. He's jealous of you — you've got a good education and he hasn't. You ought to be on deck, anyhow, not in the galley."

He paused a moment, rather thoughtfully, before he concluded, "I'll tell you what — you get the sailors' messboy to change jobs with you and I'll give it my blessing."

Next morning I represented to the sailors' messboy that he had a great opportunity to learn a profitable occupation, even possibly to become a famous international chef in a great hotel ashore, and the idea pleased him. Dirty little Tom Meadows, an undersized, pimply faced young boy from the waterfront of Montreal, was glad to become third cook, and since

Scotty promised to teach him the trade of cooking, the transfer was happily consummated. So I moved into a cabin with a French greenhorn, a sleepy Spaniard, and an Italian boy who slept with his shoes on, befouling the cabin's air. Thus far, my seafaring career had gone steadily downhill but at least I was still on my feet in the struggle. I thought wryly of my disregard of my father's advice.

By the middle of the afternoon in this third day the *Amphitrite* was ready to put to sea. The sky was the color of slate and streaked with shreds of windtorn cloud. Over the surface of a gray sea, bursting with froth in the middle distance, blew a wet wind heavy with the smell of great space. Billows of black smoke poured from the *Amphitrite*'s funnel and rolled in opaque clouds down into the road between the bleak houses, making them look doubly bleak. With the boom of her whistle throbbing in the wind, her propeller churning chunks of mud from the bottom to the foaming surface, and the wharf pilings screaming as her great hulk crushed against them, the ship rumbled out into the bay. On the fo'c's'le head and fantail the sailors worked like demons over their dripping hawsers. A rhythmic clash of steel sounded from the pistons in the engine room; from under the fantail could be felt the beat of the propeller and the drumming of the steam steering gear as its engine cogs moved the ponderous quadrant back and forth.

The gray clouds scurried faster and hung lower over the bay. Heavier blew the wind and wetter, until the dismal horizon was blotted out in a deep shroud of mist. With a hiss and rattle, flurries of rain struck the ship. Alongside bounced the pilot boat in a desperate dance with the combers, until a dark

figure, heavily muffled in oilskins, clambered down a rope ladder and his little white boat fell astern in the thickness.

Now, above the wash and hiss of the sea foam flying from
the turbulent water, came the dull moaning of a steamer's
whistle ahead, and slowly an unkempt, rusty hulk bore down
to port of the *Amphitrite*. She was a French tramp, high out
of water and fresh from the long sweep of multitudinous seas,
riding in with her head up, triumphant from her conquest
with the vast powers of the Sea Gods. I prayed that we might
come home as proudly, though fear was choking up my throat.
And in the ever-deepening darkness with the wind moaning
across the funnel top and humming in the rigging, the *Amphitrite* drove streaming to sea in a squall of wind and rain, lost to
all sight in a dank void of flying fog, with a night of storm and
misery just ahead.

3. All in the Day's Work

"RUN, DAMN IT, RUN!"

The third mate leaned out over the flying bridge to yell at a seasick coal passer down on the forward well deck. The man barely heard the cry over the roar of the storm. Down from the crest of a great wave slid the bow, down and sideways until it seemed as if the ship would stand on her beam ends, down as if to dive beneath the mound of black water that was shooting up into the clouds ahead.

"Run!"

The coal passer roused himself from his lethargy. He wiped a mop of dank yellow hair from his eyes, looked at the stream racing down the deck between his feet, and leaped to the shelter beneath the fo'c's'le head, leaped barely in time to escape the avalanche of water that poured over the *Amphitrite*'s starboard bow as she rolled and twisted upward again. The sea roared and hissed about us; it rushed about on the deck churned into a mass of foam level with the bulwarks as the vessel dove, reared, and shuddered, finally splashing over the port side when the ship rolled over. When his grimy figure had reached the forward fo'c's'le Bill Sullivan turned and waved a grateful hand to the mate, for he was sick, nearly too sick to care whether he survived the storm or not. Then he forced the fo'c's'le door and stumbled inside.

While I watched this episode from the forward main deck, shivering in the biting cold, the second mate approached me from behind, unobserved.

"Nearly got that poor devil," he shouted.

I turned round. Mr. Leighton, the second mate, whose sparring partner I had become, put his hand on my shoulder and squeezed it to show his regard for me.

"Oh, yes! Poor cuss was too sick to move," I shouted back.

"How do you feel?"

"Me? Rotten!"

Why lie about it; I did feel bad. The motion, the stuffy fo'c's'le, the smell of stale food had drained my strength and afflicted me with nausea. I had never been seasick before, but I certainly was now. Some sailor I was!

"That's all right," the boyish Leighton replied, "we don't often have it as choppy as this. You'll feel better pretty quick. Drink a bit of salt water — whew!"

At that moment a whole surge of water toppled over on the deck, dousing us with spray. Simultaneously the ship lurched and threw us heavily against the cabin. As the water poured out of the scuppers and the bow staggered up again, a small ventilator cowl and a remnant of the iron railing on the fo'c's'le head tumbled down blocking up the firemen's fo'c's'le. The mate clumped aft bawling for the bosun.

The day passed slowly, a delirious confusion of a day, and suppertime found me again in the sailors' messroom aft, a soup tureen rolling on the deck, myself sprawling in a corner. It found me endeavoring to keep tin plates on the blanketed table, tin plates that slid off and clattered on the deck as fast as I picked them up. It found me cursing my very existence in that filthy hole, the walls daubed with catsup and coffee, the deck strewn with greasy chops, the sink spattered with garbage. The room shot upward with the speed of an elevator car and my stomach followed close behind. At some indefinite point in the upper atmosphere it lurched violently from side to side and before I could embrace the sink or the garbage can dropped off like a stone from a precipice, down, down, down. Crash! It struck bottom at last, bounced everything from the table, and knocked me to the deck where the garbage can clattered over me like a steamroller.

"God!" I swore incoherently in my misery, rose dripping out of the filth, and rushed up the ladder to throw myself flat on the poop deck in the fresh air. By such precipitous ascents up that ladder I had averted several gastronomical tragedies that day. This time I had reached my limit and I indulged in a splendid relaxation. Why had I ever come to sea! Damn fool! I simply had to learn better. All right, I would have to face my troubles now. I *would* get that supper for those seamen. My will power reinforced, I propped my legs beneath me and clambered back down the ladder.

Tescula, the short, thickset, lame Lithuanian, was staring at me sympathetically at the bottom. "What's the matter, mess? Sick?" he asked.

"No!" I howled, "no!"

He watched me comprehendingly from under his bushy brows, and his curly towhead wagged approval as I picked up the great coffee can and nested the soup tureens.

"Be careful as you cross the well deck. You might get washed off, you know, and we want you should stay awhile yet. Wait! I was go up and tell you when to run."

He pushed me up the ladder, watched the sea carefully for a minute, then cried, "Now run! Here is the time."

I trotted unsteadily along the weatherside of the deck and scrambled up the forward ladder hardly in time to avoid a great wave that thundered over the bulwarks behind me.

When my soup tureens were filled in the galley I started back. The little lame man still waited on the poop deck. Presently he beckoned to me and I climbed down the ladder to walk aft. All at once I looked up. Never shall I forget that grimace on Tescula's face, distorted with helpless fear, frozen in its fixity. Before I recovered from my shock the familiar crescendo of approaching waves sang in my ears. I looked behind — up, up it mounted, hesitated, and toppled over, smothering me in a mass of foam and spray. My next sensation was one of prodigious confusion. All creation was upside-down. Vaguely I realized that I was being swept over the hatches. Not a thought, neither of regrets nor hopes nor fears, flashed across my mind. It was entirely blank. Ah, what did it all matter! The Nereids would mourn me and care for my body. And I had rather die out here than among men where gawking strangers would stare at my carrion as it rolled in the backwash of the tide, rotten and stinking. Live a bit longer? Why, I was too miserable to appreciate life just then.

Presently a sharp blow on my head aroused me. I started to laugh. How funny all this was! Here was I sprawling in a furious turmoil of swirling water, grasping a bunch of soup tureens in one hand and a coffee can in the other, while the *Amphitrite* wallowed in a gigantic whirlpool of foam a few feet away. I opened my mouth — the saltwater rushed in and choked me. I looked toward the ship again — oh, the fool! There was Tescula standing on the rail and clinging to the shrouds. His square shape loomed up large against the racing sky and the gale tore at his blue clothes. With his heavy brown whiskers silvered from spray, his pale eyes gleamed out at me as from a mask. He was reaching his hand toward me. Didn't he know he might be drowned! What was he thinking of! Mechanically I dropped the coffee can and swam a stroke toward him. He caught my hand just in time. Up, up soared the ship, and I dragged along on the strake. My weight was nothing to the iron strength of the little lame man. Hanging by one hand on the shroud he hauled me over as if I were a child and floundered aft to the poop-deck ladder. And I — I cried like a child and swore blasphemous things at him. O, Tescula! It needed a man from the unknown, who would return again before the end of the voyage to the unknown, to teach me thoughtlessness of self.

It was night. The wind roared and moaned as loud as ever; the waves still lashed the *Amphitrite* as she stumbled along in the rain and spray. I lay sleepless in my bunk, tied in to prevent my falling out, occasionally dozing off to dream a chaotic nightmare of shipwrecks and, strangely enough, of home, into which drunken sailors constantly intruded. My fantasy then placed me in the messroom. The motion of the vessel rolled me up on the wall — it was nothing, I tumbled down again. It threw me up once more *and I stuck there.*

I awoke in chaos indescribable. The *Amphitrite* was apparently lying on her side and I could hear the waves washing against the cabin. Down in the engine room roared a blast of escaping steam. Firemen were drawing the fires down there in the depths and faint yells emanated from time to time. A series of terrific rumblings shook the ship from stem to stern as if something would rack her to pieces. One of the messboys was swearing with terror. Another whimpered like a dog shut out in the cold. Then I heard the seaman on watch staggering down the companionway and screaming, "All hands to the boat deck!"

The messboys fled and left me alone, apathetically fumbling with the rope I had tied about my body. The seaman thrust his shaggy head in the door. It was Pete.

"What's the matter? Ain't you comin' out?"

"No hurry is there?"

"Hurry hell! This damn grain shifted! She may roll over any minute. And if the stuff gets wet and swells — come on, you poor bitch, I don't wanta see ya drown."

He strode in and slashed the rope with his knife.

"Here's your pants. Put 'em on, damn ya. Pretty cold out — may need 'em, ya know!"

He hurried away and I followed after him at once.

Up on the boat deck a few of the crew had gathered. They had stripped back the tarpaulins over the boats and were handling the gear like a crowd of children. No one thought of launching any boats; the danger was less aboard the *Amphitrite*. Those on starboard would have been smashed under the ship, and the port boats could not swing clear. Pete poked his head over a gunwale and chuckled at me.

"You look hungry," he said, "want some lunch?"

Presently he jerked a small keg of pilot bread from one of the stern lockers.

"Put that back, you horse thief," bellowed the second mate.

And Pete dropped from sight again.

Somewhere behind me the skipper shouted, almost beside himself with wrath, "Well, I'm a son of a whore!"

He was shaking his fist at the wireless man.

"Why in the name of all that's holy didn't you tell me your antennae had been carried away! Hey?"

The white-faced radio officer stammered a reply.

"Oh, never mind, mister — you'll have to fix it —"

The captain's voice trailed away in the wind. Then it burst forth again, strong as ever, "Mr. Schultz, take some men and see if you can repair Spark's aerial."

The chief engineer, a small black figure soaked to the skin and slimy with heavy grease, appeared over the top of a ladder. "The old hod's dry as a drum, Captain," he panted. "Anyhow, if she makes water now her boilers won't blow hell out of her."

"How are your men, Matthews?" the captain shouted into the storm, eyeing a livid patch of flesh on the chief's forearm.

"Very well, sir — one fireman burned his foot badly."

He pointed to a lank figure lying half under a boat on the lee side.

"You might put some of that salve on it, Matthews."

The third mate beat his way up against the sheer force of the gale that was now screaming through all the braces and guy ropes on the *Amphitrite*.

"Do you want the sailors to stay here, sir?"

"If they like, MacDonald; one place is as good as another. I'll not risk the boats."

The captain bent against the wind and clambered to the lower deck to find the mate.

A voice yelled faintly from under a lifeboat, "When they heaved her to, a wave pooped her and washed out the fo'c's'le — yeh, one of them damn green ordinaries didn't make the door fast — come right in three foot deep — oh, hell, yes, all our gear's washed up together in the messroom — yer right — damn sight drier up here — naw, I don't want any crackers — helluva note, tobacco all wet, too — where did —"

A snoring comber drowned out even the roar of the wind when it came boiling up under the starboard boats and washed clear across the boat deck. Then a jumble of voices.

"Put Rosario in a boat —"

"— know about that."

"Jeez, that could have finished the fo'c's'le."

"Did all the men get out, Mr. Schultz — thank God for that, anyhow!"

"Well, I guess we stay up here awhile, Edwin."

Never shall I forget that night on the boat deck. The roar and swish of the water deadened all other sounds. Awful black gulfs opened and yawned far below the ship. The sea anchor that had been rigged held her round into the gale in such a way that the spray, driving aft from the bows and rich in phosphorous, provided us with a ghastly half-light, our only illumination.

Then I began to think about the mystery of the sea, if there is any such thing; I thought of its vast power, of the power of solitude, the immensity of creation, and the inconsequence of man. By a recognition of his unimportance man begins to achieve his greatness. And it is at sea, far from the sight of men, that he can survey the visible round world, finding himself the strongest if not the happiest being in it. It is conducive to real philosophic contemplation, which the ancients regarded as the best and greatest happiness of all. Often inchoate emotions not to be expressed in the medium of words. The sea brings a sense of infinite peace to those who follow it, though most cannot tell why.

I don't believe it occurred to any of us that we might be lost, that the ship might roll over the rest of the way and capsize from her heavy list to starboard. Probably I should have been thinking of home where all was serene and quiet. Instead, I was wholly concerned with the wetness, the cold, and the sickening rolls of the ship in the immense waves and the seamanship employed to save her.

Paul crawled over to where I clung just forward of the radio house. He was a huge man, muscular as a gymnast, whose thirty years looked like fifty in the creases of his leathery face. In his eyes burned an egotistical, sometimes cruel, sometimes kindly look born of conceit over his physical power.

"You ain't afraid are ye, Emery?" he cried.

"Afraid? What good would that do?"

"Haw!" A laugh roared from his large red mouth. "Now ye talk like a sailor."

Chips, the German carpenter who had been asleep, untangled his head from a mass of sweaters and oilskins and looked at me.

"Cheer up, boy, this is all in the day's work! It ain't no use to be scared. Why, Paul and me was drove up on the coast of Australia once in a bark and no one was saved except us — yah, that's right — but it didn't do no harm. We knew the old sea would take care of us."

The sea, his idea of infinity, of unlimited spiritual strength with supernatural power of life and death, coincided with his idea of God as a benignant deity.

From eleven at night until the gray dusk of a new day reminded us of our stiffness, we huddled there, waiting for the *Amphitrite* to roll over and confirm to us that there would never be another dawn. But that culminating lurch that was to be the end-all never happened. When the smutty daylight returned with its fresher hopes and fears and its cold and aching we determined to contend with the mystery of another day's work. For the *Amphitrite* had won her first real skirmish with the old sea, cheated it through the staunchness of her frames and plates and perhaps her deistic name. Some of her plates in the after well-deck were warped, the short length of wooden mast above the foremast crosstrees was adrift and wobbling, parts of her rails were gone, ventilator cowls crushed and missing, but the hatches had withstood the storm and the grain was still dry. According to the skipper's orders, by noon steam was up, and with a heavy list to starboard we churned on our way for ten days more across the heavy swell until the Pillars of Hercules rose nobly out of that silent sea.

4. Fine Weather

THE STORM might have been well forgotten a few days later had it not been for the *Amphitrite*'s twenty-degree list to starboard. That was an ever-present reality. Since the ship would normally roll about twenty degrees to each side when steaming in the trough of heavy swells, the list greatly magnified the roll to starboard so much that before we got accustomed to it we feared that we might roll clear over. We dreaded the thought that if the grain shifted farther the ship might be unable to recover her stability, and there was nothing we could do about it. But the wind continued to drop and the seas flattened with the coming of sunny warm weather as we steamed steadily at ten knots toward the southeast.

The sheer beauty of sea and sky raised our spirits and we began to see other ships. One day we passed to port a large gray American tanker in ballast and pitching heavily as she steamed westward. A few hours later there flew by a four-masted schooner on starboard, also sailing west with all her headsails and topsails set and drawing like the wings of a gull; she must have been making at least as much speed as we. But the most beautiful and romantic vision of all occurred the following morning when we passed a large four-masted bark, hull down on the southern horizon. Since she must have been about ten miles away her presence first became visible as a compact mass of white clouds growing on the rim of the sea; as it continued to grow the tall outline of her masts and rigging became evident, so lovely that one could not take one's eyes away from the snowy mass. I thought of a fairy castle with towers and turrets built on a rock in the middle of the sea. As the graceful thing flew rapidly astern the angle of her sails changed to make her appear slim and taller, and she soon sank below the horizon more romantic and beautiful than ever.

To one to whom a ship at sea is a thing of great beauty, some of these vessels were lovely almost beyond belief. In 1922, sailing vessels were in the twilight of their epoch but were still employed in large numbers on the Atlantic trade routes. Every day we passed or overhauled a few of them. One day there was a five-masted schooner soon followed by a three-masted barkentine. As we neared the entrance to the Mediterranean we were constantly in sight of smaller, two-masted vessels — usually brigs and brigantines. These smaller square-rigged sailing ships were mostly running between the Mediterranean and such places as the Azores, the Canary Islands, or West African ports. They could at that time still haul certain cargoes as cheaply as small steamships.

The mid-Atlantic sea life was also fascinating. *Amphitrite* was always followed by a flock of small black-colored birds with a gray streak across their tail feathers — Mother Carey's Chickens. They swooped and darted in flight like swallows and lived on garbage thrown overboard into a ship's wake. Like the gulls they never seemed to rest, but they occasionally would alight in the rigging and ride along facing only into the wind.

A pair of sharks will sometimes follow a ship for hundreds of miles, each with its tall fin cutting through the surface. But the porpoise is really the sailor's companion. This playful and blunt-snouted, torpedo-shaped fish grows up to six or seven feet in length; its favorite sport is to appear from nowhere in any part of the ocean, race along with a ship, and joyfully leap from the surge across its bows. Sailors have a superstition that the porpoise is their best friend, that if a man falls overboard the porpoise will fight the sharks away, or if he falls into the sea not too far from land the porpoise will tow him ashore, dead or alive, and that when the porpoise is caught on a hook and line he will cry like a child until his life is dispatched or he is released. To all this, any old-time deepwater sailor will swear.

Some five years later, I found myself in a Gloucester fishing schooner on the Grand Banks. One day, when the men were out in the dories and only the skipper, the engineer, the cook, and I were aboard and chasing swordfish, the skipper harpooned a porpoise. It promptly sounded and drowned and we soon had it aboard. Later we hung it in the rigging to cure for four days because, being a mammal, its flesh is vermillion-colored and we feared it might taste fishy. But when the crew came aboard with their dories full of halibut and cod, they were aghast at what we had done.

"Oh, this is a wicked thing," they said. "No good can come of eatin' a porpoise. We're goin' to have bad luck — you'll see."

Four days later we had the first of several meals on porpoise meat. The steaks were cut two inches thick, were as tender as could be, deep crimson in color, and absolutely devoid of any flavor whatever. None of the older fishermen would have anything to do with it. As for their foreboding, a week later we were caught in the August hurricane of 1927 in which five schooners were lost with all hands, about a hundred men, including the *Columbia*, the queen of the Gloucester fleet. We didn't call a storm a hurricane in those days — it was only a big "breeze o' wind." We were hove to for three days, the deck seams opened from strain, and when we finally reached the Boston Fish Pier we found that half our catch of halibut had spoiled. So much for superstition.

When *Amphitrite* was in the longitude of the Azores on one clear morning, along came a school of whales. There were about a dozen of them and they didn't approach too close to the ship. But they made a fascinating spectacle. The only indication of their presence was their spouting a fountain of seawater blown up six to twelve feet into the air where the wind shredded it into a spray of white mist visible for a long distance.

To mention ship's routine, although I wasn't exactly proud of myself and my lowly job as sailors' messboy, I did have a lot of time to follow my own devices. I was called out at six o'clock in the morning and could clean up the breakfast by nine. At eleven o'clock I attended to dinner and could wash up the dishes by one. Then I worked from four to six for supper. In addition to procuring supplies and food, I swept the messroom after each meal and washed the table, benches, and bulkheads when necessary. Twice a week I washed all the decks and bulkheads of both the fo'c's'le and the messroom, and each morning after breakfast I washed the lavatory, shower room, and toilets. It was a pretty easy job, for which I was paid forty-five dollars a month.

The job would have been even easier had the feeding customs of the sailors been a little more civilized, but I had no complaint because by comparison with the black gang the sailors were all epicures. One man strewed his swill in a ring around his place at the wooden table instead of piling it up on the edge of his plate. Gus was more fastidious; he neatly hid his under the broad edge of his white enamel plate. Paul always poured a few drops of his coffee or tea on the table before tasting it. Edwin enjoyed both catsup and sugar on his potatoes, regardless of whether they were baked, boiled, or fried. As the saying is, all of them were "bird lovers," being very generous with crumbs and crusts; a robin could wade around knee-deep in bread crumbs on the table after every meal.

At my first meal I discovered that I did not have to wash everybody's dish, cup, and utensils. As soon as I brought the hot water for washing and rinsing, about half the sailors washed their own and then stowed them in separate niches in the dish rack, where each was identified by the owner's name. In 1922, from a quarter to a third of the crew of nearly every merchant ship on a long cruise was afflicted with venereal disease all the time, although not all at the same time, so the men took their own precautions with their dishes.

Each meal followed a routine something like this typical breakfast: at seven-thirty in the morning I call the sailors who are not on watch, eight of them. They arrive at once — hungry, still sleepy, unwashed, and talkative.

"Well, mess," someone says, "what we have today?"

"Is the breakfast any good this mornin'?"

"Hey! What the hell is this? Pork chops?"

"No," somebody replies, "it's beef stew."

"No, it's not. Those is liver."

"Ah, look at this — eggs!"

"Coffee, mess, hurry up with my coffee. Ah — that's the stuff."

"Now, boys — say where is the damn potatoes? Bah! I never seen such rotten potatoes!"

"Say, mess, d'you call this slop coffee?"

"Well," I reply in self-defense, "don't blame me. I didn't make it."

"Bah! It is slops."

"Say, what they think we are down here, bloomin' pigs? I won't eat this nasty swill!"

"Take this damn egg up to the cook and tell him to eat it. Look! Somebody stepped on it!"

"Well, I won't eat this damn lard on my bread, mess. Pass the jam. That's the stuff."

"What did you do to this milk, mess? You got too much water in it. Give me those milk out of the can."

"Well, I am finish. You can have what's left, mess."

And they noisily rise and depart, leaving the messroom in a stinking clutter. The wooden table, formerly scoured with sand and lye, is littered with swill; it drips with coffee, is strewn with overturned cups and dishes, and is plastered with oatmeal. The wall near the coffee can is spattered yellow.

Even the deck will be unsafe until it is swept of greasy steaks and fried potatoes. Edwin has contaminated the sugar by dipping his coffee spoon in it several times. Paul has spilled tomato catsup over his dungarees and the bench and left it there for somebody to sit in. Victor has taken a vicious delight in deliberately soiling the wooden bulkhead with his greasy hands, leaving a series of large, black handprints on the white paint.

Now Macaroni, as Alessandro is known, comes down from the wheel to get his breakfast. This morning I have forgotten to leave his plate at the galley for a special ration of hot food. The food still in the soup tureens is nearly cold. "Well, what's to eat!" he demands loudly. "What the hell! Cold! Hey! What's this, mess! I won't eat this damn cold swill. Come! Up to the cookhouse and get me hot! Hep!"

I soon return with a platter of steaming hot meat and potatoes. Macaroni begins again, "Say, the meat is like leather. Did you eat any?"

"No," I reluctantly observe. I had eaten oatmeal and eggs long ago and had not wanted meat and potatoes, but I saw nothing to be gained by imparting that information.

"Well, then how d'ya expect me to! Bah! Put this away!"

Soon I have cleared up the table, filling a large garbage can in the process, and am returning to the galley for hot water and to take back the unused potatoes in order that they may be warmed over for supper. My way leads through a corner of the fo'c's'le.

"Hey, mess, where are you going with those potatoes, huh?" someone yells. "Now look here, mess, you ain't goin' t' take those back t' that damn galley. Go tell the cook t' chase hisself. We don't want them damn things down here again."

"All right," I lie, "I'm going right out and throw them over." And then I escape to the galley with my pot of contraband where I am loudly upbraided by Scotty for not bringing it sooner.

On the eleventh day out of North Sydney, a white lighthouse and cluster of houses appeared at the seaward end of a flat tableland atop a high shoreline of miles of sandy cliffs — Cape Saint Vincent in Portugal. It was soon lost in the fog, but not before I was thrilled at the thought that we were not far from Trafalgar. During the day we passed three steamers and three sailing vessels, all of which indicated our approach to the Mediterranean. That evening the sunset was particularly beautiful it seemed to me — a hazy salmon glowing up into the blue twilight of a cloudless sky, a gorgeous display of Halloween colors.

Next morning I awoke at five o'clock to look out the porthole by my bunk at a distant mountain, the roughest and most jagged I had ever seen, I thought. It was on the coast of Africa. I was so excited that I slipped on my dungarees and shoes and walked out on the wet deck. Although the mountains on the Spanish side of the Strait of Gibraltar were similar, they did not seem so harsh and menacing as that mammoth pile of frowning blackness partly concealed by several strata of clouds on the Moroccan shore. And around on the European side, just a few miles farther along, arose the enormous mass of Gibraltar out of a green sea. We steered directly for its seaward face and wondered what adventures would be concealed in the orders that would soon be flashed to us in the predawn grayness.

5. Yarns in the Dogwatch

JUST BEFORE SUNRISE *Amphitrite* hove to close aboard the signal station perched high on the seaward mass of Gibraltar. Soon a flashing light transmitted orders to us to proceed to Algiers to discharge our cargo of grain. Then the bells clanged in the engine room and soon we again heard the rhythmic pounding of the pistons as the ship's triple-expansion engine attained its standard speed. Gradually our course diverged from the Spanish coast, which was obscured by low-lying clouds, until several hours later when suddenly we caught a glimpse of the mountaintops.

Far astern, high over the sea, rugged and barren slopes of mountainside shone through rifts in the tumbling clouds. Because the horizon was hazy, the Andalusian coast could not be seen; only bright patches of high land resplendent in casual filterings of sunshine appeared, and they like visions of a wonderland glimpsed through rents in the billowing pageantry of cloud-castles.

It was late in the afternoon in the dogwatch; the sailors had eaten their supper and now sat smoking and talking on a hatch on the after well-deck. After the toil of the day they were weary and for greater comfort had changed into clean shirts and pattens. Their talk was mainly of the small things of the day, inconsequential, possibly boring, of many-told adventures in the last port, reminiscences recent and distant, and inevitably of hopes for a better order of things when they individually would arrive at some mythical land and possess a faithful wife, a tiny plot of land to plant and harvest, and a vine-covered cottage on a bluff overlooking the sea and the silver sails and plumes of smoke passing on the skyline.

From the very first I looked forward to this short time of rest and dreaming, surrounded by the beauty and majesty of a quiet early evening. I soon discovered that it was always the most cherished part of the day in the hearts of my shipmates. Fancy a world wholly clean and fresh and bright with only the sun and stars and blue depth of space to light it! Fancy a lifetime of lonely seas and skies with the mountains of the land ever rising and sinking in the distance like unreal visions and one may better understand the hunger for love and companionship as well as the deep spiritual satisfactions of most of these professional old-time, merchant ship sailors.

No tale of the sea can omit mention of their stories and the manner in which they are told without losing some of the essential flavor of life at sea. Some stories start spontaneously. Others grow from the most unlikely chitchat, such as the following:

"Hey there, Gus — yes, you — hope you can get up to the

wheel to relieve me before five tomorrow," the peevish Pete complained to the imperturbable Norwegian. "Every morning you're ten or fifteen minutes late! You might think this was a passenger ship."

"Aw, shut up — and leave Gus alone," old Edwin drawled. "You'll be cursing at the mate next for putting aluminum paint on the rails."

"Well, why not," Pete returned. "White paint would do just as well and cost a sight less, too!"

"Well," Edwin began, with a faraway look in his bleary eyes, "when I first went to sea, we didn't have no aluminum paint. No-o! We used to scrub and scrub with our hands on brass that always was getting green again by the next watch. Aluminum paint saves all that scrubbing around — all you have to do now is paint a thing once in a while and then wash it off with suji when it is getting dirty, and when the white paint is all washed off just paint it again. Look at all the work it saves you!"

"Aw, it would be better to have brass nowadays and paint everything else black," the ordinary seaman declared.

"Yes, p'raps it would. In the old square-riggin' days everything was painted or holystoned or shined. There wasn't no halfway business about it in my first ship, I tell you. She was a old bark, you know, a windjammer that sailed to Zanzibar, a town out on Madagascar, east of Africa. Yaw —"

The old red-faced sailor began to dream away toward those mountain vistas in the clouds and we edged a little closer, divining that a yarn of some sort was coming.

"I was thinking of the time I left home — that was a long time ago, thirty year, no more than that — well, it don't make no difference. I lived in a little town called Nor — a pretty little place with only stone houses, up a fjord where the big cliffs stood way up above the water and the wind was always blowing in the pine trees like you hear it sometimes in the distance when a storm is piling up the black clouds out on the edge of the sea.

"My mother, who was a little woman, didn't want me to go to sea because my father, he fell off a t'gallan' yard and got all busted up and squashed on the deck of a big ship when I was little boy. But I didn't want to work in the woods cutting trees and I got tired of the sawmill so I think I was go to sea and make my fortune, too."

Here, the old man grunted and paused to light a pipe that he had been cramming with black plug cut from a chunk carried in his dungarees. After prodding it and lighting it and prodding it some more, he began to puff out little thin clouds of blue smoke that vanished in less than no time in the wind.

"Nor was a funny little town — all gray. The stones in the streets and the sidewalks and the little houses was gray. Everything was gray, the grayest gray you ever seen. And the day that I went away my mother and my little sister cried a lot, and then they put on clean white aprons and walked down to the landing with me. And I remember that day, that the sky and the sea was all gray too, and it didn't make me feel good because my mother and my little sister was crying and I was afraid I was going to cry, too. Then I didn't want to go, but I was afraid not to because they might laugh at me in the town, so I kissed them goodbye and got in the boat to go out to the ship.

"We sailed in about an hour and my mother and little sister was still down to the landing waving their kerchiefs to me. Well, I promised to write often, and I did for many years, but they was always wanting me to come home and I never was able to get there. You know how it is — sometimes you lose all your money in a gin mill, and sometimes the whore takes it all before you wake up in the morning, and sometimes you is on the beach so long that you has to spend it all on lodgings before you is getting on another wagon. Yah, we gets so damn little that we can't do nothing. Well, I was ashamed to go home with nothing so I didn't go at all. And then I begun to write not so much, and then I never heard from them because they didn't know where to write — and how do I know but that they isn't all dead? So I didn't write no more for fifteen years yet."

The strong afternoon light began to fail. Already a golden haze had spread over the west where the great Sierra Nevadas peeped through the castlelike clouds, and the silver sails in the distance caught the glow like mirrors. The day was mellow and overripe. Old Edwin's memories had cast a wistfulness, subtle yet strong, over some of the men lolling on the hatch. Some of them were plainly thinking back across the years to the beginning of their own wanderings, possibly to other gray skies and tiny villages nestling between a pearly sea and lowering cliffs.

"Haven't you ever been home since you left?" I inquired somberly.

"No-o. I am too old and poor to go now. That's all right. That old sea has kept me away more than thirty years and I guess he won't now pile me up on the beach all drownded in my old clothes so that all the people could see what a ragged old beggar I was."

While Edwin was concluding his words, a newcomer had

sauntered up to the hatch, the Liverpool Irishman, Pat Mahoney. Being a great boxing fan, Pat had taken a strong paternal
interest in me and frequently came aft where I might often be
found after supper. He was considerably more civilized than
most of the black gang who lived in the firemen's fo'c's'le forward, and one of the few who occasionally consorted with the
men "on deck." He ate with a knife and fork at mealtime and
he used the toilet facilities for the purposes and in the manner
for which they were designed. He slept in his drawers instead
of his working clothes, and he washed his head and hands
every time he came off watch. His life had been spent almost
entirely at sea in ships of many nations since he started out
from Liverpool at the age of ten. He was a cheery character
who had survived several shipwrecks and torpedoings and was
now in his fifties. No one enjoyed life more than Pat. When
he was off watch he spent his time habitually in a semirecum-
bent posture on number one hatch smoking a pipe and enjoying every breath while the wind blew his red hair down into
his shaggy eyebrows and whipped the lower part of his faded
blue dungarees. When he opened his broad mouth a broken
set of black and yellow teeth grinned out diabolically.

"Hullo, maties," this newcomer thundered from the cave in
the middle of his face. "Who's passin' out drinks t'night?

"And how's my boy, the modern John L. Sullivan?" he
added, addressing me.

Then he displayed his teeth and gurgled somewhere down
in his throat at his own joke. Uninterrupted, he hurried on.

"By gorry, I almost forgot to tell you the story of my life.
Sure now, and do you want to be hearing of it? Well, you
know once I went on the beach down in the Panama Canal,

and there was a lot of work there going on while they was building it. So I up out of my favorite barroom one day and started to see what I could do. Well, I went up the road alooking for the head carpenter."

The head carpenter gave him promise of a job and an advance of fifty cents since Pat assured him he was nearly dead "from no vittles to eat in me belly these three days." Next he found the head blacksmith who also gave him fifty cents because he was so hungry "he couldn't stand on his two legs."

He then invested in a bottle of whiskey but remembered in the night to climb in a window of the hiring shack where he was found sleeping on the floor under a settee in the morning. Disclaiming to be either a carpenter or a blacksmith, he announced that he was really a tourist. So he was put to work firing a boiler, which satisfied everybody, and he remained on the job six months before he got aboard a ship again.

Pat's tale evoked much laughter in the telling, so upon its conclusion he was encouraged to tell another about his adventures in providing victuals for himself, as was customary in some British ships at the time, in the 1890s, on a six-day voyage in a ship bound from Cardiff, Wales, to Lisbon.

Receiving from the captain an advance of ten shillings he promptly squandered it all on liquor save for a penny's worth of tea and a penny's worth of sugar. The first day at sea he ate nothing, he said, as a consequence of being drunk. But thereafter the cook fed him out of the captain's rations for the rest of the voyage.

Upon arrival at Lisbon he again presented himself to the captain and was given a further and rather princely advance of twenty-five shillings only upon threat of leaving the ship. This

time he got as far as the head of the dock when he met another Irishman who persuaded him to relieve a countryman's
overpowering thirst. This adventure ended up at a bullfight
where Pat's friend became ill and had to take a nap outside
the bullring under a palm tree.

On his way back to the ship Pat remembered the victuals he
had gone ashore to buy and stopped in at a farmer's market
where he bought a goat, which he led back to the ship. Following his efforts at getting the animal aboard and down into
the fo'c's'le, where the goat soon proceeded to eat a shoe and a
leg of his dungarees, the following day he butchered it and
"cut it up in chunks, fur and all," and gave it to the cook to
make into a chowder. The not unlikely result of this exploit
was a culinary disaster — "After we ate the stew it give us all
the diarrhea."

Victor then told a typical story of an escape from a mob in
Mazagan many years ago, following a barroom brawl during
which he had broken a bottle over the head of a muezzin, a
sort of Mohammedan clergyman.

By this time the sun had fallen behind the great sawtooth
range of the distant mountains. Vivid red sky glowed over the
west, shooting long streamers of fire and blood-colored cloud
over the crimson sea. Twilight had succeeded the bright afternoon and was slowly dwindling as dusk began to steal upon
the world from a somber east. Now the water was like purple
satin; the tiny sails upon it shone dimly in the gloom of the
distance and the *Amphitrite* seemed all alone in the whole of
creation. Bright coals of burning tobacco glowed in a dozen
pipes scattered on the hatch and scented the raw air delicately;
one or two men paced restlessly to and fro on the deck beating

out a regular tread on the steel plates, but save for the grinding of the propeller it was very quiet.

Was this sort of thing the real seafaring life, I wondered to myself. Frustration compounded by irresponsibility and nourished by too much liquor? Otherwise, how can one account for the fact that these older man never got out of the fo'c's'le? They may have started out in what one today calls an "underprivileged" status, but that was no excuse because many of the officers also started out on the same level and had the ambition and drive to improve themselves, and were steadily moving up through the chain of command on deck and in the engine room. I would see too much of failure before this voyage was over. But I was fast learning about all sides of a sailor's life at sea.

The *Amphitrite* rumbled along her course, rolling slightly with the uncomfortable list, quivering like a living thing with the throb of her propeller. One by one, the men who were sprawled over the hatch on the after well-deck knocked the ashes from their pipes, wearily drew themselves to their feet, and wandered away in the darkness.

"Good night," they yawned to each other. "Guess I'll turn in — good night."

And the responses sounded indistinctly through the dark, "Good night — good night."

6. The Glorious Fourteenth

Two DAYS after passing Gibraltar *Amphitrite* arrived with her twenty-degree list to starboard off the busy harbor of Algiers early in the afternoon. The offshore breeze smelled sweet, shadows of clouds played across the brown and green patches on the hills, the white city looked rather picturesque, and all in all it seemed like a pleasant place in which to spend a couple of weeks while the cargo of grain was being discharged. The crew was properly pleased.

When the pilot came aboard, however, he brought some mail that introduced a bit of uncertainty. One letter notified the captain that the ship would not be able to go to a discharging berth for two more days; meanwhile we would lie in the roadstead. Since the present date was July thirteenth, the delay meant that the crew would be able to help the French celebrate the night before the fourteenth. And that was to-night. Glorious!

I soon discovered that the ideas of the *Amphitrite*'s crew were about what one would expect of a crowd of men of diverse origins in such circumstances. Only dimly aware of the patriotic significance of the celebration, they knew there would be fireworks, martial music by brass bands, and much drinking. The crew might even get a day off from routine work to compensate for loss of the American Fourth of July celebration when we lurched and pounded in a smother of flying spume and rain off the Newfoundland Banks. If so, we could use the day as we wished — recuperation from alcoholic hangovers for some, sightseeing tours for others.

That evening in Algiers was a strange affair to me, accustomed to similar celebrations in New England before the time of the First World War. The official pyrotechnic display was a continuous performance at full intensity that lasted for hours. It was conducted in a very large, stifling, dusty square closed in by pungent shops and cafés, one of the central bazaars. Everything was gaudy with colored-paper draperies and festoons of incandescent lamps — the tiers of balconies on the yellowed buildings, the minarets and church towers, the ragged coconut palms. In the middle of the square was the equipment for igniting the fireworks — skyrockets, pinwheels, snakes, colored flares, and a large smoke balloon. A huge mob surged everywhere, jabbering, shoving, eating, and drinking — mostly nonalcoholic beverages. About twenty seamen from *Amphitrite* settled down amid a clutter of beer tables on a sidewalk and proceeded to fill themselves with the spirit of the fourteenth.

There was a great crackle of firecrackers and swallowing of
beer! The latter was more impressive than anything else. Everyone seemed to be in good humor — the Arabs, the Europeans, the sailors and soldiers. A short distance away two
French officers, fastidious in dress, smiled over their absinthe,
quietly observing the tattered people from the countryside as
they clumped by. Presently, a little wizened-up hunchback, a
miserable, drunken bundle of flapping rags, staggered against
one of them and fell across his lap. The officer roughly pushed
the wretch down, lifted his baton, and struck him hard across
the buttocks as he crawled away. It seemed unnecessarily bru-
tal.

"Look at that! Gee, let me get a crack at him."

I caught Pete by the arm, his face flushed with excitement,
just as he started for the officer.

"Come now, don't be a fool — you're only going to get
yourself in real trouble," I said. "Mind your own business.
You'd better take a walk with me. Let's go see what that
crowd is doing over there."

We pushed our way across the bazaar, jostled and jostling.
In a circle formed by the crowd, two men were playing leap-
frog; two men of large stature, serious, entirely oblivious of any
spectators. Pete exclaimed, "Well, I'll be damned — it's Mahoney and Louie." Pete and I stared in amazement. There
they were, Mahoney, the big, frowzle-headed Irishman, and
Louie, the immense Russian fireman who looked and carried
himself so like a gorilla.

"Hi there, Pat, what are you doing?" I called.

Mahoney, about to vault over the crouching Louie, turned
around abruptly. Then, instead of jumping, he fished a quart

of cognac from the hip of Louie's dungarees and advanced, glowing with affability, to offer us a drink.

"What do you think you're doing?" Pete asked him.

"Us doing? Sure now, we're demonstrating eight star cognac, best stuff on the bar, guaranteed to knock you out in three drinks." In circus-announcer tones he continued, "Right this way, ladies and gents, right this way to see Louie, the spotted Wampus. He is the wildest animal in the circus —" Louie growled as he thought a lion ought to. "He holds all the rum he drinks. What's that, lady, does he ever get enough? He don't, lady, that's what makes him wild. Here, Louie, take your bottle." Louie, still crouching on his hands and knees, allowed Mahoney to pour cognac down his throat until his eyes fairly popped.

"Say, Pat, why don't you climb over the ropes and give a show in there," suggested Pete.

"Fine, matey," boomed Mahoney, "I'll do that. That we will, won't we, Louie?"

The mob, enjoying this sideshow with obvious delight, formed a passage to the roped-off area. Then we got into trouble, becoming too much a part of the central attraction. All about us rockets, red lights, and firecrackers were flaring and rattling. After a vociferous announcement, which no one understood, Mahoney, keeping his legs stiff, fell forward on his hands that Louie might vault over. Suddenly, like a falling star from the sky, there was a hiss, a report, a yell. Like a kangaroo, Mahoney leaped high into the air. A well-directed Roman candle had hit him squarely in the buttocks and exploded.

"Howly hell! Some bloody bum plinked me in the seat of

me best balbriggan drawers. Put it out, put it out! Water, water! Can't you see they're burning. Git water! Cost two bob in a rummage sale, too! Water! Water!"

"Drag your ass in the dust, you damn fool," yelled Pete.

Everybody roared with laughter, everybody but Mahoney, who yelped like a poodle and dashed frantically about leaving a thread of smoke in his wake.

"Va t'en! Va t'en! Dépêchez-vous!" It was the gendarmes hurrying to push us out. Pete and I scrambled under the ropes to lose ourselves in the crowd, and Mahoney tried to conceal his embarrassment behind a coconut palm while he buttoned his denim jacket around his hips.

"Say, boys, I want to go up in the balloon," exclaimed Louie when he had recovered his wits, pointing toward the fire balloon, now nearly ready to be cast away.

"Well, why don't you get Mahoney? He'll help you," I mischievously suggested.

"That's a thought. By Joe, I will."

Before they started for the balloon, Louie and Mahoney reinforced their courage with another stout drink. Someone in the grotesque flicker of the lights attempted to stop them. Louie, with one swing of his ponderous arm, struck him once, and the man fell flat. They continued unmolested until their caper was all over in just another minute. Arriving at the balloon, Louie stood guard while Mahoney investigated the tube leading down to the inflating apparatus. By this time the gendarmes, in their preliminary maneuvers having created a riotous scramble among themselves, advanced from all sides. Louie started to run; Mahoney, clinging to the inflating tube, would have started also had he not fallen. There was a huge puff of smoke, a confusion of shouts and screams, a wild surge in the mob, and the bazaar became filled with choking fumes. Pete groaned. "Mahoney's busted up the fireworks!" We looked at each other in surprise and disappointment. Then we shouted with laughter. "Well, come on," I said, "we better move along."

The *Amphitrite* was a quiet ship on July fourteenth in Algiers. Only a skeleton crew remained aboard; some had not returned from the previous night. The third engineer, the radio officer, and I went ashore and took a long tour on a sightseeing bus and had a good meal at what seemed to us to be a very expensive restaurant. Algiers, although still festive, was also fairly quiet for such a large city. It was just as well. And so our holiday passed.

Early on the morning of the fifteenth, the American consul and the ship's agent appeared with an order to proceed at once to Piraeus with our grain. The consul had in his custody Louie and Mahoney, a battered pair. Mahoney's face was still smooched with soot, and his eyes, badly bloodshot, peeped out like tiny red globes. "Never again," cackled Mahoney tenderly touching a blister through the copious rent in the seat of his dungarees, "never again will I touch cognac. Do you know, it's give me an awful headache."

The skipper was eager to put the *Amphitrite* to sea, but he was reluctant to leave several of his crew behind. Now that the firemen had all returned, where were the sailors? Where were Pete and John?

About eight o'clock John arrived.

"Have you seen Pete?" we asked.

"Pete? Sure. He's coming right along. Do you know what

he did? He give his coat and shirt to a poor feller with a hump on his back. Sure he did. He always gets took. He'll be along pretty soon."

Since he could wait little longer, the skipper ordered the sailors to heave the anchor cable in to short stays. Then a motor-driven bumboat was seen splashing rapidly toward the ship. Pete stepped off at the gangway and climbed to the deck clad in a T-shirt and dungarees.

"Say, you're a damn fool," scolded Macaroni. "What if you went on the beach, what? Do you know what it is to live on swill for a month? What? Yes, and sleep on the lumber piles all because you was too stinking drunk to come back to the ship, what? And then you sober off and give all your clothes away. What you are, what?"

"Aw, go soak your head."

At that time, I thought this act of Pete's was creditable, although unintelligent generosity. As time passed I discovered that it was characteristic of the breed and more common than not. It occurred in almost every port. I was fast learning a little about typical seafaring men.

7. Shipboard Diversions—The Bible Class and the Heavyweight Championship

ON THE MORNING of July fifteenth, when business resumed in Algiers, we soon knew we were not to unload our grain there. Had I suspected such a turn of events a day earlier I would have used my excursion ashore even to better advantage. The cargo had been sold once more and the ship was ordered to Piraeus where we might presumably discharge it unless it were sold again somewhere else. With the cargo out of her holds she would again float on an even keel and become a more comfortable place in which to live. Eventually we would arrive at a final destination. Accordingly, we still churned our way into the east, past the sloping olive groves of Sicily, the arid crags of the ancient Cythera, past quaint fishing boats with patched orange lateen sails, past a small fleet of brigs and schooners that bounced along toward the west.

Late in the afternoon of the day before we arrived in Piraeus
I was sitting in the shade on the deck amidships near a steel
hatch cover over the port coal bunkers. Bill Nadeau, the
baker, Scotty, the chief cook, and Pat Mahoney, the fireman,
were quietly smoking their pipes while sitting on the hatch
and I was reading aloud to them selections from the Bible.

All this had come about one sunny afternoon in the Atlantic when Bill had noticed me reading some poetry. He had
stopped and looked at me quizzically. "Read me something,"
he had commanded.

"What would you like?" I asked.

"Well, have you got something there by Kipling?"

It happened that I had bought a cheap anthology of Kipling's in North Sydney to supplement the meager library of
three volumes with which I had left home, so I began by reading "The Mary Gloster" and then read "The Last Chantey."

"I like that," said Bill, who had sat down on the hatch,
"read some more."

So I had kept on until eight bells struck and the second
mate had come down from the bridge and wanted to box.

Thereafter, whenever I brought my books out on deck I always acquired an audience to listen to my reading, something
I would never have believed possible. I thought back to the
previous September at Harvard when I had been admitted to
Professor Charles Townsend Copeland's class in creative writing. On the occasion of the second class, Copey, as we were
allowed to call him, had appeared in the classroom doorway
looking at us with feigned distaste while hissing through his
mustache. Then he closed the door carefully, hung his derby
hat and his umbrella on the hatrack in the corner, marched
stiffly to his desk, and deposited his green felt bag of books in

front of him — all the while without uttering a word and continuing to glare at us.

Then he ceremoniously emptied his green bag, book by book, regarded them for a few minutes in silence, and then opened his Bible and began to read the first of several passages in his rich, deep voice.

"And he went out from his presence a leper as white as snow," he intoned as he completed the fifth chapter of the second book of Kings.

Suddenly he looked up at us and quietly asked, "How many of you young gentlemen read your Bibles daily?"

No one felt qualified to reply.

After scowling at us in the complete silence of the room for several minutes more, Copey slowly replaced all his books in his green bag, marched deliberately to the hatrack, reached for his umbrella, clapped his derby squarely on top of his head, and opened the door, glaring and hissing.

"You young gentlemen all aspire to be writers. How do you expect to write good English when you are unacquainted with the greatest writing in the English language? Good day, gentlemen!" he thundered, stepped out into the corridor, and slammed the heavy door behind him.

A few months later he asked us to name the three books we would select to take with us, assuming that we could take only three, in the event that we might embark on a long sea voyage or take up residence in some place such as a desert island where books were not available. Thus it came about that I had taken with me on this voyage a Bible, Palgrave's *Golden Treasury of Songs and Lyrics*, and a small dictionary.

All this I had explained to Bill Nadeau, Scotty, and Pat Ma-

honey on the occasion of my first informal "reading" that afternoon when we were steaming along serenely in mid-Atlantic. Pat had come by and sat down quietly beside Bill and
Scotty on the hatch cover. Noticing my Bible he asked,
"Now, what are you going to read out of that?"

"Well, what do you want?" I retorted, "history, philosophy,
poetry, genealogy, ethics, adventure stories, mystery, prophesy
— you tell me."

"Is all them in the Bible?" asked Pat. He cleared his throat
and spat on the deck. "I ain't been in a church for some
time," he explained.

"Let me try some poetry on you," I suggested, and proceeded to read a few of the Psalms.

Bill Nadeau, who had been brought up in French Canada,
recognized them.

"Yes, I remember all of them," he said, "but I never knew
they was poetry — or so beautiful."

Just then Mr. Schultz, the first mate, stepped out of the
forward house and approached.

"What's this," he asked whimsically, "a Bible class?"

Mahoney took his pipe out of his mouth, "Yes it is, you
heathen, and it's time you learned a little something besides
how to tie knots. Sit down and keep a civil tongue in your
head and you might enjoy yourself. The cooks and me is having a good time and you might, too."

To my surprise the mate did sit down and I explained to
him the meaning of the fifth chapter of the second book of
Kings and then proceeded to read it.

When I had finished the passage, the mate was visibly impressed. He was silent a moment and then said, "Mahoney's

right. I've been missing something. Keep on with these Bible classes, boy, and I'll drop in when I have a chance."

That was the way my "readings" started. On sunny days I usually went out on one side of the deck, depending on where the sun was shaded, and began to read to myself. In those few volumes there was so much to read or study or memorize! I never invited anyone to join me. Seeing me there was enough of an invitation, and I was constantly amazed that four or five usually came to sit down. I always read aloud when I had an audience of one. It also surprised me that sometimes a man would bring a book or a magazine story and shyly ask me to read a certain passage or story to him. Sometimes the selection was rather dull or second-rate, but I always complied. And I marveled that none of the men appeared to feel self-conscious. Could my pugilistic games with the second mate have made the pursuit of learning respectably masculine?

On this particular afternoon while *Amphitrite* was quietly rolling along with the coast of southern Italy in the distance, Scotty appeared with a copy of Sir Walter Scott's *Ivanhoe*, which had been in the ship's library and then had been hidden by one of the crew for some time until it came into Scotty's possession.

"I want you to read this masterpiece by a great Scottish writer," he said. "But first I'd enjoy to hear some of that Limey, Kipling, to get me in the right mood to appreciate it."

The time passed so quickly that I had not had time to begin on *Ivanhoe* when eight bells struck and the second mate arrived.

"Well, Scotty, if you like, I'll start in with a couple of chapters of *Ivanhoe* after supper," I offered.

"That will be good," he replied. "You keep the book so nobody'll swipe it and come and get me when you're ready."

Leighton, the second mate, and I then climbed down to the forward well-deck and had our gloves laced on to begin our sparring exercises. The third mate, MacDonald, held his watch to time us for two-minute rounds because we didn't believe in wearing ourselves out. Pat Mahoney had long ago appointed himself my second and trainer and Louie, who considered himself the greatest rough-and-tumble fighter afloat, performed the same service for the second mate. While we boxed, Pat and Louie, the two big men, sat on each side of the third mate on the edge of number two hatch in a space reserved for them because nobody cared to dispute their choice vantage point.

This afternoon we had our usual audience of about thirty strung out in a large circle sitting on the deck or the hatch. For some reason, Louie, who usually had plenty to say on any occasion, was more voluble than ever.

"Come on, second," he called, "he's pushing you all over the deck. Put some steam in your mitts. Hit 'im! Aw, you better go to the shower!"

After a few rounds of this comic abuse, Mr. Leighton became annoyed. At the end of a round, he finally placed his hands on his hips and stared at Louie, who was still heckling him.

"All right, Jim Jeffries," he said, "since you know all about it, you put on Emery's gloves and try a round or two with me!"

Louie was momentarily taken aback. All the spectators shouted happily, "Come on, you big ape, put the gloves on! Let's see what you can do!"

"Oh, no, you don't," Louie called, "I ain't having nothing to do with either one of you."

"Then put the gloves on with Pat," I suggested. "You and he are well matched."

"Well, he's my friend, too," said Louie, "I ain't going to hurt him."

Pat spat on the deck in consternation.

"What d'ye mean, hurt me!" he shouted, his blue eyes flashing under his mop of red hair.

"Aw, you're no match for me," Louie growled, with his face thrust across the third mate's toward Pat on the hatch.

"Begorra, we'll find out!"

Pat slid off the hatch and approached me, waving the dirty towel with which he always equipped himself on these occasions, as did Louie, just in case — The second mate and I always forbid them to touch us with the towels, preferring to sweat down our necks into our T-shirts, but Pat and Louie always appeared with the towels, which they draped around their own necks, presumably to make a more professional appearance and strut in the reflected glory of the main event.

Handing me the towel, Pat unlaced my gloves and then I laced them on him. Meanwhile, Louie had swaggered up to Leighton where the same office was performed. While this was going on, excitement rapidly mounted among the crew, every man in the ship having arrived to take up a vantage point except those in the engine room and the man at the wheel. There was a great hubbub — cheering, yelling, and the placing of various types of bets on one gladiator or the other.

Leighton and I attempted to give Louie and Pat some advice but we might as well have saved our breath. Pat adopted a stance with his feet nearly a yard apart and his fists out in front of his stomach where they would be useless to him, either offensively or defensively, reminiscent of a formal studio pose affected by his great hero, John L. Sullivan. His only accommodation to the impending event was to remove his pipe from his mouth and hand it to me for safekeeping.

"Now, Pat," I began, "put your feet closer together in a natural way. And lead out with your left and hold your right in front of your face to ward off his blows."

"Keep a civil tongue in yer head, boy," Pat said. "I know what I'm doin'. I'm one of the old-time dock-wallopers of Liverpool."

I shrugged my shoulders and gave up.

"Louie," said the second mate, "if you try to box Pat without any guard at all you're going to get into trouble."

"Aw, leave me be," growled Louie, "I'm goin' to kill 'im!"

Louie crouched about ten feet away from Pat with his left fist waving vaguely in front of him, his right swinging in a circle behind him in the area of his bent knees as if he were about to hurl a discus. His filthy plaid cap remained attached firmly to the back of his head. Leighton and I looked at each other hopelessly. Then the third mate yelled "Time" and Pat and Louie rushed at each other.

At the moment of imminent collision each delivered a mighty right swing at the other's head. Both missed. The impetus of the blow was so great that each lost his balance, spun in a complete circle, and crashed heavily on the deck about ten feet apart, and there they lay. Without receiving a single blow each man was knocked out cold.

A tremendous roar of laughter shattered the comparative

silence of the previous moment. Men slapped each other on the back, rolled on the hatch, and laughed uncontrollably. As the noise began to subside, the mate shouted down from the wing of the bridge, "If I hadn't seen it with my own eyes, I'd never believe it." The captain was still laughing too hard to comment.

Fortunately for Louie his cap had somehow adhered to his hair and probably prevented a concussion when the back of his head smashed on the deck. For a couple of minutes, he was unresponsive to the efforts of the second mate to get him into a sitting position.

Pat was equally fortunate in falling. His head had struck the folded edge of the tarpaulin clamped over the hatch covers, and he lay crumpled against the hatch coaming, completely dazed but not unconscious. I hoisted him into an upright posture.

"What a smacker!" he gasped. "That Louie knocked me out."

"Well, look what you did to him," I said.

Pat's wits slowly returned as his eyes beheld Louie being propped up also. "What d'ye know!" Pat ejaculated. "I knocked him out!"

Then he held up his gloves to me and said, "Here, boy, take 'em off! I'm quitting while I'm ahead."

Louie slowly got Pat into his range of vision and began to smile incredulously.

"So I knocked him out, did I! That Pat, he fights too rough. This is the first time in me life anybody ever knocked me out. He must have had a horseshoe in his glove. Here, take 'em off. This ain't for me. I ain't young enough for this racket."

"Well," Leighton replied, "if you two had been willing to listen to us neither one of you would have got knocked out. Now get up on your feet and shake hands with Pat. You two fought a draw and you won the joint championship.

"Here we are, ladies and gents," he shouted to the crew while holding up the arms of the big men, "the joint heavyweight championship of the *Amphitrite*."

On other days once in a while we were able to get some of the other men to put on the gloves, but they were always seriously respectful of the rules and willing to take our suggestions. The exhibition of Pat and Louie had eloquently convinced everybody that skill was more effective than brute strength.

8. Piraeus and Athens

ON OUR FIRST EVENING in Piraeus I went ashore alone. It was my first real eastern port, still quite primitive in 1922, and the quays were filled with brigs and brigantines and very, very old small steamers. Ashore it was a bizarre place — crooked alleys through which tiny donkeys staggered under the weight of sloshing water casks. And there were four-wheeled electric cars. A heterogeneous populace all seemed to be wandering aimlessly in the streets and swinging prayer beads! As I picked my way among the legion of tables and chairs scattered over the sidewalk, slipped through the sewerage, collided with the polyglot crowd, and stumbled through swarms of flies, suddenly I bumped squarely into Mahoney. So fast was he moving that we had to embrace each other to keep from falling.

"Why hullo, matey," he shouted. "You're just in time to go to the banquet."

"The banquet?" I asked. "What foolishness is this?"

"Follow your Uncle Pat!" he commanded.

It was useless to resist. Fastening a mighty grip on my arm he dove into the crowd, knocking the people to right and left as he towed me along in his turbulent wake. Presently he stopped before a café, drew a fireman's cap from his shirt and laid it tenderly on top of the bristles of his red head, turned, and pushed me through and out into a beer garden in the rear. At sight of us some of the *Amphitrite*'s crew who had already assembled there burst into protracted cheering. I judged they had done considerable drinking within a comparatively recent time. Mahoney acknowledged the receptions by lifting his cap and bowing elaborately.

"Nine more beers," shouted the genial and grizzled old carpenter, Chips.

"Well, I thought you was a regular guy," called big Paul, whose face looked very large and very red tonight. "How much money have you got?"

"Haven't got any Greek money yet," I answered. "But I've still got some American."

"That's all right. We'll pay tonight. When we're broke, we'll change your kopecks. Hey waiter, bring nine vinos too — ya, cognac, that's it — vino!"

"Well," I thought to myself, "this is a long way from old Newburyport."

Pete was reeling on his feet sentimentally and ostentatiously proposing a toast to the American merchant marine, when a bottle skimmed by his head, smashed on the garden wall, and showered us with bits of broken glass.

"Limeys!" yelled Pete, blinking in a befuddled manner around the garden.

In those days most Europeans, especially English soldiers and sailors, still had a fairly well justified idea that all Americans thought they alone had won the war. Many waterfront brawls started as easily as this.

I stared across the garden, around the potted palms, toward a mixed group of sailors who were as inebriated as my companions and who glared back at us. As both groups rose to their feet a perfect fusillade of bottles and glasses rained upon the other sailors from some point behind me. Turning, I saw Mahoney with the lust of a fight shining in his eyes, his shirt opened to his hairy chest and a corner of his cap peeking out safely from within his underwear. He was snorting with artificial ferocity and hurling everything within reach promiscuously toward his current adversaries. Pete recovered from his stupor long enough to cry, "Come on! Up and at 'em, boys!" leap to the top of a nearby table, slip, fall awkwardly to the ground, and pass away into a dense bacchanalian blankness.

Louie, the big Russian fireman, lumbered rapidly forward. Presently Louie charged, or stumbled and failed to regain his balance; two men toppled to the ground and lay prone under his weight. Three more of our antagonists attempted to climb over the wall and two more dashed into the café, leaving a broad path of overturned tables, shattered glassware, and a horde of other sailors yelling and splashing about in puddles of wine and beer.

Someone began shouting for the police. The tumult was awful. I paused long enough to see Mahoney, with his jaw drenched in blood, lose his balance and collapse under the attack of a small and determined sailor. Then I fled, leaving the German carpenter hurling broken chairs at a solitary intoxicated seaman marooned halfway over the back wall, his body hanging headfirst on one side, his legs on the other.

Just as the police were arriving I wriggled through the crowd at the street entrance and ran down the road. Some distance further on I saw one of those antediluvian ancestors of the electric streetcar and ran on after it. Finally I caught up with the rear end as it bounced and jolted along a serpentine track, and I clambered onto the rear platform and clung to the door, panting. Only when the conductor began poking me to obtain the fare of one drachma, which providentially I did possess, did I recover sufficiently from excitement and fatigue to collect my senses.

At length I reached the end of the car line in the central marketplace and started out to walk the remainder of the distance to the ship. One or two carriages that trotted past me made me wish I had at least enough local currency to afford a ride when I was so tired. I was surfeited with sailors-ashore excitement for that night; my only ambition was to get back to my bunk. When I reached the towering stern of the *Amphitrite* I clambered up the rope hawsers that held her to the quay. Someone on the fantail steadied them for me as I wriggled along.

To my amazement, Mahoney himself helped me over the rail. He was breathing hard and mopping a cut on his chin with his shirttail.

"I thought you were knocked out and arrested in that gin mill," I panted.

"No, I sneaked out before the bobbies got there and just got aboard myself."

"Well, how?"

"Me? Oh, I hired a hack and then beat the driver running down the wharf. Cheap transit and good exercise combined, my boy!"

He sighed languorously, spat over the rail, and sauntered forward. And I sought out the messboy's room, quite disgusted with myself for a wasted evening.

The following day, Friday, I could think of nothing but a visit to Athens. From pictures, I knew it would prove to be a beautiful place — quite different from the port city of Piraeus with its shabby warehouse areas and waterfront slums and miserably poor people common to waterfronts. Moreover, I had already had enough of watching drunken sailors brawling in beer gardens. From now on I was determined to try to see the historical places that might become available in the course of this voyage and act more like a partially cultivated man than a bum. So I worked steadily all day at washing up the messroom and the fo'c's'le and even pared a couple of buckets of potatoes for Tom Meadows, who had made my new free time available by changing jobs with me.

Getting away from the *Amphitrite* as soon as supper was out of the way was no problem because everybody shared the same idea. By five-fifteen the messroom was empty and Bob and I were washing and wiping up the dishes. Because we had decided to visit Athens together, he had volunteered to help me get away quickly. Somehow, he felt that he would learn a little by going to Athens with me because his curriculum at Worcester Polytech had not included any classical studies. Five minutes later he and I were climbing into a bumboat and heading for the railroad station to go to Athens.

The ten-mile journey between Athens and Piraeus was

made in fifteen minutes in an electric train of small, low, four-wheeled open wooden cars. The train ran quietly and seemed to be very fast; the rush of air through the cars was delightfully cool. We felt as though we were traveling in an open crate. But the green plain across which we sped seemed perfectly beautiful — a level, irrigated country of small farms growing corn, grain, melons, and many types of vegetables.

Soon the Acropolis came into view — a rectangular body of dark stone rising high above the city and crowned with the familiar mass of graceful ruins on its crest. At first glimpse, one feels that one has seen it before, especially the Parthenon with its fluted Doric columns and western façade gleaming white in the late July afternoon sunlight. One senses that this is truly hallowed ground, and at once I felt a relationship with those clear-thinking ancient men and women who built the Greek civilization and whose works I had so recently been studying in college. I began to tingle with excitement.

We hurried toward the Acropolis as soon as the little train stopped at its terminal, steadily rushing up narrow streets and lanes in an effort to reach the top before the gates might be closed. With all our panting, sweating scramble over the cobblestones we found the iron gates locked.

Then an old woman in a black shawl and long black dress hanging to her ankles appeared from nowhere to sell us some postcards. For a few drachmas we each bought a quantity of cards that were better than any photographs we might have taken, and in gratitude she showed us where we could crawl under the fence and climb up to the top because all the guards had long since gone home to supper.

The view over the countryside from various directions was

awesome, especially in the mellow tones of light from the sunset. We gazed down silently toward the city and the almost perfectly preserved Theseum. In the side of a hill toward the sea were three black holes cut into the rock, the prison where Socrates was finally thrown for his heresies.

Just above the prison was a level place where Demosthenes conducted his school, which he taught while walking about in the open air. On the southern side we looked down directly into the very well preserved Odeum, or Theater of Herodes Atticus (which was partly built in a hollow in the side of the Acropolis).

In the gloom of the east I could see the Stadium, a long, well-preserved structure that looked exactly as I had expected it — not as high as American college stadiums in general but perhaps more graceful — and it could obviously be used today for field games as it had been some two thousand years ago. In the east there was also the Temple of Jupiter, little more than a cluster of columns today, a poorly preserved jumble of ruined stone since it was smashed by Turkish artillery in 1833. Everywhere were remnants of age-old glory — ruined temples, defaced monuments and tablets, traces of fountains, wells, and walls. Picking our way among the rubble we walked around to the western façade, where we sat down at the base of the beautifully preserved Erechtheum to watch the first twinkling of lights in the great city below.

At last we went down into the town, and the street debouched into the Square of Ceon, adjoining the graceful Theseum, the most perfectly preserved of all the old temples. On the side of the square opposite the temple there was a rather prosperous-looking restaurant with tables and chairs on the broad sidewalk in front of it, and to this we made our way. A waiter in a long white apron soon arrived with a bill of fare, but he could speak little English and we were having difficulty making it clear that we wanted a thirst-quenching rather than an alcoholic beverage. As we argued and explained without much success, two Greek gentlemen in light hot-weather suits and straw hats drew abreast of us on the sidewalk and stopped. Presently, one of them said, "May we be of help to you?"

"You certainly may," I replied. "We'd like something like a lemonade, and a big glass of it."

"Ah," he answered. "We have here a carbonated lemon and lime drink which is quite cheap and very good. May I order it for you?"

"Thank you so much," said I. "Would you by any chance be willing to join us?"

They looked at each other as if to say "why not," nodded, and then the older held out his hand. "My name is Peter Nicolopoulos, Nicholson translated into English, and this is my brother, Spyros. We have lived in England and so have some ability with the language. We will gladly join you, but only as your hosts."

Then began one of the most delightful evenings in my life up to that time. The brothers Nicolopoulos operated a department store in Athens and apparently were men of considerable means. They were a fertile fountain of fascinating information about modern and ancient Greece, knew their history well, and enjoyed talking about it. We each drank two large bottles of carbonated lemon and lime drink while the sunset faded out and night eventually hid the Acropolis and a light, sweet-smelling breeze wafted fragments of distant orchestral music played in a minor key. It sounded quite melancholy and romantic.

But eventually — it must have been as late as eight-thirty — Bob and I decided we should find the railroad terminal and take the next train back to Piraeus and the *Amphitrite*. I shall always remember Athens as it was in 1922 when it was less than a third the size it is now, but even then was memorably a clean, modern, and prosperous city, its streets paved with asphalt and its sidewalks of cement shaded by palm and locust trees. It looked neat and smelled good, resembling a Californian or Floridian city even then. I decided it was one place I should like to visit again and, in spite of a long passage of time, perhaps I may.

9. Pat Mahoney Leaves the Ship

THE QUALITY of resourcefulness is not altogether rare and it permits many people to enjoy life to a degree some never experience. My friend Mahoney had it in a highly developed state. Life was a joyous thing to him, although fraught with one crisis after another. My last memories of Pat Mahoney are etched in the outline of his bold resourcefulness.

On a Friday the *Amphitrite* lay in Piraeus all day, her stern made fast to the quay and her bow secured to a large mooring buoy some five hundred feet out in the harbor. She lay there tranquilly awaiting orders to unload her cargo of grain into lighters that would come alongside. Meanwhile, the crew had drawn half their wages due, as was the custom, and when not on duty they went to the town, some shinning down the stern lines and others being ferried to and fro in a native bumboat for a fare of one drachma.

In his rich mixture of Cockney and Irish brogue, "My gear is deplorable," Pat observed of his dungarees and shirt, although to me they looked to be in good condition. "I must have a new outfit before I go ashore this evenin'," he said, and went off in search of the third mate who had custody of the slop chest, that seagoing variety store carried in all deepwater ships for the convenience of the crew.

The slop chest purveyed articles of work clothing, shoes, tobacco, cigarettes, candy, oilskins, needles and thread, nearly everything a man needed on a long voyage. In the navy this establishment is known as the "Ship's Service Store" and is operated for the financial benefit of the Ship's Welfare Fund, to be spent for recreational and social purposes, and goods are priced at cost plus fifteen percent — or less. In the old merchant ship days it was never quite clear for whose financial benefit the slop chest was conducted. The prices were reasonable enough, slightly below the ordinary retail markup and without taxes. Even so, it was possible to run up a considerable debt, which could later be deducted from wages due. In those days a coal-burning fireman got sixty-five dollars a month. Were he not careful he would have a considerable portion of a month's wages deducted at the end of a voyage. But, after all, a gentleman is entitled to live as luxuriously as his income permits.

"If ye don't mind, Emery," Pat said later, "I'll not be taking you ashore with me tonight. D'ye see that big Limey rust-bucket down at the foot of the harbor? Well, that's one of the Clan Line pots an' I think I've got some friends aboard of her. I'm after goin' visitin' tonight."

So he elegantly descended the gangway and took a seat in

the stern sheets of the bumboat with all the dignity of a skipper. He was arrayed in a brand-new outfit from head to foot, labels still attached. New army shoes were on his feet, a new black-visored fireman's cap perched jauntily on the great mass of unshorn red hair, and he carried a new jumper on his arm. "It might turn chilly before I get back," he had explained.

I knew he had no intention of paying his bumboat fare and, sure enough, about halfway to the landing the boatman stopped pushing on the heavy oars and demanded his money. A noisy altercation ensued and might have continued indefinitely had not a couple of our Scandinavian sailors appeared at the gangway and begun shouting for transportation. Pat was quite unruffled when the bumboat put back. "Well," he called, " 'twill take a trip and a half to make it this time, Emery. Patience does it, my boy, patience!"

Pat didn't return to the ship that night. But next morning, Tuesday, at seven o'clock sharp, when the crew were about to have breakfast, there was a loud commotion on the quay. Pat was discussing terms to have himself conveyed back to the ship. "By the holy saints, I swear it," he bellowed, "I've got plenty of drachmas aboard the ship. You'll get your fare when I get back aboard."

Pat's appearance was remarkable. He was naked except for his underdrawers. Barefooted and bareheaded, thumping on his vast hairy chest and flailing his huge arms, he towered over the circle of screaming boatmen. Apparently he was well-known in Piraeus. It required no less than five minutes of vociferous bargaining to reach a settlement, which in itself was a notable achievement since Pat had nothing with which to bargain.

At length he appeared at the top of the gangway, dancing from one foot to the other on the hot steel plates. Since I was his friend he failed to notice me but his eye lighted on a generous Swede.

"Olsen, my dear boy, could you be loaning of a drachma to a shipmate?" he called to a seaman.

"Sure, Pat," Olsen said, "as much as you want."

"One is enough, my friend," said Pat. "And you may be sure I'll never forget your generosity."

Having thus reestablished his credit, probably to the surprise of the boatman who had pursued him up the ladder, Pat trotted forward to enjoy his breakfast.

Just before eight o'clock, Pat had again sought out the third mate and made a considerable purchase. He had also learned that the ship would cast off and sail for Salonika at nine o'clock. This intelligence agitated him a bit. I was sitting on the midship hatch when he joined me. "Emery," he said solemnly, "it's not a good thing for a man to be away from his home too long at a time. Now me, I've not seen dear old Liverpool for three years, it is. So I'm after leaving you. Mind your manners, keep a civil tongue in your head and your dukes up, and you'll grow up to be a happy man."

He might have dropped other pearls of wisdom but just then the third mate came along. "Mahoney," he shouted, "what are you doin' amidships? For'ard is where you belong."

Mahoney chuckled, patted me on the head, and ambled forward. The third mate looked worried. "He's overdrawn his wages due at the slop chest," he grumbled to me. "Guess I better get that gangway up before he jumps ship. Bosun," he shouted, "bosun, let's get this gangway up to the rail right now. We'll lower a ladder for the pilot when he gets here."

Each of the mates was a busy man at sailing time. The third mate's duties kept him on the bridge where he could not watch Mahoney as carefully as he would have wished. Pat obliged him, however, by sprawling out on number one hatch forward, serenely smoking a new pipe and keeping a new pound tin of tobacco hard by. He didn't appear to be a man about to launch an exciting new adventure.

In the general activity of casting off the lines and winching them in, with men furiously hauling, the winch and windlass thundering, and orders shouted through megaphones, Mahoney disappeared. I next saw him on the after well-deck, feverishly making a spare piece of line fast to a bit. Pat was already too late to reach the fantail where the lines were being hauled aboard. Then I heard profane shouting behind me as the third mate galloped down from the bridge, picking up a piece of board on his way, and racing aft. He was not quite quick enough. Pat had clambered over the rail and lowered himself down into a waiting bumboat — the only one in the flotilla where his credit was good. He pushed off from the ship with a mighty heave, pulled up a floorboard, and began to paddle vigorously while exhorting the boatman to supreme efforts. The ship's propeller began to churn. The third mate flung his club ineffectively after Pat in his bumboat and we slowly moved out into the harbor.

"You lousy, double-crossin' skunk, you Irish wampus!" the third mate yelled. And half to himself he called, "I'm ashamed to be an Irishman myself when I meet with the likes of him."

The last I saw of Pat Mahoney he had just leaped out of the boat at the landing and was running up the quay with the boatman in hot pursuit.

In such manner he ran out of our lives with all his wit and resourcefulness. I would miss him at the "Bible classes" and his shouted encouragement, whether needed or not, at the boxing exercises. Could we but have been shipmates a little longer I think I might have profited greatly and grown faster in worldly wisdom.

10. Salonika and the Greenhorn

WHILE OUR erstwhile shipmate Pat Mahoney was running up the quay with the bumboatman in close pursuit, the *Amphitrite* slowly rumbled out of the inner harbor of Piraeus. She passed the hospital and the cement factory on the opposite shore and soon was abreast of the tall round shaft, at the end of Salamis Island, commemorating the destruction of the Persian fleet by the Athenians in that narrow channel just 2400 years ago. As we steamed slowly by, I clung to the rail transfixed with excitement at the thought of the great battle fought in that small body of water.

Soon we dropped the pilot and gathered speed to our full deliberate ten knots, steering into a powerful easterly breeze of very hot, dry air.

Gray dawn found the *Amphitrite* in the long gulf approach-

ing the city of Salonika. At six o'clock, with the dew still glistening on the heavy foliage in the city streets, *Amphitrite*
stopped, let her chain roar out of the hawse pipe, and anchored on the eastern side of the bay a half mile off a large
flour mill, a modern brick building where at last she would
discharge her cargo of grain and slowly careen back to an even
keel.

In World War I, just four years earlier, Salonika had been
the Allied base for the Balkan campaign. A city of about two
hundred thousand people, now ninety percent Greek although
for almost five centuries (until 1912) it was Turkish, it is a
place of yellow-white buildings, red roofs, minarets, and
domes, all amply shaded by palm and locust trees growing
thickly everywhere.

When supper was over and cleaned up that evening most of
Amphitrite's crew piled into bumboats to go ashore at the
nearest landing, which was about a long mile from the city's
center marked by the white tower. This landing was on the
premises of a large beer garden–restaurant, with an outdoor
vaudeville stage called "Hanatoah," meaning "eastern," the
whole known as the "Parc Roi George."

The Parc Roi George seemed like a particularly beautiful
spot and was designed to represent a typical Levantine garden.
Although there would still be a couple of hours of daylight, I
decided to remain there that evening and visit the city itself
the following afternoon when I would have more time. So I
seated myself with my shipmates and ordered a dish of
"glace," which turned out to be lemon sherbet. After the sun
had set behind Olympus and it became dusk and the patrons
who had come to eat had finished their dinner, the stage of

Hanatoah began to glow with naked electric bulbs and an orchestra began to play. One could turn one's back on the orchestra and contemplate the bay and the lingering sunset, or one could face the stage curtain and study Hanatoah, who was painted as an ancient Greek stonemason with a huge nose and a wreath of holly decorating his angular brow.

The vaudeville show would have been more interesting to us had it not been delivered entirely in Greek. Even so, it kept one's attention. It had a few acts of pantomime, some acrobatic and tumbling stunts, several vocal efforts at classical music by two attractive ladies, and was concluded by the antics of a troupe of clowns, one of whom was arrayed to represent an American Indian. This act elicited tremendous laughter and applause from the patrons and I wished I could understand what it was all about.

On the fourth day in Salonika I had an accident that terminated my sightseeing activities for ten days. It also terminated my boxing exercises with the second mate for the same period.

While carelessly filling a tureen to carry back from the galley to the messroom, I spilled a ladle of scalding soup on my left foot. It raised a blister that soon broke and became infected from my black sock. By the following morning it throbbed with pain, had turned black and red, and began to suppurate at the edges. Quite alarmed, I sought the services of the mate.

"Ah yes," he said, "you got the beginning of an infection and it's a good thing you got sense enough to come to me before it gets any worse. Go out and sit on number three hatch and keep your shoe and stocking off and I'll come out with the saw and cut it off for you."

He laughed and I smiled dubiously.

Several of the crew were always hanging around the midship hatch because it was near the fiddley as well as the galley, so we had an audience.

"Now, this may hurt you a bit," said the mate, waving a surgeon's saw that he had extracted from the medicine chest.

The audience pressed closer, round-eyed and with mouths agape. Mr. Schultz examined my foot soberly.

"Well, after looking it over, I think we'll postpone the amputation until after dinner. And now we'll treat it with iodine. This may hurt a bit, too, Emery," he said, "so maybe you want a towel to bite on?"

"No, I guess I can stand it, sir. Whether it hurts or not, I'm grateful for your help."

"Good!"

First, he washed the wound with a hot solution of phenol, studied it a bit, and then poured a few drops of iodine into it. I winced but said nothing, having decided to faint before I would complain before a half-dozen shipmates who, I suspected, might be amused to see me cry out in pain.

"Good boy," said Mr. Schultz. "I know that hurt. Now I'll just put on some salve and cover it lightly and it will slowly heal. I think the infection will stop, but don't you put on a shoe and you come to see me again right after supper."

Since the infection covered most of the top of my foot, it was difficult to devise any kind of footwear that wouldn't irritate it. I covered the soft compress on the top with a white sock that I bought out of the slop chest and then wrapped it in burlap tied around my ankle with rope yarn. This improvised wrapping helped me to walk on the blistering hot steel deck, but it wouldn't have stood much stress had I tried to walk ashore with it. So, to compound my misery and frustrations I had to confine myself to the ship.

After a few days I became submerged in self-pity. Each day after supper when nearly everybody went ashore I used to lean over the rail and watch the refuse float by on the tide — a typical sailor's pastime. It was always quiet except for the normal noises on the ship. As the heat diminished, in the cooler air the contracting deck plates of the ship occasionally snapped and rumbled. And all the flotsam drifting out to the empty sea fascinated me. I became very sorry for myself because it didn't occur to me that most people live perpetually with disappointments that they have learned to surmount.

One evening I stood by the gangway ladder watching the crew fight for places in the only bumboat alongside at the time. There wasn't room for everybody, and presently Frenchy, the pantryman, was eliminated in the struggle for survival of the most aggressive. It was his usual misfortune, and he clambered slowly up the ladder to lean on the rail beside me and gaze bitterly at the city as its lights began to twinkle. He seemed ready to weep.

The bumboat pulled away with the crew still jostling and shoving each other, shouting like a gang of buccaneers. Presently Frenchy moved away and Pete came and stood beside me. Pete was thinner than ever and he looked worried and sick. He should be, for he had got drunk in Algiers and spent the night in a house of prostitution and now he had a first-class venereal infection.

"Well," he began, "you ain't as bad off as I am. You'll be all right in a few days but the mate says I'll never again be as good as I was."

"I don't know what to tell you," I replied. "I'm no authority on venereal diseases, and this last month I've lived with more of it than I thought existed in the whole world. But you're supposed to feel better after the first symptoms clear up."

"You're not much help," he growled. "Look, here comes that damn frog again."

Frenchy rushed out of the forward house with his bulging eyes agleam with eagerness. "Hey, Emery, you want go rowing with me?"

I looked at the poor man, so pitiful in his enthusiasm, and felt a peculiar sense of compassion, which was odd, because I had been thinking of little but myself recently. As he stood there so pathetically I thought back to the morning off Quebec City on which he first came over the side, tall, thin as a rail, and with a hungry, bilious expression on his pinched face. A rather unexpected odor of violet perfumery exuded from his stylish, tailor-made suit, which was cut from a Parisian pattern, and his fedora perched awkwardly on top of an oversized head. He looked like a post surmounted by a pumpkin. The steward was with him, and the first sound he made was an insipid cackle exchanged for one of the steward's witticisms.

Emile, or Frenchy, as everyone chose to call him, did not really distinguish himself until the *Amphitrite* ran into the storm off the Grand Banks. In North Sydney, to be sure, he had achieved a ludicrous notoriety by attempting to entertain on board ship a girl whom he had found at a soda fountain. Even then the matter would have attracted no attention had not the steward locked Frenchy in the pantry and entertained the girl himself.

But when the *Amphitrite* began to roll and toss in the cold

fog of the Banks he became a memorably unsanitary spectacle.
For two days, except for the night on the boat deck, he
sprawled in front of the fiddley door groaning and retching, a
cumbersome nuisance, a pitiful horror, this brassy creature
who had boasted, "I won't be sick. I am very good sailor."

"Huh, you're a great sailor," the steward jeered. "What did
you come to sea for?"

"For my health," Frenchy moaned.

"For his health! Ho! Look, he came to sea for his health!
That's what we go ashore for."

And we all laughed abusively while Frenchy squirmed in
wretchedness at our feet.

When the storm diminished and Frenchy recovered, like
the rest of us, he began to exhibit his aggressive qualities. One
night he tempted the mythical Howling Cerberus by invading
the skipper's holy place and requesting that the foghorn be
shut off as it disturbed his sleep. His naiveté was monumental,
and he had little sense of discipline or of the proprieties because he had been brought up as the only boy in a family of
seven girls. Since we were quartered in the same room with
two others I had a good opportunity to observe his habits. He
was essentially modest, completely honest, and a thoroughly
decent young man, but the rest of us simply could not understand why he loved to sprinkle himself with very feminine-
smelling perfumes, to fuss with his clothes, and to take an afternoon nap in sensual-looking silk pajamas. The rest of us
napped in our working clothes with our shoes on. But a sailor
in blue silk pajamas! Oh, Mother Amphitrite, what an enor-
mity! Little wonder that the sailors dubbed this greenhorn,
"the French whore."

I felt genuinely sorry for him; I wondered if I could help

him grow out of some of his old practices and earn a place of respect in this brutally masculine world into which he had thrust himself. So when he rushed out of the passageway to the mate's room in the forward house and implored me as much with his eyes as with his words — "Hey, Emery, you want go rowing with me?" — I was inclined to be helpful. I looked at him quizzically.

"What are you going to use for a boat?" I asked.

"The mate, he give me leave take old man's boat."

"Well, do you know how to row?"

"Nooo," he smiled self-consciously, "you going teach me."

Pete and I laughed.

"All right," I replied, "I hope you'll have a good time. Come on."

In true greenhorn fashion Frenchy descended the broad steps of the ladder backward, I limped down after him, Pete behind me. I pulled the boat up to the staging and steadied it, a trim fourteen-foot jollyboat with a square stern, lapstreak siding, and an immaculate coat of white paint with varnished trim.

"Well, come on, row this thing," Pete called from his seat in the bow.

Frenchy established himself in the middle seat to row and I sat in the stern and shipped the tiller. I pushed away from the ladder and Frenchy attempted to run out his oars. It soon became apparent that he had never rowed anything in his life.

"All right, Emile," I attempted to palliate his growing frustration, "take it easy and run them out at the same length on each side. Now lean forward, dip them in the water only to the top of the blade, and pull slowly toward you. Don't put the blades in so deep. That's right. Now, keep your hands together. Lift them out and lean forward again. That's right."

Try hard as he would, the learning process was slow. His oars repeatedly jerked out of the oarlocks, he twisted and caught his blades under the water, he splashed and drenched all three of us. But Pete and I didn't care and enjoyed the fun. I steered the jollyboat toward the old fort on the point to the southward of the flour mill off which *Amphitrite* lay. We were curious to see this old ruin that had been built and manned by the Turks when they held Salonika before 1912.

"Wait a minute," Pete called back from the bow when we were within a few hundred yards of the shore. "Wait. What did the mate say about an old minefield for landing parties here?"

"Said it was off the tip of the point, didn't he?" I answered.

"I think it comes around here on the inner side also," he said. "They're pretty shallow, you know. We could see 'em breakin' the surface when it was rough the other day. Fat chance we've got if we strike one."

"I don't think we need to worry," I reasoned. "This field was laid several years ago and I'll bet it's disarmed itself by now. Let's keep on a bit."

Frenchy continued splashing us nearer and nearer. Seeing a small landing and a signal station near the old British barracks I turned the jollyboat toward it. Then a surprising thing happened. We were probably two hundred yards away when suddenly a shot rang out on the shore and a bullet sang over our heads in the deepening dusk. Frenchy stopped rowing and turned to look across our bow.

"Keep it up, Frenchy," I commanded.

Before he could take another stroke a second shot sang over us. As we lay on the water indecisively a fusillade of shots rang out and whined all about us. At the same time someone ran up a red lantern on the flagpole at the landing; in its glow we could see men waving their arms frantically and hear their incoherent shouts in the dark. The Greek soldiers manning this post had finally made their objections to our coming closer quite clear to us. Just as I started to tell Frenchy how to turn the boat around Pete stood bolt upright in the bow, trembling as if he had a chill. His voice was strained and thick, "Emery, you damn fool! Get us out of this! For God's sake."

Then Frenchy was seized with panic. He dropped his oars and fell forward to grasp my knees. His fear had rendered him totally inarticulate. Although I still didn't believe we were in any danger from mines, the rifle shots disturbed me, but I retained enough composure to recognize that the oars were in the water and drifting away.

Viciously I pushed Frenchy away and leaned out of the boat just in time to catch one oar with the tip of my fingers. With it I reached the other, and shipped them in the oarlocks. By this time the bullets whined steadily and the shouting continued. Frenchy seemed paralyzed by fear and his bulging eyes rolled with terror.

"Come on, Frenchy," I began. "Get back on your seat. Hold your right oar steady in the water and row with your left. Don't dig deep."

He grasped the oars but didn't move.

Then I lost my composure all at once. I wrenched the tiller from the rudderpost and waved it over Frenchy's head.

"You get to work fast," I yelled, "or I'll smash your head and throw you overboard!"

Frenchy shivered and began to turn the boat as I had explained to him. Then he dug straight down and nearly lost his right oar. At the same time something bumped heavily against the bow. Pete shrieked and fell over backward in a dead faint. Frenchy stopped again and looked at me with horror in his eyes.

"Now, Frenchy, do you want to live forever?" I asked calmly. "If that had been a mine we wouldn't still be here, would we? Stop worrying and pull yourself together, boy. I can row this boat out to the ship and you can, too. We've got a lot of time and you haven't had much practice rowing yet, either. Now, come on!"

He took another stroke and a waterlogged beam slowly slid astern.

"See, Emile," I encouraged him, "that was only an old log. We're in no danger except maybe from those fools ashore and that's because I'm afraid of their marksmanship."

He didn't speak but he continued rowing. The firing ashore and the whining bullets soon ceased. Splashing, missing strokes, catching crabs, jerking his oars from the oarlocks, he zigzagged out toward the open bay where the *Amphitrite* swung at her anchor, an indistinct blotch against the lingering western light toward Mount Olympus. With each stroke, Frenchy's courage returned bit by bit. So did his self-confidence.

"Emery," he said after a time, "do we have to stop this little trip now?"

"Not as far as I'm concerned," I replied, "unless maybe Pete's had enough."

Pete replied from the floorboards in the bow where he had recovered from his fainting spell and made himself comfortable, "No, I'm in no hurry, now that we're out of that damn minefield." Then he added, "What damn fools we were to get mixed up in something like that."

"It was my fault," I said. "Just the same it doesn't reflect much credit on any of us. We knew we had no business trying to land at an army post. And I think we'd better not say anything about it unless we're asked."

Frenchy spoke up again, "Well, Emery, if we don't go back to ship now, will you please row. Both my hands are sore."

After that row in the captain's boat, Frenchy's self-confidence flourished to an unprecedented degree. He borrowed the boat almost every evening, even finally daring to go out alone if he couldn't find a companion. His self-assertiveness grew also and he put away the silk pajamas, although he couldn't get along without his perfumery.

"What is difference," he would say. "Everybody puts good smelling lotion on his face after he shaves. Well, I like smell good to myself."

The greenhorn was growing slowly into an awkward conformity with the other men, possibly catching up on a delayed maturity. A couple of weeks later off the coast of Cyprus one evening he acknowledged his awareness of the changes that were taking place in him. "You know, Emery, this ship she is hell afloat, but I think she is best thing ever happen to me."

11. Sailors Ashore — Brawls and Misadventures

EVENTUALLY, after ten days, my foot had healed enough so that I could wear a pair of white sneakers that Bob had bought for me in a shoe store in the city. If I didn't try to exert myself or walk too fast I could again get about without much pain or interference with the healing process. So I used to take the electric car up to the White Tower after supper and wander on the waterfront watching the small sailing vessels that were secured stern first to the quay. Many were schooner-rigged, but some were square-rigged brigs and brigantines, and I enjoyed tracing their running rigging against the sky.

My leisurely progress one evening brought me to Hanatoah about nine o'clock when it was in full swing. The vaudeville show was going on and the place was comfortably full, many of the crew of *Amphitrite* being present and in an inebriated condition, to put it politely. As I approached the restaurant area I was intercepted by two of our petty officers — Hugo, the deck engineer whose main job was to look after the winches and auxiliary machinery, and Sammy, a Greek oiler. They were returning from the lavatory and in a mood to continue their search for euphoria. I joined them at their table in the shadows at the outer edge where we could watch the performance without being too conspicuous.

Near us two tables were occupied by some of our black gang. One table was headquarters for four Mexican firemen, three of whom were slightly dazed and in a comatose state while the other had an irresistible impulse to participate in the show and had to be forcibly hauled back each time he staggered toward the stage. Two of the A.B.s, Paul and Edwin, sat at a table by themselves near another occupied by the steward, the second engineer, and the third mate, who seemed bewildered and inarticulate and was buying Paul and Edwin glasses of cognac as fast as they could consume them.

Soon another of the *Amphitrite's* men appeared, Louie, the big Russian fireman. Louie was dressed in a dirty white shirt and a cap that hung precariously on the back of his head. He rolled along with his head thrust forward and a straight black pipe clenched in his teeth. His arms swung almost down to his knees and in each paw he carried two bottles of whiskey and cognac. One of the bottles was half empty and it was easy to surmise where the rest of it was by the manner in which Louie weaved across the front of the stage in full view of the entire audience. This spectacle struck Hugo as very humorous, and he laughed long and loud enough to drown out the vocal efforts of the two ladies trying to sing on the stage.

At the same time the other firemen caught sight of Louie and his bottles and shouted until he joined them. Louie lurched to a chair, placed his bottles on the table where they loomed up like monuments, and proceeded to share the half-empty bottle with the others as it was passed around. After a while two of the firemen slid off their chairs to assume a recumbent posture on the ground. Then Louie discovered our table and covered a good deal of space while negotiating the few feet separating us in order to demonstrate his generosity. Sammy took a long, gurgling draught and soon became more garrulous than ever.

Louie then proceeded to visit Paul and Edwin who obliged him by taking a liberal potation. Next he arrived at the officers' table. At first they offered excuses. But Louie demonstrated the liquor's quality.

"See, it's all right," he shouted several times as he adjusted the bottle to his lips.

This proof having allayed any suspicions of contamination, the third mate decided to take a drink, and the bottle gurgled ominously before it was lowered. But the steward consistently refused — he'd had enough, he said — and Louie moved down to sway in front of the stage for a better view of a juggling act. Soon he returned to his table, bottle in hand, after wandering through most of the restaurant area, and discovered that his two remaining bottles had disappeared. Nobody seemed to know anything about this pilferage and all the firemen who were still sitting upright maintained a mute silence. But not Louie. He shouted threats and obscenities, promised to wreck the place, scared two waiters out of their wits, chased the manager and the bouncer into the dressing rooms behind the stage, and completely disrupted the show until he finally sat down quietly by himself at a distance from all of us and proceeded to imbibe the contents of his last bottle before he disappeared altogether.

While this was going on, in another part of Parc Roi George Paul and Hugo put their heads together and contrived to procure some drinks without paying for them. They installed themselves at a bar on the other side of the place and ordered two whiskeys for a starter. More followed. At length they were presented with a bill. Ah, how to pay! Paul had no money; "Deck" did not remember ever having had any. Then Deck had an idea; the captain will pay for the drinks.

"Send the bill to him," said Deck, pointing out the steward.

This temporarily appeared to satisfy the bartender and the two carousers tottered off.

All this time I had remained at my table seated with Sammy, surrounded by the dishes of three "glaces" apiece that we had consumed. Across the front of the stage, group after group of *Amphitrite*'s crew sauntered past on their way from the town to the landing. Finally the captain, the chief engineer, and the ship's agent paraded wearily by and seated themselves at a front table. Soon the Parc's manager accosted the captain with the bar bill incurred by Paul and Deck. The culprits were identified and the captain agreed to advance the money for the bill, thereby winning points for good conduct by the crew.

The third cook, Tom Meadows, staggered in under the influence of much more cognac than he could manage. He discovered the firemen and joined them. Then he discovered me, crossed over to borrow some money, but upset the table as

soon as he arrived. With a terrific clatter the dishes and enameled metal tabletop flew in all directions. Sammy was
knocked over backward in his chair among the spoons and
plates and Tom fell on top of him. The waiter helped us find
our dishes and the tabletop and I paid the bill. Remembering
the disastrous brawl in Piraeus a few weeks ago, I decided the
police would be summoned fairly soon and I had better clear
my decks to get back to the ship. But we didn't need to leave
just then.

When next I looked for the third cook he was lying on the
ground, stretched out full-length under the firemen's table
while the steward was attempting to revive him. Abandoning
the effort, the steward picked him up, slung him over his
shoulder with hands and feet dangling fore and aft, and carried him off to the landing.

In another section of the Parc, the second mate, the third
mate, and some engineers had by this time become quite hilarious, to describe their condition by an understatement. There
was a warm discussion that all enjoyed because all talked at
the same time. Then the two mates became so incensed with
each other's point of view that they started a fistfight, but
were immediately separated by the engineers. Finally, after
vociferous apologies and much handshaking they started removing the enameled tabletops and rolling them about the
premises like hoops. Pandemonium and disorder were ram-
pant all over the Parc as other patrons joined the fun while
some became frightened and began to leave. This time
Sammy and I quietly left and walked the short distance to the
landing where we soon embarked for the *Amphitrite* with the
skipper and the chief.

"Well, sonny," asked the captain, "what do you think of all these drunken sailors ashore?"

"They don't seem to have grown up. I just can't compete, sir," I replied.

He laughed. "That's one way to look at it. I notice you know when to get out of a place, too. Don't try to compete with these fellows, boy. Don't get mixed up with them too closely."

Next day I piously wrote in my diary, "Of course, in the opinion of the natives all Americans are similar to these unrepresentative drunken sailors. No wonder we increasingly lack respect in foreign countries."

The next evening I wrote a long letter to my mother and decided to take it directly to the post office and mail it. It was quite dark when the bumboatman rowed me in and I mused contemplatively on the beauty of the scene.

Splash, splash — the boatman's strokes beat a steady rhythm as he rowed toward the blackness of the shore and the flickering lights of the harborfront cafés. Splash, splash — I dreamed as the bumboat slid through the quivering water — from the great deep to another great deep, from the mystery of the outer ocean, of the long sweep and the heavy swell to the mystery of this strange yellow city on the mountainside, seething with the emotions of ordinary people in their struggle to exist. Splash, splash — the shore lights grew larger; now they illuminated contiguous objects in progression, dimly, plainly, brilliantly, with a grotesque effect of mingling shadows and distorted proportions. Stronger and stronger grew that stale, piercing stench as of open cesspools or gutter sewerage common to many Mediterranean cities of that time.

Gradually, the square, pyramid-roofed buildings of the city became visible, the locust trees with their leaves all aglitter with reflected light, portions of streets and people walking in them; now the interior of the beer gardens and the puppet shows, now the yellow, crumbling plaster wreaths that garnished the window frames. Bump — the boat touched the little landing and I was ashore.

As I passed the boatman a two-drachma note he smiled wearily and wished me a pleasant evening, "Kale nihto, Kyrie."

"Kale nihto, Kyrie," — "Good evening, mister."

I walked up toward the street along the end of the Parc Roi George and felt in the hip pocket of my dungarees for the sixth time to ascertain that the letter to my mother was still there. Being reassured for the sixth time, I raised my eyes to look across the clutter of tables in the Parc toward the outdoor stage, Hanatoah. At this little distance it all looked quite attractive. A melodious tintinnabulation jangled softly through the trees from the orchestra to mingle with a hum of voices and a tinkling of glasses, a sound vaguely reminiscent of light rain pattering on the surface of smooth water. Bright lights, the glitter of rhinestone jewelry, the whiteness of bare arms and shoulders were dazzling me, as if I were half awake somewhere near a garden pool upon which rain was falling, where people were laughing merrily on the other side. Should I stay? Or should I get on with the business of mailing my mother's letter?

As I paused, a familiar voice called my name, "Hey, Emery!"

Not far away I saw Sparks, the radio officer, seated alone at a table. He was only a few years older than I, tall, good-looking, and intelligent, with all the openness of the Nebraska plains in his face.

"Come over and have a beer with me," he cried.

"I think I better get down to the post office and mail my mother's letter," I replied.

"All right. See you when you come back."

On past the lights I walked, on among the vine-grown trunks of the trees; into the denser shadows of the outer garden I moved through the fragrance of flowers. Presently, I reached the gate and stepped out into the vile-smelling street.

It seemed as if I had walked a long distance when I stopped daydreaming abruptly. Actually, I had walked but a few hundred yards from the gate to this boisterous crowd that I suddenly encountered. Under a streetlight they jabbered and yelled, attracted by a common object of interest in their center. My natural curiosity provoked me to shove my way in so that I could see better. Of all the sights! I joined in the laughter of the mob. For there was Mike Lang, the oldest of *Amphitrite*'s coal passers, flat on his stomach, propelling himself down the gutter with a swimming motion. He would squirm a few feet forward, turn on his side, take a draught from a bottle of cognac that he carried in his hip pocket, and then start off again on the breaststroke. He was an amazing sight — covered with dust, spotted with dirt, and soaked in sweat.

"Hullo, Mike," I shouted, slapping him on the back, "how's the water?"

He stopped his exertions at once and turned his grizzled face up toward mine. He was a short man, muscular, covered with hair all over his body, and his chest was enormous. His mind was uncoordinated with anything.

"Huh," he grunted. "Say, been swimmin' all night — ain't got out to that — that bloody coal hod — yet. Where is she — tha's the trouble. Dogs! Couldn't get aboard of a 'lectric car to save me shirt so, says I, there's nothin' but to swim. Well — here I be."

"Come on, Mike, get up and walk," I said. "I'll take you back to the bumboat wharf."

"Huh! Emery, yer — ye — damn nice guy — but I'll get there quicker swimmin'."

I raised him, lifted him to the cobblestone sidewalk, steadied his steps. The crowd began to move away, vanishing in all directions. In a few minutes we were nearly alone, stumbling, reeling, staggering through the darkness of the hot July night from one streetlight to another.

"I won't walk, damn ye, I won't. Go ahead, Emery — yer good guy. Me legs ache terrible. Let me dive off here. I'll show ye. Let me swim. No! By God, I'll kill ye. Leggo me arm!"

He struggled as his gray eyes, shot through with red streaks, clotted with white scum in the corners, blinked eagerly up into mine. His voice whined and grated.

"Come on, let me dive off here. Just once?"

Oh, well, I thought, perhaps another good jolt will sober him up, so I released his arm. One, two, three — thud! He landed flat on his chest on the cobblestones. Just at that moment a clamorous crashing and clanking sounded up the street, growing louder and louder as it rapidly moved toward us. It sounded like a Greek army patrol wagon — and it was

— a battered, squealing Ford lorry that the British army had abandoned four years before. With a screech and a clang, perilously close to Mike's head, it rattled down to a stop and a whole provost guard of Greek soldiers piled out of the rear, half enveloped in the darkness and a cloud of dust and vapor from the exhaust.

With a great deal of conversation, they lifted Mike from the road and pitched him into the van, while I prepared to resume my walk to the post office. As I turned away I felt a grasp laid on my shoulder. Did they think me intoxicated, too? Was I to be arrested?

"Pardon, monsieur," I politely explained, "je suis sober — pas ivre. Savvy?"

They did not "savvy," but surrounded me and attempted to push me into the van. I resisted, and shook off their clutches. Then, out of the corner of my eye, I saw one of them raise his rifle to club me from behind. I ducked and the blow caught one of the other soldiers and knocked him sprawling. Then from behind I was hit a solid blow on the head and shoulder! A light seemed to explode and I fell, not quite unconscious, and found myself lying on the ground, bleeding from a scalp wound and aching. I recall being dragged over the stones and thrown into the van on top of Mike. Then I became aware of the old vehicle jolting and pounding as it climbed up through the city.

At last it stopped and the silence was heavy. I had regained most of my senses as I was pushed out of the van into an open place. At once I knew where I was — it was the walled yard of the medieval fortress prison of Yedi-Coulé. The thought was most discomforting for I had heard stories to the effect that prisoners might lie there for months awaiting trial.

Presently, another squad of four soldiers came and pushed me away. We passed from the clear starlight into a broad low doorway in the base of the great tower, into a putrid warmth, into dismal stone corridors that reverberated with our footsteps. Down damp stone stairways we went, down into the bowels of the hill. At last we stopped before a solid iron door. One of the guards fumbled with a ponderous key that didn't seem to fit the lock. At last the door creaked open and I was shoved into a small stone cell where I sort of fell down on two planks that I saw in the light of the lantern. Then someone fastened a heavy something around my ankle and I lost consciousness before they locked the door.

While I slept a nightmare seized me. I dreamed that an indistinct incarnation of evil was hovering in the murk by the door, leering at me with red eyes and stretching poisonous claws toward me. Reality or fantasy, it was utterly frightful. I could not see it so much as feel its presence — suffocating, consuming me. My heart raced like an engine out of control and I awoke trembling and aching.

A very dim light filtered through a tiny barred window above the door, filling the cell with a pallid murk. Morning must have arrived. I looked about the tiny place, which was scarcely eight feet square and as high. I was lying on two six-foot planks raised at one end by a billet. Near my feet stood a square, five-gallon oil can — the latrine. Everything was damp and moldy, but I knew I would not suffocate, even though the hole stunk like a sewer, nauseating and rank enough to take away one's breath. Then I discovered that my right foot was shackled to the wall at the end of a fairly long chain. That frightened me and I closed my eyes again, while my head and shoulder throbbed with pain.

While my mind was racing through a jumble of ideas to relieve my predicament I heard footsteps in the corridor and the door squeaked on its hinges. A burly soldier handed me a can of a thin bean soup and a generous chunk of black bread, which had a chafflike consistency but tasted good. This surprised me because I had not expected to be fed well when the army was trying to feed swarms of completely destitute refugees who were crowding in every day from Smyrna. It gave me hope and I felt calmer.

After the guard had returned, taken the soup can, and locked the door again I began to examine my injuries. Feeling the great ridge that the rifle butt had raised along my skull over my right ear, I discovered that it had been bleeding, that my hair was matted, and my torn blue shirt was still sticky with black congealed blood. No, my shoulder was not broken but it was badly bruised and almost numb with pain. I had to lie on my back and I thought how fortunate I was that my left foot had healed from its infection.

The enforced rest and absolute quiet were an ideal prescription to help me recover rapidly from my injuries. After I had lain there for hours, sleeping most of the time, toward nightfall when the light from the inner corridor had nearly failed, an elderly guard brought me more soup and bread. In the light of his lantern I could see in his eyes and by his demeanor that he felt sorry for me. Uttering a few softly spoken words in Greek, he went away wishing me a good evening, "Kale nihto, Kyrie."

I slept all night, still plagued by the same nightmare, but it was not so horrible as before. Then I heard marching footsteps coming down the corridor. It couldn't be a guard sent to

fetch me for I had adjusted my expectations to incarceration
for at least several days more. But it was for me. Clank!
With a screech the great iron door swung open and I saw
three soldiers slouching outside. A corporal entered, unlocked
the shackle on my foot, and reached down to help me up.
Feeling as if I had been pulled from a sickbed, I followed the
corporal out of that stench into the moist tepid air of the corridor. The two privates fell in step behind, and we marched
briskly back up all those stone steps and corridors until we
arrived in the guardroom.

My captain and the American consul sat with the commandant of the prison. They all looked very grave when they
saw me, and the captain pursed his lips and wagged his head.

"Fine, Major," said the consul in Greek to the military
warden, "now where's the other one?"

At that moment an outrageous burst of waterfront profan-
ity sounded far down the passage. Soon Mike appeared —
such a sight! The captain laughed aloud and the others
grinned. Mike stood before us, naked except for a garment
resembling ladies' silk panties.

"Ye know what the bloody bastards done?" he shouted at
once. "Put me in a yard with forty other bums an' they stole
every bleedin' thing I had on! It's a bloody shame, I say. I
want me rights! Where's me dungarees? I ain't goin' out in
the street in only the drawers what somebody stole off'n some
old whore so's they wouldn't have to send me up here in me
bare arse!"

"Did somebody see them take us away?" I asked the consul.

"Yes," he replied. "It's a cut and dried pattern. Happens

to just about every ship that comes in here so we know just where to find people who disappear."

Then he added, "You'd better get back to your ship and take our friend with you. I think I'll get a carriage for you because I don't want either of you showing up in public in your present condition."

He and the captain shook hands with the commandant, exchanged felicities, and let us out into the street where he engaged a carriage, took down the driver's license number, ordered him to take us to the Parc Roi George, and paid the fare in advance. After our recent experience we really enjoyed the luxury of riding down through the baking hot streets in the July sun. We did attract many curious stares as we drove along, and Mike brazenly enjoyed the sensation he caused.

When we arrived at the Parc we were both hungry, and since breakfast had long ago been cleaned up aboard *Amphitrite* we managed to get something at Hanatoah. Because I still had my money intact, I was able to buy Mike four bottles of beer and a box of very good local cigarettes, so that when we climbed up the ladder to *Amphitrite*'s shelter deck, Mike felt so good that he marched around the hot deck exhibiting his costume. He became somewhat of a temporary celebrity. As for me, I determined to go ashore again that evening, but I would take no less than two other shipmates, of the sober variety, to act as a bodyguard and assure that I would finally get my mother's letter mailed.

12. On to Cyprus

ON THE MORNING of our last day in Salonika we hoisted anchor and steamed over to the inner harbor formed by a mile-long breakwater and tied up to one of the long quays that ran out from the shore at right angles to it — the customhouse pier. Our spirits were high because we had been told we were to sail in ballast directly for Boston. And it was a great convenience to walk down a gangplank when one wanted to go ashore. Soon we began to take on water and provisions while the winches rattled and clanked and the great red buckets of grain swung up from the depths of *Amphitrite*'s holds to be dumped into lighters alongside. The last of the grain would soon be gone.

That evening Gus brought aboard a gray cat and installed him in his own berth in the sailors' fo'c's'le. The cat was obviously accustomed to ships because he acted completely at home from the first, found his way into the messroom, and voraciously ate up the remnants of some roast beef that Gus provided from the "shack" locker. He then investigated the stray pup that Gus had also brought aboard earlier and that was now stretched out under Paul's bunk in some distress, having made himself sick by eating too much too fast.

"Hey, Gus, what for you want so many animals aboard?" Paul objected.

"Well, I only got one of each," said Gus.

"Aw ya," Paul continued, "and the firemen got a nice black kitty up in their place, and the old man has a cute little brown pup, and if the mate hadn't put Tescula's lousy dog ashore this afternoon we wouldn't have enough to eat ourselves."

He alluded to an obviously unsuitable little cur brought aboard by Tescula just after the noon meal. The animal was sickly and very dirty; moreover, it had a white coat and anybody should know that a white animal does not properly belong in a ship. But when it demonstrated that it was not housebroken by committing a nuisance just outside the mate's door, Mr. Schultz forthwith ordered Frenchy to carry it far up into town before turning it loose. At least the dog had consumed a good meal before it was banished.

That last evening at supper we noticed a strong, brackish taste to the water.

"Oh, well," we said, "some damn engineer turned the wrong valve and put boiler water into the drinking water line. It'll clear up."

That night some strange events occurred aboard *Amphitrite*. The night was hot and sultry alongside the pier, and we missed the breeze that usually cooled us down when we had lain at anchor in the open bay. I was sitting on the boat deck with Bill Nadeau, the old second cook, and Sparks just outside the radioman's shack. About ten o'clock we heard a truck stop on the pier close to the ship and just abaft the afterhouse. Bill Nadeau walked across the deck and peered down from the shadow of the davits of one of the boats. He stood there quite a while before he quietly returned to us and said, "If you want to see somethin', come with me."

We cautiously followed him back to the edge of the deck and looked down. There on the pier and in the forward corner of the ship's after well-deck were several Greek laborers and Scotty, the chief cook. They were lowering slings of canned food, quarters of frozen beef, crates of eggs and chickens, and other stores of provisions. After a half hour, during which we remained completely silent, the ship's steward appeared from the refrigerated storeroom, leaned over the rail, and softly called down, "That's it. Take it away fast." The truck started up and drove away up the pier, and Scotty and the steward locked up the storerooms and were heard no more.

Sparks, Bill Nadeau, and I were almost too dumfounded to talk, but Bill said, "Well, I guess the less said the better. It ain't any of our business yet, but it might be, so I think we better keep it to ourselves."

That was not the last of the strange events that night. An hour later the captain chanced to leave his cabin to walk on the dock, possibly to try to cool off before attempting to sleep. We watched him walk down the gangway to the pier and start up toward the ship's bow. Suddenly he stopped, and then we noticed something we had not seen before. A horse-drawn dray was standing under the flare of the ship's bow and a long, brand-new six-inch hawser was being snaked out of the bosun's stores just abaft the chain locker under the firemen's fo'c's'le. The captain began to shout, the movement of the hawser ceased, and soon the mate appeared at the gangway. From our vantage point above on the boat deck we saw the bosun and Victor quietly sneak by in the darkness of the far side of the deck and make their way aft.

There was a commotion on the dockside as the captain ordered the dray to unload the hawser, which it did by driving away while the line uncoiled out of the rear end. The mate went aft and turned out the sailors who were aboard, including the bosun and Victor, and they all went forward, complaining loudly, and hauled the long hawser back aboard by hand and stowed it back in its locker.

"What a bunch of thieves!" exclaimed Sparks. "And I'll bet there won't be a thing about any of this in the saloon at breakfast tomorrow mornin'."

"The skipper'll have to turn detective for the rest of the trip," I ventured, "if he wants to take much of the ship and her stores back to Boston."

"Well, the hawser is bad enough," said Bill Nadeau, "but stealin' the ship's grub is somethin' I won't put up with. If I get hungry before this trip's over, I know just what to do — and somebody's goin' to be mighty sorry."

The following noon *Amphitrite* sailed. But not for Boston. In midmorning the captain returned aboard and announced that the ship's orders had been changed and we were cleared for Limassol, Cyprus, to pick up seven thousand linear tons of carob bean pods in bulk and take them to Barcelona.

"Gee, this ship won't get back to the states until Thanksgiving," Bob worried. "What'll I do! Classes begin about the first of October."

"Well, it looks as if you'll miss a semester, but you can make it up," I sympathized.

"Well, you had no business comin' to sea nohow," Gus assured Bob. "The old sea is so wide and uncertain that you never can count on it."

It was such a relief to get moving again that the rest of us didn't care where we went. So we enjoyed watching the triangular-shaped city fade into the distance and the old fortress-prison of Yedi-Coulé disappear behind the hills as we rounded the point and laid a course toward the southeast.

Late in the afternoon of the second day on the wings of a strong easterly breeze we pushed our way into the bay of Limassol and anchored in the calm, clear water fairly close to the town's waterfront. We were the first American ship to touch here for thirty-nine years. Limassol lay on the southern coast of Cyprus, on a narrow plain running along the shore for several miles, a belt of green fields and orchards shut in by a range of jagged rough mountains. It was a pretty town with its red roofs shining through a thick cover of palm trees, quaint with its cobblestone streets and stuccoed houses, and there were two mosques with minarets and an imposing Greek cathedral with three mosaic domes. Although the waterfront was largely sandy beach, a part of it was a long quay abutted on the inner side by an almost continuous line of stuccoed sheds and warehouses, small shops, and a few houses.

Stretching up the long slopes behind the town were vast orchards of carob trees, the pods of which we were to load aboard *Amphitrite*. These trees looked exactly like apple trees from a short distance, and the countryside seemed to be one large apple orchard. The fruit of a carob tree, however, is quite different from an apple. Carob beans grow green and hang from the branch in the shape of a pod that grows up to twelve inches long, a couple of inches wide, and nearly an inch thick. When ripe it is colored dark brown and contains five to fifteen hard brown seeds shaped like lima beans and enclosed in a sweet pulp. I recalled buying the whole pods for a penny apiece and eating the honey-flavored pulp at a circus when I was a child. But the commercial value lies in the seeds, which are processed into stock feed and carob gum, which has a variety of industrial uses.

The *Amphitrite* lay in Limassol only four days after arrival, loading from tubby little lighters with lateen sails that made their own way between ship and dock without the aid of a tug. Although this type of cargo handling may have been inexpensive it was very slow because the bean pods were first put into large burlap bags ashore and then dumped in bulk down the hatches when they were hoisted aboard. The lighters are the same today as they were two thousand years ago; they have a small deck in the bow and in the stern, an open hold taking up most of the ship, and a semilateen rig. Although very beamy, they sail well and are surprisingly seaworthy.

Between Limassol and the three neighboring villages of Zyyi, Efdimo, and Pisuri along the same stretch of coast, *Amphitrite* would spend nearly three weeks loading her cargo, finally completing it back again at Limassol.

13. Heat

A QUIET WIND blew out of the east. It changed the color of the sea from a light blue to a dense purple and drove away the suffocating heat and all its burden of rank smells. Swinging round at her anchor off Zyyi, the *Amphitrite* seemed to move away from the shore. The lateen-rigged lighters, which hitherto had been fastened on the water between the rickety wharf and the ship, received a new breath of life, keeled over with the breeze, and resumed their voyages.

I slid down a rope over the *Amphitrite*'s side into an empty lighter just as it prepared to cast off and sail ashore to load another cargo of carob beans for the ship's holds. The spot for which we steered was the tiny village clustered around the end of the rickety wharf. I was stealing ashore to make a little pilgrimage up into those tumbling white hills of Cyprus that I had watched for three days from the hot deck.

The chunky little lateen caught the breeze, listed slightly to port, and began to rock forward over a purple sea scintillating with sunshine. It was precisely the kind of boat that had borne Paul the Apostle to that same shore nearly twenty centuries ago. Like an ancient Minoan seafarer sailing from Knossos or Palaikastro I braced myself in the bow, drank in the approaching scenery with long ecstatic breaths, trembled with the thrill of high adventure.

Behind Zyyi rose a dreary wilderness of limestone hills, almost totally deforested and covered only with sparse clumps of a dry, lavender-colored bush. Twisting up over the white hills, hazy with heat waves, wound a deeply rutted road. In places it was completely washed out and disappeared for yards at a stretch in a treacherous mass of loose gravel, for the desert rains are severe there and wash away entire hills, form new plains, and dig out strange stream channels. Along the very road where Paul had trudged preaching the word of God from Limassol to Larnaca I intended following a short distance behind the dust of the mail caravan.

When the lateen wallowed up to the swaying wharf I jumped ashore and hurried up into the village. The heat of the afternoon was terrific, well over one hundred and twenty degrees in the sun, heat almost unbelievable to a stranger like me, laden as it was with a choking dust that poured from the warehouses like thin smoke. Emaciated laborers, nearly naked and carrying enormous bags of carob beans on their backs, staggered by with the sweat dripping in streams. Before I had tramped fifty feet between the mud buildings up that gorge of a road my own body was oozing sweat in every part. With that strength-sapping heat and the stench of swill and sewer-

age evaporating on the pavings my head began to reel. I tried
to quicken my pace in an urge to get beyond the smell of hu-
mankind. Just then the eight dromedaries that comprised the
mail caravan swung out from behind a shed and ambled into
the rutted road to begin the winding ascent up into the interior of the country. Soon they disappeared over the brow of
the hill and the dust began to settle again.

On up the road I walked, leaving behind the fumes of the
mud village and entering a new kind of atmosphere, fragrant,
thick like the air in a hothouse. Orderly rows of carob trees
stretched endlessly up over the rising ground. Days earlier
their long brown pods had been harvested, but the sweet
brackish smell lingered behind. Soon the road left the stagnant carob orchards, dropped over a hill into a desiccated river
valley luxuriant with a heavy growth of corn and wheat, and
finally emerged on the baked clay surface of an utterly barren
land. After I had followed its wheel marks a mile or more into
a parched wilderness of stony hillocks, the heat had drained so
much of my strength that I had to sit on a boulder and rest
while I dazedly stared at the narrow coastal plain, the village,
and the distant sea. The sun poured down its enervating heat
without mercy, and there was not a cloud in the sky to provide
relief. My clothes clung to me like rags dipped in warm water;
my body ached with fatigue.

In my trance I failed to observe the sooty-looking clouds
that were beginning to drive pell-mell down the range of hills
in the northeast, tumbling over themselves, swallowing each
other in their haste to hide the eastern horizon before they
might be seen. Not until they had spread along the west and
begun to wave their ragged shadows across the now reddening

sun did I sense that a storm was brewing. Quickly I got to my feet, glanced apprehensively around, and hastened back downhill. My excursion into the desert had suddenly ended.

As soon as I had returned to the *Amphitrite* and carried down to the sailors the soggy steamed potatoes and carrots and boiled salt beef together with the rice pudding that comprised their supper, I cleaned up the messroom and climbed up to the fantail to settle on a hatch beside my friend George, the third engineer. He was frail and slender, with a mild open glance, and his face, hollowed by undernourishment, worry, and the excessive temperature of the engine room, was haunted by a kindly melancholy. We were both homesick, so sick that eating had not only become repugnant but almost impossible and our morale had sunk to a point of hopelessness. Only a dull ache remained, and its weight was expressed in his eyes.

With an appalling suddenness the sun dropped into the furnace it had prepared for itself among the tumbling clouds on the mountaintops. It seemed as if another burden had been loaded on my shoulders, and I began to shiver in the rapidly cooling air beside George. The twilight that followed only lasted a few minutes, reveling in a brilliance of orange colors to compensate for its brevity. Rapidly the dusk filtered through the carob orchards. Had it not been for a solitary palm that stood on a hilltop silhouetted against the smoky flames of the sky in the west, I should have thought we might be lying off the coast of Maine, the rocky headlands of home. In the cooler air the hot steel plates of the ship snapped and rumbled, sending faint vibrations throughout the hull. At a day's end, when the world has begun to grow pensive, twilight is naturally an hour for reflection, a time briefly to remember the laughter, the futile cursing, and the weary toil of the past and to conjure better hopes for the morrow. Yet George and I did little reflecting, for in the eastern sea the twilight is too short. Rapidly now, the brilliant west faded into a general paleness of evening; it glowed for a moment, deepened, thickened into murk, and lo — nothing remained but a silver haze that gleamed through infinite moth holes in the garment of night.

Though the evening had at first begun to grow cooler, presently we became aware that the wind was blowing with a queer warmth and smelled of the carob trees. Brackish gusts tore across at us from the restive village where already the number of swaying lights was beginning to dwindle. Stars still shone overhead, but those around the horizon were hidden under shreds of haze.

After a while I noticed the change and spoke up, "Say, the sky looks funny tonight! Look at those clouds in the north'ard — rolling like smoke and black as ink. I'll bet we're in for rain or something."

"Not in the dry season," George replied shortly. "Don't worry about rain — 'twould be a blessing. Well, time to turn in!"

He rose stiffly from the hatch coaming on which we had been sitting and stretched.

"Don't hurry. It's time for me, too," I said.

He joined me again after I had taken my mattress from the messboy's room, and together we strolled past the group lolling outside the galley and spread both our pads on the midships hatch among several other men. Preparing to turn in was a simple task with us, consisting of removing one's shoes and loosening one's belt.

For a long time we lay there among some of the other men, too warm to sleep, watching the stars and a thin wisp of smoke that swirled out of the *Amphitrite*'s funnel. A stuffy wind, blowing strong now, chased myriads of fluffy clouds across the new moon so that it shed its faint light through a purplish murk. Down in the depths of the ship an iron door clanged as a fireman threw some coal into his furnace, sending up a belch of smoke from the funnel, and then it was quiet again. Even in the sticky and strangely warm air, my fatigue was finally sufficient to permit me to doze.

"This *is* a queer breeze — warmer than usual, ain't it?" George asked, thinking me still awake.

"Yes — a warm night."

"Aw, pipe down or you'll lay awake all night," someone growled.

In a trice I really was asleep and heard no more.

When I began to awaken, it seemed as if I had been sleeping for eons. Something was wrong. My heart was thumping. I was too worn to be dreaming, but I felt conscious of a vast roaring sound through which faint shouting pierced, scarcely audible — conscious of wild disorder, of dizziness. Something was suffocating me, shaking the blanket in which I had rolled myself. Ah, I knew. I was in my old room at college and my roommate was trying to pull me out of bed. But it was too hot! Was there a fire? My roommate delaying to awaken me? Oh, goodness, yes! The heat was terrific. I could hear the roaring of the flames.

"Hey! Cut it out! Stop pounding me!"

"Hey, Emery, wake up —"

Someone tripped and stumbled over me in the dark.

"Damn it — get out of my way," a hoarse voice growled.

"The port side!" the first voice cried again. "Come over on the port side — sheltered —"

As my eyes blinked open I felt a terrific blast of heat on my face and cringed under its force. What in the world! I was too bewildered to think. There was physical pain in that blast. This was not my college room. Here there were men stumbling about in the darkness, hiding their faces in blankets, their shirts, in anything they could find. A fierce torrent of gale that tried to blow me from the hatch ripped away the blanket that stuck to my streaming body and plastered it against the afterhouse.

"George — George!" I shouted.

"Yes, Emery!"

"What's the matter! — what's wrong! — where are we?"

"God only knows — awake now? Take your blanket — where is it? — Oh, never mind —"

Again I struggled to sit up. Something struck my face and stung like a swarm of hornets. A blast of the gale nearly knocked me to the deck.

"Look out — all right!"

I had stumbled over my shoes. Silly of me to forget them. The deck pricked my bare feet.

"George!" I shouted again.

"Yeah?"

"What's wrong here? Are we afire?"

"Fire? No! Desert blow — sandstorm or something —"

Out of the east roared the gale, stifling hot, laden with particles of dust and sand from the desert, sand that stung one's face fiercely. Squinting toward the shore I could see a few lights flickering wildly in the town — an unusual thing at midnight in Cyprus. The sea was lashed into a fury of foam. It swirled, boiled as in a kettle, and leaped into the air. Blasts of wind blew the wave tops completely off and whipped the water near the shore into a mad rush for the open sea.

"How hot is it getting?" a man yelled.

"What d'you care!" another answered.

"That damn east wind! He'll have us on the rocks!"

I heard the mate's voice call, "Hundred sixteen."

"Don't believe yuh!"

"Who the hell took that pail of water!"

In the jumble of shouting someone began to laugh nervously.

"Cheer up! It's a damn sight better here'n ashore."

I discovered that sweat was oozing from my body as freely as it had that afternoon up in the hills. Listen! Distinctly, through the screaming gale and the slamming of blocks, came the sound of church bells — the bells in a minaret ashore. Bells of another world, they seemed. What palliative effect could bells have on folks when for all we knew the ship might be about to part her cable and drift on to the shoals off the point behind us in the blackness! Louder, louder roared the wind! It screeched through the wires and guy ropes and howled around the *Amphitrite*'s wheelhouse and smokestack.

"Hey, you guys! Come here a minute, will you!"

Suddenly a faint voice down on the after well-deck could be heard, cursing and screaming like a terror-stricken child.

"It's Macaroni," a voice I recognized as Pete's, shouted.

"He's had a fever all day — don't know where he is. Somebody must of forgot him."

"Go down and help him up here!"

"Let him help himself! He ain't no better'n I am."

"Aw, get out of the way! You can't leave a sick man out in this."

It was George. The frailer man elbowed the others aside and pushed out into the stream of driving sand. In the murky glare of the phosphorescent spray we could see him buffeting his way down the deck to a spot where someone groveled on the plates. He helped the other to his feet, ducked his face away from the stinging wind, and dragged the helpless one back amidships. Several men who had hung back now stepped out to lift the delirious Italian up the ladder. Macaroni was all right anyhow. It was not important to make oneself uncomfortable to help him. In a matter of life and death it would have been different —

The storm was growing worse. It bellowed ferociously across the top of the smokestack. With unbelievable violence the eastern fury swept hot gases over from the desertlike land, screamed in the shrouds like a horde of ghouls, even rolled a mattress across the hatch and hurled it out to sea. I thought I would suffocate. Every now and then a man in the shelter of the cabin sank wearily to the deck, gasping for breath. Before long the steady roar lulled me into a coma and my head rolled back on the steel plates in a stifled dream.

Hours later I felt the rays of the sun scorching my face. Although still in a stupor, I dragged myself to my feet and looked about the deck. They lay where they had thrown themselves, sailors, firemen, and officers twisted together in groups. At the other end of the deck stood the skipper and the mate looking as if they had been without sleep for a week, pinched, wan, and purple under their eyes. As the sun burned hotter and hotter the crew began to writhe like worms coming out of the ground and to pull themselves up, still bewildered at the terror that had passed in the night. Some of them leaned on the rail and muttered ear-splitting oaths to the water. It was time to set about the drudgery of clearing hatches, chipping rust, and washing out latrines.

When I entered the after-messroom under the poop I found a loaf of bread, originally of a generous size, now shrunken to a third its bulk. I threw it out of a port and listened as it rattled over the deck.

"Humph! Guess it was pretty hot after all," I murmured to myself.

Heat! Now I should know what men meant when they talked of heat. Not even the Red Sea could make me cringe after this.

Shortly after the *Amphitrite*'s arrival in Cyprian waters an accident of far-reaching consequences took place. The refrigeration equipment broke down. And before the engineers could machine a new part to replace the vital one that had been destroyed, several days had elapsed during which nearly all the meat remaining in the cold-storage compartment became unfit for consumption. The crew went on short rations.

Three weeks would pass before we would terminate our visit to Cyprus. Three miserable long weeks of parching heat and sickness and loneliness. But at last the *Amphitrite*'s cavernous insides would be filled with carob beans — a nasty cargo that filled the heat of the day with that sickish, stale smell and the air of the night with swarms of insects — filthy, flapping things that clustered around your head and squirted slime in your face when you squashed them. By the time we left we felt that a few weeks longer in Cyprus would drive us mad.

The *Amphitrite's* crew was in poor condition. Every man on the ship had dysentery; half of them had a fever, and a good dozen suffered with venereal disease also. So short-handed had the firing room become that the sailors had been drafted to keep steam in the boilers. The fresh meat had become spoiled and rotten and had been thrown overboard. Fortunately, we had a small supply of salted beef. There had been no fresh drinking water at the taps for nearly a month, the flour was alive with worms, and the vegetables were punky and soft.

In Limassol, I made an acquaintance just before we sailed for Malta who turned out to be quite interesting. Several of us had gone ashore to get haircuts because we had discovered Limassol to be a very clean place with modern shops. The sidewalks appeared to have been swept, the streets were well lighted after dark, and there were no piles of rubbish or swill. The barber shops had marble washbasins and modern chairs and, of course, were wide open to the street for ventilation.

While Bob was having his hair trimmed, I sat in a chair smoking my pipe quite placidly. Presently, I was approached by a well-groomed young man in his early thirties. He was well tanned, of medium stature, and had a pleasant, open face.

"Would it be possible to buy passage in your ship to Spain?" he asked. "I've heard that part of your cargo is going to Spain."

"I really wouldn't know," I replied. "You might find it a bit rough in a freighter."

He smiled.

"It isn't for me," he said. "It's for my sister and her husband."

"Oh, then you'd better talk with whoever represents the ship ashore, here. Or, if you don't get anywhere with them, why don't you come out and talk with the captain?"

He thanked me and was turning away when I suddenly called out, "Where did you learn to speak English so well?"

He turned and smiled rather broadly at me. "I own a store and live in Detroit."

Then we introduced ourselves and I learned that his name was Silvas, that he had lived in the United States eight years, including a year in France with the 14th Army Division, and was now on a short visit to his family in his birthplace, Limassol. When he learned that I had taken several courses in geology in college, he promptly drew up a chair to a table, produced a specimen of long fiber asbestos, and unfolded several field maps.

"Here is something that may interest you," he said. "This asbestos comes from an area near Mount Troodos about one hundred ten miles away from here near the center of Cyprus. Troodos is about six thousand feet high — the largest mountain in the island. It's filled with great veins of this stuff, from four to eight inches thick. Now, why don't you take a couple of days off and come with me at my expense and look at it. I don't know whether anything can ever be done with this deposit, but it's worth thinking about."

I would have given anything to be able to go with him, but the idea was entirely out of the question, aside from the fact that *Amphitrite* would sail in another day or two. At any rate, Mr. Silvas took Bob and me on a little walk around Limassol, pointing out places of interest that otherwise we would have missed, especially the crumbling ruins of the Church of Saints Peter and Paul, for centuries the original Christian cathedral here, built very early in the Christian era as a result of Paul's evangelizing efforts.

Next day two events of minor importance occurred. The first was my change of jobs from sailors' messboy to pantryman, replacing Frenchy, who became third cook. This was made necessary when Tom Meadows, the ex-third cook, was sent ashore to a hospital to have diagnosed the nature of the open sores that now covered considerable parts of his body. The second was the captain's agreement to transport Mr. Silvas' sister and her husband to Spain.

On our last evening in Limassol the steward brought Tom Meadows back from the hospital. Yes, his malady had been diagnosed as an advanced and virulent case of syphilis. Rather than leave him ashore in Limassol the captain had decided to carry him to Barcelona where better provision could be made for him. Meanwhile, he would be isolated as much as possible. And meanwhile, we would all continue to suffer a few hours longer from bad food and water and the terrific heat of Cyprus in August. What a nightmare, on the whole, my sea voyage in a blue-water freighter had become!

The next morning we hove up our anchor and steamed into the west. It was a vivid relief to watch the white hills of Cyprus sink beneath the horizon. At last the *Amphitrite* was bound for Malta for coal, food, and fresh water. The waves sparkled as I had remembered them from recent time that seemed ages ago. Now a gentle wind blew out of the east, the prevailing, inescapable easterly. And once more I had the old thrill of feeling the deck rise and fall gently beneath my feet, the new thrill of contemplating from afar shimmering heat waves on a baked mountainside, contemplating them as in a nightmare, and I had the simple joy of again confiding my trust and love in the good God of the deep blue sea.

14. At the Setting of the Sun

THE *Amphitrite*'s ACTUAL DEPARTURE from Cyprus had not been without an aspect of humor. Since the ship had no fresh vegetables whatever, nor any eggs, it was imperative that the steward try to buy stores in Limassol. Accordingly, he and the captain had gone ashore for supplies while the great number two hatch was being topped off. They were successful in obtaining a considerable supply of melons and garden vegetables, and a boat soon arrived and sent them aboard. But they ran into a snarl of red tape with the eggs.

From the deck of the ship we could see the British and Cyprian officials, the farmers and merchants in their shirts and baggy pantaloons, our officers and 100 dozen eggs in crates on the dock. The officials declared the eggs to be contraband, the steward later informed some of us, because they had been taken from one town to another — hence, they had been smuggled and were obviously intended for export. The ranking British official made the gratuitous assertion that 100 dozen eggs would be too many even for a British warship. The steward said that's one reason their ships were second-rate — they starved their crews. As tempers arose the official threatened to arrest the steward and the steward started to throw him off the dock and had to be restrained by the captain. Finally, the steward told the man to go to hell and stuff the eggs in an unlikely place, apologized to the Cyprians for being unable to complete their deal, and returned to the *Amphitrite* leaving the eggs sitting on the dock. We then hoisted our anchor and sailed immediately.

At the setting of the sun we were steaming across a glassy sea, leaving the mountains of western Cyprus astern. Although the heat had been terrific in midday it had already abated with the approach of evening and the sailors were lounging on the fantail looking forward into the west as the sun dropped behind the edge of the sea. A deep salmon color spread over the cloudless sky, filling the world and all its creeping, crawling things with thoughts of survival that lie outside our human knowledge. Standing alone on the after well-deck I heard someone humming a facsimile of the words of an old roundhouse song, one of those that the chanteymen of bygone years used to sing in the ship's waist at the end of the day when it might be calm and quiet:

> "At the setting of the sun,
> When your dirty work is done,
> Heigh ho, the wind and the sea.

You won't need your bit o' pay
For Davy'll take you far away,
At the setting of the sun,
When your dirty work is done,
Heigh ho, the wind and the sea."

I had not heard those words for a long time and their poignant melancholy made me shudder. Who aboard this ship would have known that song? It made me feel lonely, too, so I walked across the deck and peered into the fo'c's'le, which was filled with a mellow half-light from the glow of the sky. It seemed empty except for Gus's gray cat, which was sitting on the long table in the center and turned to look at me. He made a little tentative questioning chirp and then turned his eyes back toward Gus's bunk.

"Anybody there?" I called.

Since no one answered I was turning away from the door when I noticed in the dusk a thin trickle of water meandering along the steel deck. Following it to its source with my eye, I could barely discern Gus in his bunk.

"Oh, dear," I mused as I strode in, "he must have spilled his coffee cup."

But as I leaned over him a queer feeling of fear swept over me. My knees trembled and I felt afraid. Looking closer I saw something that froze my muscles. Instinctively I shrank back uttering a choked cry and stood quivering with horror. When I recovered sufficiently to move again I dropped to my knees to look more carefully. A knife lay on the deck by the berth and his throat was slashed from ear to ear. Out of the ghastly wound the blood still dripped, and the chords and membranes were beginning to protrude. At that moment Bob entered the fo'c's'le from the steering engine room.

"Bob," I gasped, "go get the skipper!"

He took a step nearer.

"Oh, God!"

"Hurry up, will you!"

"I can't. You go."

Hardly conscious of what I was doing, with my senses swirling I moved up the deck and up the starboard ladder to the captain's bridge. He was standing just outside the door to his office and turned upon me in surprise, recognizing from the look on my face that trouble had brought me to him.

"Captain," I panted, "Gus — committed suicide — would you —"

He had moved to clatter down the ladder before I could finish. Following him aft to the fo'c's'le I switched on the light and stood in the doorway while he stared down at the corpse.

"Yes," he said finally, "afraid this might happen. We noticed he'd been acting queerly. A few weeks ago when he was at the wheel one night he told the mate that he was going to do away with himself — saw no use in going on. Now he's done it. Too bad! Too bad." He shook his head. "He was a good guy."

After a pause, he added, "Well, I'll send the mate down here, sonny, and you call the bosun and the carpenter."

As I left, he turned to the gray cat still sitting on the table and stroked its head. "Well, kitty, now we'll have to find somebody else to look after you."

The body was removed to a spare room amidships in the afterhouse. Late into the evening the carpenter and the bosun sewed up a canvas shroud to serve as a coffin for poor Gus. The coal passer on watch sent up some broken furnace grates in the fiddley hoist to be used to weigh down the body. The captain found among his books a copy of the *U.S. Armed Services Manual and Prayer Book* and read over the orders for a funeral service. Many of the crew talked long about the tragedy and said many good things about Gus, for he was respected and well-liked.

"Well," rasped Tescula, "now I got me a dog and a cat. You other guys didn't want no animals and the mate put my dog ashore so these is now mine. Anybody got anything to say about it?" he growled belligerently.

I lay sleepless on my mattress on the port side of the deck a long time. Gus's hollow eyes as they stared up at me from his bunk had disturbed me deeply. Although I was slowly maturing I was still a young creature of unworldly sentiment and emotion and I found it difficult to sort out my thoughts in a constructive way. So much had happened to impinge upon my ideas and ideals in the last two months — the storm in which only the watchfulness and courage of a shipmate had saved my life, the stupid brawls in Algiers, Piraeus, and Salonika, the filthy prison of Yedi-Coulé, the torture of the midnight sandstorm in Cyprus, and now the suicide of a kind friend. Had I not been quite so ill with dysentery and perpetually hungry from poor nourishment during the last three weeks I might not have become quite so disconsolate. I was beginning to believe that adventure was a silly, overrated affair and that the shipping business was not worth the cost of getting into it. Then I reflected that almost every one of these outwardly rough men with whom I was working and living also had tender, generous, and wholly admirable qualities in their lives, qualities that far outweighed the unlovely parts. I concluded that my character still needed further melting in the cauldron and much more molding before I would become as strong as these men.

Clang! Clang! The ship's bell, sounding like a weird, uncouth thing that really belonged to the world of spirits and ghouls, began to strike eight bells, marking the end of the graveyard watch and the beginning of the morning. Knowing that dawn of a new day was at hand I lay sweating on my mattress until the horizon began to show and up above the stars began to fade and the mate took his morning star sights on the bridge, and a pink glow spread across the whole sea.

At nine o'clock, in a silence that hung over the satin water, broken only by a quiet hissing sound of steam escaping from the vent at the top of the stack, *Amphitrite* was rolling quietly all alone on an empty sea. With the exception of a couple of men in the engine and firing rooms, the crew had all gathered amidships at number three hatch, forming a close circle around the captain and the mate who were standing at the head of the long canvas bundle on the plank at the gangway, one end of which rested on the starboard rail. Everything was grimly quiet, the ship, the sea, and the crew. The captain quietly took his place at its inboard end and removed his uniform cap, and those of the crew who were wearing any hats did the same. Then the captain opened his *Armed Services Manual and Prayer Book* and began to read:

> *"They that go down to the sea in ships, that do business in great waters, these know the glory of the Lord and His wonders in the deep —*
>
> *"I am the Resurrection and the Life, saith the Lord: He*

that believeth in Me, though he were dead, yet shall he live:
and whosoever liveth and believeth in Me, shall never die.

"For we know that if our earthly house of this tabernacle
were dissolved, we have a building of God, an house not
made with hands, eternal in the heavens —

"Forasmuch as it hath pleased Almighty God, in his wise
providence, to take out of this world the soul of his deceased
servant, we therefore commit his body to the deep; looking
for the Resurrection of the dead, and the life of the world to
come, through our Lord Jesus Christ; at whose coming in
glorious majesty the sea shall give up her dead; and the
mortal bodies of those who sleep in Him shall be changed,
and made like unto His own glorious body; according to the
mighty working whereby He is able to subdue all things
unto himself."

When he had concluded his reading the captain stepped
back and the first and second mates grasped the inboard end
of the plank and slowly raised it, inch by inch. Presently, the
bundle began to slide faster and faster until it slipped off and
fell with a loud splash into the pellucid depths below —
down, down, down. The instant that the body struck the
water the crew made a noisy rush to the rail to watch it sink,
but they saw only the long trail of bubbles that shot up toward
the surface. Then we dispersed and soon the pistons began to
pound again and the ship gained steerageway.

I moved aft to sit on number four hatch on the after well-
deck to be by myself and think. The little ceremony had so
much dignity, yet was so pathetic that I was quite moved.
Chips, the old German carpenter, had followed me to the
well deck, and seeing in my face that my mood matched his

own, sat down beside me staring wistfully off to port. Chips was an elderly, sandy-haired, frail-looking man, with a narrow face tanned and wrinkled like old leather.

"Well," he began to say in his broken English, "this is bad business, this funeral stuff. It makes me feel too much like wanting to run away and be somewheres else. Gus was a fine boy, a fine boy!"

"Yes," I said, "I can't get over it."

"Neither can I," replied Chips. "These funerals always put me in mind of one in the old days when I first went to sea. It was rough."

"Tell me about it," I suggested.

He looked at me suspiciously, "You want to know too much, what?

"Well, no matter. I tell you anyhow. It was a old Dutch ship called *Luna*, out of Rotterdam, bound for Surabaya with rails and general cargo. We was slow — eight knots, but we didn't know no better in those days. She was a pretty ship, painted yellow with white topsides — and a workhouse at that. Well, about three weeks out of Suez the old mate up and died. Got a sunstroke from being out without a cap on his bald head. Dummkopf, that's what he was.

"Well, in those days, the nineties it was, the Dutch ships had a custom of passing out schnapps to celebrate the burial. So the old man, he gets out with a good-sized keg of schnapps and ladles out a big cupful to each one of us. 'The mate was a good man,' he says, 'so you drink to his spirits.' And every time he ladled out a mug for one of the crew, he took a drink hisself."

Chips snorted with gleeful memory and lighted his pipe again.

"Well, by the time we had all had a drink and got the mate all sewed up in a sack and ready to be buried, the old man was pretty drunk. So he come out with his Bible and he had it upside down. Couldn't see a thing. He wiped his glasses and turned the Bible around and then he began to sweat and his glasses got all steamed up again, so he bangs the Bible shut and hollers, 'Well, you know what it's all about anyhow. Throw him overboard!'

"So we tilted up the plank and the old mate slides off and lands in the water with a big splash, and we all run to the rail to look over and see him sink, and by chimminy, he come up again. Yes, there he was floating around in the water because we was all so drunk we had forgot to put any ballast in him.

" 'Oh, by gee,' the old man hollers, 'we can't let him float around like that. Lower a boat and fish him out.'

"So we lowers the small boat off the bridge and us geezers on the afterfalls let the line go too fast and the stern comes down straight in the water, and the boys in the boat fell out and the boat come down on top of them. Well, there was a lot of hollering, but the guys in the water got sobered up and all climbed in the boat and rowed aft to where the mate had drifted. The ship didn't have no way on her, but y'know, she drifted a little in the wind. Well, they finally got the old mate in the boat and started to row back after the ship. And when they got to the stern they says, 'Aw, this is good enough. Lower a line and take him aboard here.' So we lowered a line and they made it fast to the mate and we hauled him aboard on the fantail. Then we stuffed him full of slice bars so he would sink and we sent for the old man to come and have another funeral.

"Yaw, the old man come down with his Bible and he says,

'Well, if any of you think you is getting another drink, you is wrong because you had too much already and if we have to bury anybody else we'll only have enough for a little drink anyhow.'

"And then he looks at the corpse and he looks at us and he says, 'I ain't going to go through with all this all over again.' So he puts down his Bible on the capstan, picks up the old mate in his arms, and chucks him overboard with a big splash. Yaw, and this time the mate sunk all right so we got under way again and in about a week we come to Strait of Sunda.

"Well," Chips concluded, "that's all right. When the sun goes down we get our pay, don't we?" After a pause, he drawled more seriously, "Yaw, and sometimes we don't."

Then he laughed and walked away, trying to look unconcerned and humming the tune that had puzzled me the other night:

> "At the setting of the sun,
> When your dirty work is done,
> Heigh ho, the wind and the sea."

So it was Chips who knew that old song. I wondered where he had learned it.

15. She of the Black Eyes

ON AND ON through the darkness plodded the *Amphitrite*. The hissing waves swept far astern, jostled and smashed by the huge black bulk that wallowed through them. At dawn we came to a strange new land, to a mighty city of towers and terraced roofs, a city of walls and fortified high places reared upon the sea cliffs — Malta.

The ship responded to a clanging of bells in her depths and slackened her noisy pace. Thinner grew the dusk, blown into the east by a strong west wind, and firmer the outlines of a looming apparition beyond. It stretched out dead ahead like a great serpent floating on the waves, its belly bulging with an angular object it had swallowed. A serpent — no, it was land, land at last, gray and rugged, rising out of the morning sea. In the west lay a grim rocky shore, stretching low along the water but for a ragged mass of pinnacles and walls in its center. Barely perceptible, a tiny blue pilot boat with an orange sail tossed in the offing. With more clanging of bells and a morose booming on her whistle, the ship slowed her march until a cockleshell boat was diving along by her side and a swarthy pilot in a red shirt and curled black mustache was struggling up a rope ladder.

While the ship had been occupied with the pilot boat the delicate color of morning had spread over the whole world. Now a great and strange city appeared where had towered the pinnacles and terraced roofs on the crests of some cliffs against which the white sea thundered and hissed. There it lay, like a fairy castle on an enchanted rock, all pink and gold in the light from the red sun hanging over the eastern sea, its windows gleaming like scoured brass and its towers and steeples partly shrouded in pink mists that rose from the waves to swirl about them in garlands. Dead ahead danced a fleet of fisherboats bound for the day's catch, a brilliant fleet of flashing hulls and patched orange sails. Now the sky deepened into a blue once more, the swirling garlands of mist vanished in the stronger light, the ethereal gold of the windows began to tarnish, and many of those walls, studded with tiers and tiers of old iron cannon, frowned out upon the glistening sea. This was the citadel of Malta, high-towered and yellow, resting implacably upon the sheer cliffs of its narrow harbor.

In a tumult of shouting, clanging of bells, and thundering of the propeller, at last the *Amphitrite* came to rest, stern in against a Maltese quay in the Grand Harbor of Valletta. Before long she was surrounded by a fleet of blunt-nosed coal scows and her decks were alive with scores of miserably ragged

Maltese who swarmed back and forth over the side like crowds of undesirable vermin.

After I had washed the officers' breakfast dishes and cleaned up the pantry and tidied up their staterooms, I walked aft to see how Tescula's cat and dog were getting along. Macaroni stood in the fo'c's'le door.

"Well," I called, "how do you like this place? You been here before?"

"Ah, Valletta — she is a big city, beautiful city," cried Macaroni. "I was here once. Much fine girls — aah! I knew one — Muratelli the name of her — she fine girl. I spend every night for a week with Muratelli — aah!"

His brown eyes widened with an animal pleasure and he puckered his mouth into a grimace by which he meant to depict the highest state of ecstasy. Macaroni was of medium height, quite ordinary in his physical proportions, and he had a shock of light brown hair. He was unusually intelligent. Many long hours he passed in reading the chief engineer's set of Shakespeare. He could quote Dr. Johnson and Mr. Furness on the disputed passages and recite many noble selections from *King Lear* and *The Merchant of Venice*. But he specialized on *Romeo and Juliet*. Often he had entertained me with his enthusiastic comments on that play upon the fo'c's'le head during the night watch while the ship pitched forward into black hills and valleys of water. This was a curious man, both gentleman and degenerate, who could love one woman with all his heart while he remained completely faithless to her.

Macaroni's real name was Alessandro Cavallo, a son of a fine old Venetian family that had lost its wealth and much of its social caste, he said. Having finished his education he went to sea, "to make travel and see what the moon looks like in other places." Once at sea, the freedom and the bigness of it captivated him, and he had continued for five years, dissipating his youth. He did not intend to remain at sea. Oh, no! Back in Venice was Maria Marti, she of the black eyes, the shining hair, and the smooth olive skin. He was going back to Maria sometime, sure he was; had he not been betrothed to her for five years? Yes, he knew that the war had ruined her father's Venetian business, that there had been many soldiers there, but he was certain that Maria would remain faithful to him. She do wrong? Impossible! Sometime he would take her to the old church of San Giovanni and lead her back under the iron balconies and through the twisty streets of the higher town to a little house in the Via Castiglia where he would raise a troop of little Alessandros and live in exclusive happiness. Employment — of course! Could he not get a job teaching school or writing for a newspaper?

He had expressed this reasoning to me, together with his hopes, several times in the past. Now we moved into the fo'c's'le where the sailors were taking a coffee break.

"Here's the Macaroni," shouted Victor. "He ain't going ashore here because he's engaged."

"Well," said Paul, "if I was damn fool enough to get engaged I wouldn't live with so many other women when I went ashore." Then he settled back on the bench and wagged his great tanned head at Macaroni.

"Ah, it's all right," replied the latter. "I only love the Maria."

"Bah!" expostulated Tescula, the little lame man with the scarred, homely face. "If you was a man you would live only with the one. You is a poor son-of-a-bitch, that's what you is, not to treat her right. What for you think she love you for anyhow, huh?"

"You don't make sleep with the girls when you are ashore, do you!"

"That's all right! I ain't got no girl for to keep away from the others."

"Say, you," Paul began, "what if you should find your woman chasing around with other men? What you would do, what?"

"I don't care about that so long she ain't got disease. You think me a big stiff, huh? Well, she don't have to be straight — but when we make for to marry, then I live with her and her with me only, see?"

Round the midships gangway sounded a confusion of women's voices, soft, musical voices that droned and scolded and swore. A dozen little cockpit gondolas, with bright decks that flashed in the sun, clustered around the landing stage seeking permission to put aboard the laundress each contained. Yanking and scratching, waving their arms, and spitting out blasphemy the women clawed each other on the landing stage, all seeking to come aboard at once. They were handsome women, olive-skinned and black-haired, with large, sparkling eyes, and they were dressed in long black skirts and loose open-necked waists. Ostensibly washerwomen who had come aboard to secure business, they carried liquor in those wide skirts and practiced the oldest of professions. It was the same in every large port. Within fifteen minutes after those eleven women had come over the *Amphitrite*'s side only one could be found. The heavy steel doors of the firemen's fo'c's'le up forward were shut and battened, the sailors had barricaded themselves in a similar manner aft, some of the officers had disappeared, and only Scotty was much in evidence. The chief cook was seated on the midships hatch where I had taken refuge.

Scotty, the red-haired, wiry Scotchman who was suspected by the sailors of being financially interested in a nefarious scheme to misappropriate their rations, was squatting on the hatch, holding his freckled face in his large red hands and attempting to seduce the single laundress who remained on deck. Scotty needed to practice seduction. No woman would ever admire him for his beauty, for he had baleful, leering eyes, an immense drooping mouth, and a great wart on his chin. But Scotty was shrewd. Presently, he drew out a cake of yellow soap from within his apron and held it under the beauty's nose.

"What d'ye say? Like the looks of it?"

The woman tossed her head disdainfully, while traces of a sneer played across her mouth. She was young, scarcely more than a girl, with an appealing if not an artistic beauty. Of medium height, she was still slender and fresh. The striking thing about her was her brown hair and the light color of her skin. Although her nose was a trifle large, her mouth was small and pretty, her skin sleek and ruddy, exuberant with youth and health, and her large black eyes looked out from profound depths, mystic and clear as a black pool of water with the sun flashing on it.

"Well," Scotty continued, "we'll add this to it." And he drew out a can of condensed milk.

"This lass is hard to get," he observed in a side remark to me.

"Ah!" The girl's eyes widened, but still she hesitated.

Scotty set the soap and milk on the hatch and scratched his red head. Then, as the woman made a quick movement to seize them, he snatched them up again. She replaced her hands on her hips, grinning.

"No you don't, you little poodle," he said, shaking his finger at her. "What do you say, take 'em and this here bottle of olives and come in me room?"

She turned her face to watch some gulls wheeling high over the harbor, then tossed her head. "All right, I'll take them. You very cheap — pooh!"

Then she followed him into the afterhouse, for he would not give her a chance to take the bribe until she was securely locked in his room.

While I remained alone on number three hatch, presently the second mate stepped out of the captain's office with some papers and descended the ladder to my side.

"Do you know, Emery," he said, "this ought to be a good time for you and me to do a little sparring. I'll bet, for once, we wouldn't have much of a gallery and could get in some serious work."

"Well," I replied, "I doubt it. Give them five minutes more and we'd have a ladies' cheering section in addition to the usual."

He laughed.

"Yes, you're right. I never before saw a bunch of whores take over a ship so completely all at once. These guys have been to sea too long. Well," he added philosophically, "if we want peace aboard we better leave them alone."

Then he moved off toward his own room with his papers.

A short time later the door of the sailors' fo'c's'le down aft was pushed open and a number of laundresses, still with no soiled clothes, stepped out and sat down on the edge of a hatch to preen themselves in the breeze. Following them came some of the sailors, among them Macaroni, looking quite flushed and pleased with himself. Macaroni continued his stroll forward, climbed the after midships ladder, and swaggered along the main deck. Just as he reached a corner of the passage he ran plumb into the chief cook who was climbing over the high sill of his room, followed by the black-eyed laundress whose capacious skirt bulged with various articles the cook had given her. Scotty beamed with satisfaction and radiated good will in every direction.

"Well, Wop," he shouted at a glimpse of Macaroni, "thanks for the cognac you give me this morning. It went smooth. Here, if you want a fine lass take this one down in me room and give her a couple of shillings. I'll give you me keys."

Macaroni did not answer. He stepped forward, lifting the girl's chin with his finger, and looked down into her face. Then he blushed and dropped his hand, but her eyes continued to study him.

"Sure, I'll take her," he replied at length. "Looks like good stuff."

"You're about right, my lad. Here, take me keys."

"No." He addressed the girl. "Wanta see you tonight. Where you live?" And turning again to Scotty, "I'll take her on tonight, Chief. Don't bother the keys."

She whispered her address in good Italian, drew her shawl over her head, and swung briskly toward the gangway. Scotty and I stepped to the rail, watched her climb into the boat and the boatman row her away with her canned goods and soap.

Then he alternately stroked his wart and scratched his head, as an indication that the bright Wednesday morning, the strong breeze, and the world in general pleased him mightily.

Evening came after a long, hard day and two much improved meals. The *Amphitrite* was grimy with coal dust — thick, dirty particles of soot that leaped up in little whirlwinds when a gust of wind rustled across the deck. The dust had deepened the color of the stew that Scotty produced in his galley and had mixed itself in the mud-colored frosting that the baker spread over a gritty loaf of cake. Having left black hand marks over the white walls of their messroom the sailors were beginning to soil the clothes in which they were dressing to wear ashore. It was the dirty end of a dirty day. Not preparing to dress like the other sailors, Macaroni lay in his bunk whistling a quaint little Venetian tune and beating time with his foot.

"Macaroni," observed Tescula with a quizzical smile in his old bloodshot eyes, "he ain't going up in the town with the rest of us. He don't like the Maltese girls, I guess."

"What?" Macaroni stopped whistling.

"Sure he does, didn't he once sleep with his Muratelli here for a week?" the big Paul shouted.

"But he don't like her no more," Victor jeered. "I guess she give him more than a good time."

Macaroni sat up and started to glare at Victor's sour face, forgetting for a moment that the latter was an ex-gunman and a fugitive from justice. Seeing a fine chance to bully the less courageous man, Victor sidled up to the bunk and snarled down, "What's the argument, huh? Am I a liar?"

Macaroni meekly lay back in his bunk and feigned not to

notice the insult. "Ah, I go ashore later," he cried, trying to appear unconcerned although the words trembled on his lips. "Got a new girl now. Much smooth stuff. Go up later and spend the night."

Victor sneered, "For cripe sakes, what are you going to do with a woman! They oughta put you into a Sunday school kindergarten for little kids, that's what they had, hadn't they fellers? You with a woman — whooo!"

Macaroni joined weakly in the laughter and Victor strutted across the fo'c's'le, content with having picked on the only man in the fo'c's'le whom he dared so insult. With a whoop and a scramble the sailors piled out on the deck to start for the town, the dimly lighted cafés, and the semiluxurious pleasure palaces, leaving Macaroni alone in the fo'c's'le with me and Tescula's gray cat. When the brawling and the uproarious laughter had moved up to the main deck, leaving the after fo'c's'le in a strange quiet, he rolled out of the bunk and rested his head in his hands against the table for a long time. At last he rose, went to the door, and looked out at the overhanging rock walls of the harbor. He stared into the northwest where a mammoth outcrop of rock frowned at the satin water that appeared grotesquely black in contrast to the jumble of stone buildings on its crest, shining with a reddish-brown glow from the sunset over beyond the hills.

He was trying to remember something, stroking his wiry beard in perplexity. Just where was that house? One of the hovels in the chasm by the marina? No. But wait! It was one of those great rambling "pensions" on the summit of Barracca Inferiore. Yes, that was it. He remembered now, a five-storied building with iron balconies sticking out of its dirty

plaster and a central stone stairway that twisted up flight after
flight. It had a bad name in these days. Yes, time was when it
had been a respectable apartment building inhabited by merchants and small professional men, but it had fallen in caste
and now afforded shelter for many seedy-looking men and
women who stole in and out all day and all night long on mysterious errands under its great portal, gloomy and solid as a
door in a church. That was where she lived. But why — how
long had she been living in such a place as that? He could not
understand, persuaded himself that he did not wish to understand. Oh, well, she had changed a bit since he had seen her
the last time, but the sea is ever changing also, and he could
well understand. After he had watched the reflection of the
Barracca shivering on the black harbor for many minutes he
turned into the fo'c's'le again.

Most of this soliloquy was murmured aloud to me in a sort
of monotone that I did not interrupt, although I could have
because he seemed deliberately to invite my comments. He
looked at me quietly for a moment before he approached and
extended his hand.

"Goodbye, Emery," he said, "I've liked knowing you and I
wish you good luck. I'm leaving the ship now to find my
Maria Marti, the one love of my life. We shake hands now.
You come up to the gangway with me and don't say goodbye
there. Make as if I only go ashore for the evening."

Reaching under his bunk he drew out an old canvas sea bag,
unlocked it, stuffed in a few clothes from the tangle of bed-
ding on the berth, and snapped the lock again. Then, in the
deepening twilight he slung the bag over his shoulder and
moved noiselessly up the deck. No one was in sight. Only the

Maltese customs guard stood near the gangway. Macaroni approached him and mumbled a few words in his ear before he slipped past the gloom of the cabins and stepped down the gangway like a phantom. A native boat responded to his short whistle, moved silently out of the shadows, took him aboard, and disappeared without a sound into the unknown whence it had come. Macaroni was leaving the *Amphitrite* forever. When he reached the shore he turned, set his bag down, and stared pensively out at the murky bulk and the very few lights that marked the ship that had been his only home for so long. "Goodbye, you old bitch," he muttered, "goodbye to you and the sea for a while, you old hell ship."

I could watch him for a while as he started out and then follow him in my imagination. First he walked along Kingsway, the main business street, and eventually he began to follow one of the streets of stairs, climbing by flights of stone steps along the sea cliffs through the blackness cast by long archways and balconies. At length he paused before a great stone building, peered into the gloom of its mammoth doorway lighted by a dim lamp flickering in the breeze, drew a breath of happiness and hope, the culmination of those fond reveries that he had dreamed so many times in the lonely starlight on the fo'c's'le head, and plunged into its depths to find Maria Marti, she of the black eyes.

16. The Little Lame Man

SOMETHING UNUSUAL was about to happen. Grimy Maltese stevedores, their faces bulging with curiosity, peeked over the edges of bunker hatches and up from the coal scows bumping against the *Amphitrite*'s dark sides. Tescula poked his scraggly beard and pug nose around a corner of the cabin and stared popeyed at the strange crowd shuffling along the deck and up the ladder of the forward house. Even the Maltese traders from the bumboats paused in their business of selling silk scarfs to watch the impending drama. The firemen clambered up to the main bridge nervously, like small boys who fear they are doing something wrong, herded on by Louie, who was powdered with coal dust from his plaid cap to his shoes. They were led by a stocky, light-haired Yankee boy who alone was possessed of the courage to utter their grievances to the skipper.

Then, before the men had time to compose themselves and feign indifference, the captain, a tall calm figure in white linen, stepped brusquely out of the door onto the bridge. His face was stern and set.

"Well, men," he asked, "what's the trouble?"

The spokesman flinched for a moment, but his strong features soon stiffened again. Bill Sullivan was a gray-eyed coal passer, muscular as a gymnast and a good antagonist in a fight with any man. This gave him self-confidence. But he spoke up apologetically.

"We don't mean to make no trouble, sir, and we don't want no mutiny — so we waited 'til we got this damn ol' hack into port."

He paused and shifted about until he backed into the railing. The rest of the black gang stirred uneasily, glancing furtively at each other. This was a poor beginning. Sullivan continued.

"Y' know, a man can't work when he ain't got nothin' to eat, sir."

While the captain raised his glance slowly toward the funnel top his face remained stolid as ever. He was the very picture of authority, standing there biting on his pipe, hands folded behind him, eyes impassive, and his young, smooth-shaven features rigid. Although his thoughts may have been disturbed and troubled he lowered his gaze, still expressionless. After a time he spoke in a strong, even voice.

"Well, men, I'm eating the same food you are in this ship. I know it's no good — the meat comes out of a barrel and the cook can't cook, but I have to eat the same stuff. We're all in the same trouble and we've got to stick it out. Now get forward where you belong and forget it."

No one budged. The spokesman replied, this time in stead-
ier tones.

"Y' see, it's like this, Captain, we can't work on what we're
getting — we're all sick — and we don't wanta take this ship
to sea until we get a square and some of the food what was
stole off'n us."

Over the shadowy mass of Barracca Superiore, that great
rock crowned with a nest of stone houses that stands like a
sentinel in the harbor of Malta, the captain cast a weary smile.
He had expected that the firemen would refuse to work on
salted meat; the sailors were more docile. He had half expected trouble today, the second day in port, when the coaling
would be finished and the ship ready for sea. He recognized
his responsibility for the steward's dishonesty in stealing half
the ship's food supplies in Salonika. A sense of the seriousness
of the situation had kept him up through the black hours of
the previous night with his unfaithful officer making lists for
the purchase of new provisions this very day. He grimaced. A
thankless business, that of commanding a tramp!

"Men," he began, "the steward's ashore buying more grub
now. You'll have plenty from now until we get into Barcelona, and then we'll lay in full supplies."

"We don't wanta go below again 'til we get a square meal,"
Sullivan pronounced.

This was nearly mutiny. In that case the master must assert
his authority and punish the guilty with due severity. Yet,
these men were sick. Moreover, he himself was guilty of gross
neglect; he knew the crew knew it. To that extent his authority was compromised. He was not afraid; he wanted to be fair.
Deep within himself he felt a carking care lest the *Amphitrite*'s operators learn of his fault. Ah, these days of steam and

shore regulation when a man was no longer master of his men in the true sense! He dared not act the old-fashioned tyrant. For the first time a tone crept into his voice that suggested that doubts were throbbing in his brain to belie the serenity of his face.

"Men, the steward has fell down in his job of keeping the ship in food. The cook's no good anyhow —"

A loud murmur showed a desire to agree with the master on something, though the hapless Scotty was to be sacrificed. The captain resumed again.

"Now, I know some of you want to get paid off — this is what I'll do — we'll take the ship into Barcelona and then I'll pay off anybody who wants to go."

Guttural mouthings of approval sounded from the ragged mob.

"All right," Sullivan replied a little doubtfully. "That's a go with us."

And with a mumbling sound not unlike that of steam escaping underwater, they hurried down the ladder, having entirely forgotten their original purpose, while the skipper shrugged his shoulders and stepped back into his cabin.

Turning his ugly, genial face round to mine, Tescula nudged me in the ribs with his huge elbow and croaked in his deep rasping voice, "Well, what did I tell you! They ain't got no guts, those guys. Had him by the eyebrows and let him go — huh!"

"What would you have done?" I asked impertinently.

"Me? Why, I would have gone and sat on the seat of my pants until I saw the grub coming over the side, that's what I'd do. It don't do no good to talk about it. Sure! Those guys, they don't know what they want. They is too willing to do something for nothing."

Tescula turned and began to hobble off. One of his legs was a full inch shorter than the other, his shoulders were so round one might think him hunchbacked, and his face was long, pockmarked, and thin, and partly covered with brown beard. Only the pale eyes glinting beneath the stubble of his shaved pate were easy to look at, and they were gentle, sympathetic, and generous — quite unrelated to the rest of his plainness.

"Where you going, Tescula?"

"What?"

He bellowed savagely, hesitated, and then snorted, "Bah!"

In a low voice, as if he were ashamed to be heard, he added "I promised to help the deck engineer with a winch he can't fix alone."

I laughed to myself as he clumped down the ladder.

Halfway down the gorgelike harbor a small steamer was backing away from a quay. The smoke billowing from her skinny funnel rose straight into the heavy heat of the air like the plume on a quill pen and cast a flickering shadow over the opposite shore, as it drifted across the sun. Cockleshell gondolas painted light blue and purple and orange, with high slender prows and sterns, flashed upon the narrow waters. High over the obsolete fortresses at the harbor's mouth flocks of gulls wheeled in the air. It was a gay morning. The fleet of crude black coal scows surrounding the *Amphitrite* creaked against each other as the minute waves slapped their splintered sides and washed at the coal piled just out of reach.

Suddenly, the crew and the half-naked stevedores sweating amidships were startled by a blast of steam thundering on the

after well-deck. Within that scalding cloud of vapor that ed-
died round the winches by the mainmast someone was screaming. As we rushed aft to the ladders, the deck engineer stumbled headfirst from the cloud, cowering behind his raised arm
and dragging Tescula by the leg.

"Hey, you guys!"

He gesticulated wildly.

"Get the mate! Tescula's killed! Dead, I say — damn cylin-
der head wasn't on tight — hit him in the chest — those
damn fools in the engine room — turned the steam on —
crazy sons o' bitches — what the hell they thinkin' of — he's
killed — damn 'em!"

Tescula lay very quiet on the hot deck while we crowded
round to gape at his wet shirt, the pallid unshaven cheeks that
were beginning to redden and swell, and the livid chest. After
a while he began to writhe in his agony, not a single word
breaking the silence. Crimson blisters began to puff out on his
neck and gird it like a brand seared across raw flesh. Although
the sight was ghastly enough, not a single man was other than
childishly inquisitive. I do not mean that we did not pity the
ugly little lame man, for we all did. We loved him in our way.
Had he not stood Macaroni's watches for hours after we had
found the delirious Italian rolling on the deck of a latrine and
screaming with the pains of acute indigestion? Had he not
given his only suit of clothes to a poor devil starving on the
beach in Salonika? Had he not saved my life for me off Newfoundland? Was he not the one man on the *Amphitrite* always ready to help a shipmate with his work? Everyone loved
Tescula — just as he was always loved by the shipmates with
whom he sailed in some part of the wide, wide sea.

"Take him up midships to the spare room," the mate said.

Then a dozen men stooped to comply as tenderly as their rough hands could, and got in each other's way and cursed as they carried his dead weight forward to the room in the after-house that served as the ship's hospital.

The damage to the winch was repaired, the Maltese returned to their toil, and all went on as it had before, but Tescula, daubed with vaseline and tannic acid and swarthed in compresses, lay quiet and white in the darkened room. Detailed by the mate to look after Tescula for a while, I remained near him talking to Tom Meadows, the fifteen-year-old ex-third cook who was rotting inwardly with venereal diseases resulting from his adventures in each port we had visited. He was a sturdy boy, tousle-headed, with big brown eyes and a perpetually dirty face. Worse than that, he had an offensive habit of picking his sores and handling with his unwashed fingers everything in sight.

" 'S'all right," he would say, "I'll get over it."

I sat gingerly on a box and watched Tescula, looking from the corner of my eye at Tom lest he inadvertently come close to contaminate me. Tom was too colossally ignorant to know any better. An hour passed before Tescula was able to say a word. At last he muttered something about water and I went to fetch him a drink. For two days he lay in tense agony, his face twitching and working — the only means by which we knew the extent of his suffering.

But on the night before the *Amphitrite* made Barcelona he was able to sit outside on a hatch and take the air. It was a beautiful clear night with an old moon riding jauntily over a few fluffy clouds in the jet sky, the kind of night that may arouse long-forgotten tendernesses. A steady breeze piled up a long heaving swell over which the ship rose and fell with a comfortable, pleasant motion. The sea glowed like a bubbling mass of molten silver. Greedily breathing at the fragrant salt wind I felt supremely happy. Here I was on the eve of reaching a new strange land, the gaiety, sunshine, and beauty of which I had heard sung for weeks! Here was the simple and stalwart Tescula beside me! Ah, how little did I divine the stark adventure that lay ahead.

"You seem to have a lot of hard luck, Tescula," I mused.

"Huh!" He laughed. "Well, what harm it does to a poor old booze-fighter like me?"

"Well," I continued, "you have too much trouble. All these accidents haven't helped your health any."

"Yes, I'm wearing out I guess. I won't last much longer. And when I go I'll say, 'Goodbye nothing, and bedamned!' "

After a short silence he barked, "And what of it, huh?"

Since I had learned not to be disturbed by his gruffness, I laughed also.

The moon sailed on nearer the bright horizon; the wind blew cooler. I began to shiver, and the *Amphitrite* wallowed on her course without a care or emotion in the world — just like the unfeeling mass of steel that she was.

At sunrise we arrived at Barcelona, the gay city of the starry-eyed señoritas who preen themselves along its palm- and maple-shaded *ramblas,* the city of which I had dreamed so long, in the land of romance. Nearer and nearer ground the *Amphitrite* toward those ruby walls, past the orange-colored sails of the lateen-rigged fisher fleet bouncing out to sea on the breath of a light western breeze, past a stodgy old English tramp that loitered near the breakwater. She slipped by the mole into the jumble of spars and drying sails and a murky cloud of smoke drifting from a score of funnels until at last she lay quietly on the smooth, shimmering gloss of the dirty harbor water that heaved so restlessly, with an oily flow, as if some pulsating form of life moved and breathed beneath its opaque surface.

At the quay of the Estación Sanataria where the *Amphitrite* lay in quarantine with a yellow flag drooping at her foremast, a dingy hospital van arrived in the late afternoon. Then Tescula and Tom were loaded into a battered old bumboat at the gangway and carried to that wheezy van, Tescula quite happy to think of white sheets and a pretty Catalonian nurse, Tom worrying lest they want to open up his insides.

The last I ever saw of the little lame man was his blue dungarees and his knee-length seaboots just inside the open rear end of that old van.

One by one the crew were drifting apart, leaving the *Amphitrite* as if she were a pestilence. Scrambling in desperate haste down into a bumboat, Mahoney had furiously paddled away in Piraeus without looking back. The morbid Gus lay at the bottom of the sea, where at last it was cold and quiet. Louie had lurched his gorillalike body away earlier in the morning before the customs officials were hardly out of sight. Macaroni had slipped away in Cyprus and now Tom Meadows and the little lame man had left the *Amphitrite*. In a cloud of dust the ambulance rattled over the cobblestones away from the yellow estación and swung around a corner to lose itself in the hollow murmuring sound and rancid smell of the great city. I was left alone on the steel quarterdeck in the sultriness of the afternoon, feeling as if my world were falling from beneath my feet.

17. On the Beach

JUST BEFORE Tescula and young Tom had been taken away to a hospital in the ambulance, I had gone to the room improvised as a sick bay that they occupied to see if I could perform any last services for them. Tescula was sitting up on the edge of his bunk and Tom had gone outside.

"Say, Emery," Tescula leaned toward me and said in a low voice, "I think you is in a bad spot. I hear you is one of those who saw the steward steal all the grub in Salonika. Ya! And I hear he is going to have all of you put out of the way. He is a bad mans, boy! I think you had better get off this old hack just as soon as you can. This is from your friend."

Tescula's remarks had disturbed me rather badly. So seriously did I take them that I wasted little time in climbing up to the captain's bridge. I found him in his office and at my hesitant knock he called, "Come in."

With respect to my business I could not have arrived at a more unfortunate time.

"Sir," I said, "can I get paid off here?"

"Yes," he replied with obvious annoyance, "but it will take a while. We have a lot of trouble and we have no orders until this cargo is sold again. I don't know where we're going and we'll have to find a replacement for you."

He hesitated and looked at me with narrow eyes.

"Do you know anything about this business in Salonika?"

I answered directly, "Yes, sir, I was one of those who saw the whole thing, but I didn't say anything."

"Yes, I know you didn't. But others have talked plenty and I don't know just what's going to happen."

He shifted restlessly and seemed to have exhausted his patience with me and everything else.

"Now you go back to work and keep clear of this bridge unless I send for you."

As I returned to the shelter deck I saw the steward descending the ladder to go ashore. Knowing he would not be back in time for dinner I summoned enough courage to go to work in the pantry, and later I served dinner to the officers during a strangely silent meal. A little later I accosted my friend George, the third assistant engineer, whom I knew I could trust.

"What's the latest you hear?" I asked.

"Well, I don't know who talked," he said. "I guess everybody did and the ship's full of rumors — all about the grub and the mate trying to swipe the new hawsers and even the chief's accused of buying boiler water at a cheap price to substitute for drinking water."

He added, "But I don't believe that. I wasn't on watch at the time but I know Charlie from way back, and he's honest. He wouldn't have done that. But he'd like to know who did — he's still got dysentery pretty bad."

"Do you think I'm in any danger from the steward?"

He thought a moment.

"I really don't know, Emery," he finally said. "But I'd keep out of his sight as well as you can."

"Keeping out of sight" was not so easily managed in my position. As pantryman I was literally under the steward's thumb. And my imagination was working at a lively tempo and I was growing more apprehensive by the hour. Since the steward didn't return for supper, I survived that ordeal. Then I went ashore with a group of the sailors.

We strolled up to the monument in the Plaza Colón at the center of the harborfront, then up toward the Rambla de los Fleures, a beautifully tree-shaded avenue with a broad walk in the middle. Since I didn't have any money, I felt quite uneasy because I didn't like to sponge on these goodhearted shipmates. But there was no holding back. Old Edwin insisted on buying me a bottle of beer, which I was in no mood to enjoy. Soon Paul and Edwin and Chips began to talk about girls.

"I think we better go up to Madame Vicente's place," Chips suggested.

"Yes," rejoined Edwin, "that's the place called 'the house of the holy angels,' or is it holy innocents?"

"Well, no matter," Paul chimed in, "they is good girls and they is inspected by a doctor every day."

"Come on, we'll all go up," said Edwin. "And that means you, Emery."

"Oh, no," I hastened to reply, "not me. This ship is so full of disease I won't go near the place."

"That may be so," said Edwin, "but you don't have to do nothing. You can sit and listen to the victrola while we is out. Now come on, we don't want to lose you. And if you get lost maybe the old steward shoots you, huh?"

For all I knew, he might be right about the steward so I decided to stay with the crowd for my own uneasy comfort and safety.

There were eight of us, and the sound of our shoes as we clumped up the long flight of echoing wooden stairs to the "Abode of the Holy Innocents" brought joy to the bloated face of Madame Vicente and squeals from some of the half-naked girls who peeked around the corner at the top. We were led into a completely barren room about twenty feet square, three sides of which were lined with plain kitchen-type wooden chairs on a bare wood floor; the whole place reeked with phenol — and so did all the ladies. I imagined that these antiseptic exhalations were intended to suggest assurance against veneral disease. An upright piano and an old victrola occupied the fourth side of the room, and the walls were all decorated with religious chromoprints depicting angels sitting on clouds, the dripping heart of Jesus, and various men and women clad in decorous robes and all with painful expressions fixed dolefully on the Heavens.

Madame Vicente was an obese lady in middle life, fluent with a few standard expressions in various languages that indicated her understanding of the objectives of her guests. She waddled about encouraging the immediate initiation of sexual activity. Her "angels" or "innocents" sat in a row on one side of the room waiting to be selected by the clients who sat in a row opposite them. They were uniformly clad in a transparent black silk chemise that barely covered their buttocks, high-heeled slippers on their feet, and many wore elaborate coiffures with high Spanish combs or ribbons in their hair. None of them could be called pretty; some were cross-eyed, some very fat or skinny, and all looked definitely subnormal or moronic. Clearly, Madame Vicente's place did not attract a discriminating clientele.

Being the last to enter I sat uncertainly on a kitchen chair nearest the door, placed my brown felt hat on the floor beside me, and looked about apprehensively. I felt decidedly uncomfortable. How could I escape the attentions of Madame Vicente with any dignity at all! As the other men selected a lady partner for anticipated delights and one by one followed her down a hall leading from the far side of the room and up another flight of stairs, I remained mute and fidgeted on my hard chair.

Madame Vicente planted herself in front of me and began to waggle her huge pendulous bosoms in my face and to squirm in a manner that might be called suggestive of lewd gestures. All the time she rasped in a jargon intended to invite my attention to various of her assistants to which she pointed one after the other.

"What your name?" she cackled.

"John," I replied.

"Here, John, much fine girls. You pick."

I finally blurted out an excuse that I hoped would discourage her ministrations, "I haven't got any money," I called in desperation.

She abruptly ceased and regarded me with a puzzled look.

But then Edwin, who had continued to exercise a paternal interest in my welfare, shuffled over and reached in the pocket of his dungarees to produce a handful of pesetas that he pushed into my hand and exclaimed, "Here, boy, I lend you pesetas."

Madame Vicente looked relieved and grabbed at my fistful of money, but I successfully evaded her gesture and plunged it into my own pocket. Then she and Edwin withdrew in a conspiratorial discussion beyond my hearing. Presently they both laughed and Madame Vicente jabbered a bit and bawled "Angelita!" Turning back toward me she called, "Hey, John, I give you my daughter — Angelita. She only for high-class caballeros."

At that moment there entered a rather pretty and chubby child with rouged lips and glossy black hair. She might have been aged thirteen but was unmistakably nubile. Taking instruction from her mother who pointed at me, she suddenly raised her chemise above her umbilicus, shouted "Hey, John," skipped across the floor, and leaped astraddle my lap, calling, "Hey, John, plenty jig-y-jig, plenty jig-y-jig," during which she engaged in various gyrations doubtless intended to arouse my so-called animal desires.

But alas! Her seductive movements aroused in me sentiments contrary to those needed to accomplish her expectations. I was frightened almost out of my wits. In a flash of foreknowledge I imagined myself about to be confined in the syphilitic ward of a hospital. I panicked. Forgetting all my manners and sense of chivalry, I rudely pushed Angelita off my lap so that she sprawled on her back on the floor in a most indecorous posture with her legs up in the air. Simultaneously, I grabbed my hat and ran pell-mell down the wooden stairs, leaving behind me a pandemonium of screeches, screams, and profane threats to my very life. Even as I ran I wondered whether Madame Vicente's outraged yells were more concerned with the humiliation of her daughter than with her failure to acquire my money.

I was so agitated that I ran as fast as I could up the Rambla for two blocks until I began to lose my breath and slowed down to a walk. I was promptly apprehended by two policemen, members of the elite Civil Guard with their distinctive polished black-leather hats. Fortunately for me, one of them spoke English. After they had examined my seaman's identification card, searched me for weapons, counted my money, and returned it, one asked, "Why were you running?"

"Somebody wanted my money," I puffed, "and I need it, too."

Since I was sober and looked reasonably respectable, the officer replied, "You should not run. Next time you should call out and we would come in time. When people run away they are mostly guilty and we have to arrest them. But you can go and we hope you'll like Barcelona."

"I guess I'll go back to my ship," I said.

They slowly walked with me back toward the Plaza Colón and fortunately for me we passed Madame Vicente's place without meeting anyone who might be interested in me. At the Plaza Colón the English-speaking officer said, "Keep out in the open on the quays. This is a very dangerous place. There are several murders here every night."

About a half mile down the quay, near the stern of a Canadian freighter, I met several men sitting on a lumber pile and listening to some really good violin music coming from the ship. The radio man was sitting outside his radio shack on the boat deck, playing a violin from memory. With the bright moonlight it was quite lovely. I stopped to listen.

"Ain't you from the *Amphitrite?*" one of the figures on the lumber pile called to me.

Turning toward the group, I recognized several whom we had fed both at dinner and supper earlier in the day. It was a universal custom at that time for crews in port to feed any destitute seamen who might come aboard; they were given the food left over after the crew began to leave the messroom, the same food given the crew, and with clean plates and cutlery. After eating, they usually stayed to help the messboy clean up. These were men who were penniless and often without identification, having missed the sailing of their own ships and exhausted the patience of their nation's consuls. Eventually, they usually shipped out in vessels that had difficulty in obtaining crews, for good reasons, and sometimes they stowed away.

"Yes, I remember you," I called back. "Was the grub all right?"

"About the usual, and good enough," the speaker, who was an Englishman, replied.

"Is this where you stay?"

"Yes. Want to join us?"

I thought for a moment.

"If you'll let me," I said, "I've jumped from *Amphitrite* and I've got to stay somewhere until they pay me off. I can't go back there."

"I heard there was a lot of trouble in her. Well, come aboard."

He didn't introduce himself or anybody else, but he did explain their arrangements for mutual protection.

"We built a bit of a wickiup here," he said. "While the rest are sleeping, one of us sits outside the hole to keep guard. The gangs travel by threes and fours and they let us alone because they know there are too many of us. It's these blokes what sleep out alone that are killed for their money or their clothes."

So I joined this group of seven seamen and went "on the beach" to hide from whatever enemies I might have, imaginary or otherwise, until I could get paid off from the *Amphitrite*.

Each day somebody shipped out or never returned to our hideout and somebody new joined the group. The police were aware of us and kept a benignant eye on us to some extent. We were known to be law-abiding and eager to leave port. Life could have been much worse.

Barcelona in 1922 was an interesting port for various reasons, one of which was that there were several large, steel, square-rigged sailing ships and barks at the quays unloading guano from Chile. These were the homes of last resort for the stranded seamen who had no identification papers. Just how their signing on was arranged, I never learned. But when a man was completely discouraged he could join one of these old sailing vessels for a trip around Cape Horn and somehow become equipped with reliable new credentials. So I never fell into despair, and aside from the fact that my clothes were getting dirty and I had grown an unsightly and uncomfortable beard, at times I was almost enjoying myself.

One afternoon when I was passing the time of day while awaiting suppertime near an Italian ship that I knew would feed me, I spied the *Amphitrite*'s old carpenter wandering near a pile of crates on the quay. I called eagerly to him.

"Well, well," he cried, "if here ain't the student! Oh, my God! And how do you like beachcombing?"

"You damned idiot, can't you see I'm having a wonderful time?" I shouted. "It don't make any difference to you, does it?"

"Yes," he agreed. "They ought to give you your pay, hadn't they! My God, what a pretty sight you is! Where is the looking glass? Haw!"

Chips was slightly drunk. His blue eyes blinked vacantly under the lopsided brim of his straw hat and his long legs seemed unable to keep from getting tangled up in each other. In his hand he carried a wilted bouquet of flowers, a sad, bedraggled-looking thing that he had bought from a bumboatman.

I snorted derisively. "Ho! Where do you think you're going with that thing! Got some woman up town?"

"I'm going to take 'em up to Tescula."

"Oh!"

Then I almost felt like asking his pardon, but I was not yet man enough. Up the quay toward the richly sculptured granite mass of the *aduana* Chips reeled, awkwardly stumbling over himself every few yards and smelling of his drooping flowers.

"Poor old Chips, God bless you," I thought. Then I tried to swallow the lump that was choking me but failed.

On the fourth afternoon I took up a place near the *Amphitrite*, which still lay near the outer end of the quay. There was no sign of cargo activity at all. From where I sat I could watch my former shipmates as they disembarked from the bumboats at the landing. After a while I saw Sparks, my friend the radio officer, and I hailed him.

"Hey, Emery, we've been looking for you. I've got some good news. The steward's been arrested by the consul and, as a consul prisoner, will be put aboard a ship called the *West Caliph* bound for New York in about a week."

"Did he make any trouble for anyone?" I asked.

"Not a bit of it. He confessed the whole thing and said he was solely responsible. Took everybody else off the hook. There's just one thing though."

Sparks hesitated.

"They need an affidavit to wrap up the whole business and Bill Nadeau and I have given them all the dope they need — what we saw, you know — and we're going to sign it at the consulate tomorrow morning. They want you to sign it, too."

"I'll do that," I promised.

"Well, you better come back to the ship with me now. You can clean up and sleep in your old bunk and work in the pantry tonight and for breakfast. I told the skipper I'd try to find you so this business can all be cleaned up and you can get paid off in the morning. You got nothing to worry about and everybody feels all right about us because of all the bad feeding the crew had to put up with on account of the steward."

I returned to *Amphitrite* with Sparks. Frenchy greeted me as I came over the gangway, "Ah, Emery! How please I am to see you! I been doing all your work and my own since you been gone. Please to clean up and help me!"

Bill Nadeau, the second cook, said to me, "You shouldn't

have run away. You had nothing to fear from the steward. You remember I told you I'd put up with anything excepting stealing the men's food? Well, I turned him in and he knows it."

Scotty said with a leer, "Long ago I told you this'd break your bloody heart, didn't I?"

"Well, it didn't," I replied and turned away toward my old room.

18. All Aboard Once More

THE CAPTAIN'S GUEST at breakfast in the saloon was a handsome, intelligent young American named Jim McDermott, the port supply officer for the United States Shipping Board, which owned and had jurisdiction over *Amphitrite*. McDermott was responsible for the provisioning of all shipping-board vessels touching at Spanish ports. He was tall, built like an athlete, quick in his movements and his understanding, and fluent in Spanish and other languages. Moreover he was thoroughly dedicated to his job.

His purpose in coming aboard *Amphitrite* that morning was to escort Sparks, Bill Nadeau, and me to the United States Consulate. I felt that I could trust this man and for the first time really believed that my fortunes might take a turn for the better.

At the consulate we read over and signed the affidavits concerning theft of the food. Louie and Bob also came in; Louie had joined the crew of a Finnish ship bound for North Sea ports so he would be no problem to the consul and was paid his full back wages. Bob was reconciled to the knowledge that he would miss the opening of Worcester Polytech but believed he would be admitted for the fall term, even if he was a few weeks late. *Amphitrite* would take five of the consul's indigent Americans off his hands and the remainder he planned to ship to New York in a week as "workaways" in the *West Caliph*. The captain signed our discharge papers, the money was counted out, and I received much more than I had expected, due to some provision for "overtime" of which I had not been aware.

As we left, McDermott gave us a steer to the place where he lived, Madame DeBerque's pension at 79 Rambla Cataluna.

Madame DeBerque was an elderly, tall, very gracious lady dressed entirely in black except for a fine cameo brooch at the neck of her high white collar. She greeted us in perfect English, since she had lived in England for some years, and showed us a large, high chamber that looked out over the street and was furnished with three beds and two walnut armoires. She also showed us the parlor and the dining room and announced that luncheon would be served at one o'clock. Everything seemed so luxurious and spacious that Bob and I felt as if we had been transported into a real Spanish castle.

The very next day *Amphitrite* sailed for Glasgow to discharge her cargo of carob beans that had finally been bought by a Scottish firm. She carried a new steward and replacements for the five of us who had been paid off and left behind.

My mind would have been perfectly at ease if I could have known that the ex-steward would not bear a grudge against me. But I would be uneasy until I knew he had left port.

A week after we had been installed at Madame DeBerque's, Jim McDermott told us at dinner that the *West Caliph* had arrived a few hours earlier and he suggested that we both go aboard in the morning to make certain that the captain would take us. It was customary for a captain to accept any work-away seamen that a consul might recommend, but it was not mandatory and the shipmaster could use his own discretion.

Consequently, next morning we found the *West Caliph* docked alongside a pier not far from where *Amphitrite* had lain and presented ourselves to the captain, who happened to be standing near the gangway. He said, "Yes, I guess we got room for you. Come to the consulate tomorrow about ten o'clock and we'll sign on."

Then he looked sharply at me and asked, "Can you run a typewriter?"

"Yes, sir, I'm not a typist but I can get along," I replied.

His eyes lighted. "Ah, good, you can do all my typing. I have so much of it, I don't get time to sleep. See you tomorrow."

When we arrived at the consulate, a vice consul was reading off a list of six names, including that of the *Amphitrite*'s ex-steward, of those who were to be signed to work their passage back to New York in the *West Caliph*. When I heard the steward's name I knew I could never sail in that ship, yet I didn't want to be left behind. My name was not on the list. The vice consul promptly herded the five, including Bob but not including the steward, who was not present, into another office. I couldn't get near the vice consul to ask why I was omitted and I had the distinct impression that he was avoiding me. I sat in the waiting room, hat in hand, in frightened dejection.

Presently, the door opened and the *West Caliph's* captain hurried out. I rushed to intercept him, with a strained smile, "Captain," I said, "I thought I was going with you!"

He neither looked at me nor stopped in his hurry to leave the building, but he did say, very brusquely, "No, haven't any place for you. S'all taken care of."

I was crushed. When Bob appeared, he knew no more than I did, and my efforts to find the vice consul were fruitless. At lunch I told the story to Jim McDermott and he said yes, he had heard about it and said the vice consul had told the Shipping Board office that when the captain learned I was one of the signers of the affidavit implicating *Amphitrite's* steward, he became convinced that I was a detective employed by the government and he struck my name from the list that very morning. Jim added, "We've decided in our office that maybe something is worrying the old boy so we're going to make a fine-tooth comb examination of his inventories, beginning this afternoon."

Bob went away after lunch and I never saw nor heard of him again. The *West Caliph* duly sailed three days later. My attempts to buy a passage on any ship were useless; in 1922 immigration into the United States was at a peak and people were booked ahead for months for any available space. There was a better chance in the channel ports, it was said, because stranded American citizens up there were given a standby preference, especially in British and American passenger liners. So it was decided that I should go to Madrid to get a special ambassadorial passport because my seaman's papers did not permit me to travel overland between countries.

Returning to Madame DeBerque's pension with passport safely in hand, I met Jim McDermott leaving for his office. "Emery," he said, "you may not need your passport after all. Unexpectedly this morning a large American freighter will arrive. She's going to pick up a few hundred tons of high-paying freight and then is going right on. She's also going to put a man in the hospital so she may have a berth. But you may not want to join her — she's outbound for the Far East."

My eyes widened. "Gee, I'd like to go to the Far East. When does she get in?"

"She's probably in now. When you get cleaned up come down to the office and they can tell you exactly where she is."

By eleven o'clock I climbed aboard the *Winona*, which was lying alongside a pier on the eastern side of the inner harbor. She was much larger than *Amphitrite*, weighing 10,000 tons, and she was a turbine-driven oil burner that cruised at a standard speed of twelve knots. She was of the three-island type, like *Amphitrite*, painted black with white deck houses, buff masts and fittings, and a buff funnel with a broad blue band and a buff sphere in the middle. Her crew, all told, numbered thirty-two against *Amphitrite*'s forty-eight. She was heavily laden with case oil, automobiles, and general cargo and couldn't stow any more than she would take on in Barcelona. At once I knew I wanted to sail in this ship under almost any conditions.

"The mate's name's Crocker and he's in his room now," the gangway watch told me.

When I knocked at the mate's door a voice called, "Come in," and even in these two words I detected the mellow tone and unmistakable twang of Down-East dialect.

I stepped over the high threshold and introduced myself. "My name's Emery Cleaves," I began. "I'm regrettably on the beach here and I'd like to sail with you."

He received this intelligence in stony silence. Then he asked, "What part of the coast you from?"

I knew exactly which coast he meant. "Mostly from Falmouth and Portland and north to the Bay region and south as far as Newburyport."

"I come from Rockland," he said.

"The cradle of sailors," I replied.

"Not so much anymore," said he. "Sail is gettin' scarcer and scarcer and it ain't so easy t' ship out nowadays."

"I found that out, too," I agreed.

Our conversation languished for a while during which we looked at each other silently. He was a man in his middle forties, over six feet tall and with a weight of about two hundred pounds, very agile and quick in his movements; his brown face was lined and strong, and his thick hands said plainly that here was a man who had been raised in sail and would be a good man in any ship.

After a time he asked, "What's your ratin'?"

"Still an ordinary," I said, "but I only got two months to go for an A.B." Then I added, "I been in sail, too, in the *Kenwood* with Cap'n Grant and in the *Tina Marie*."

Again there was a considerable silence, which Mr. Crocker, or rather Captain Crocker, for he held master mariner papers and had commanded vessels of his own, finally broke with almost a flood of volubility, in a comparative sense. He said, "Well, you go ashore and get your gear and get right back here and eat dinner aboard. The consul don't know it, but the man we put ashore to the hospital is too sick to sail with us. He's on his last legs. I'm havin' the bosun pack up his gear now to send after him. After dinner the vice consul's comin' aboard to see if we need a replacement and we will, and you'll be here, so there won't be any fuss an' bother. I'd rather have a man from Maine than somebody I don't know about."

Feeling giddy, I arose and extended my hand, which he grasped with a gesture of embarrassment. Captain Crocker was not exactly a social lion in a drawing room, but he was a real man in a ship and won my gratitude and loyalty forever. I felt that now I might begin to amount to something.

That good old lady, Madame DeBerque, was delighted at my good fortune and insisted on helping me pack. Perhaps she was thinking of a son now long dead. She even insisted on darning a pair of socks for me. "Now you be a good boy and write me," she said. Then she kissed me on the cheek and pushed me out into the hall, and added, "Now hurry and don't miss this ship. I'll tell Mr. McDermott what's happened when he comes in for his lunch. God bless you!"

Aboard *Winona* I was issued a clean mattress and pillow covers, sheets, blankets, and towels, and moved into a room shared with two quartermasters, or helmsmen. The sick man whom I was replacing had been a quartermaster. This room was adjacent to the sailors' fo'c's'le on the starboard side in the fantail, and in the same passageway were rooms for the bosun and the ship's carpenter. The firemen's fo'c's'le was on the port side aft, and the oilers and deck engineer were berthed adjacent to them. A large messroom between the fo'c's'les was shared by both the deck and engine room hands very congenially. Firemen and wipers in an oil-burning ship seemed to belong to a higher order of humanity than those in coal-burning ships. Strangely enough the engine room crowd in this ship were all American born, and with the exception of myself the sailors were all foreign. Both of these fo'c's'les were scrupulously clean. I felt at home.

After dinner while I was scraping red paint from the main deck aft with the other sailors preparatory to sluicing it down with a rust-preventive "fish oil," the mate summoned me up to the ship's saloon to sign the crew list. The vice consul looked at me and smiled, but said nothing. The captain and the mate were seated at the green, felt-covered table signing other papers. "There, that does it," said the captain, putting on his uniform cap. "I reckon we'll sail at four o'clock if the pilot gets here on time."

For making and leaving port, I was assigned to the mate's detail on the fo'c's'le head, unless I should happen to be at the wheel. This pleased me because I would be able to show him what a strong and willing hand I was and confirm his hope that he had made no mistake when he hired me.

At eight bells, four o'clock in the afternoon precisely, the sailors were called to take in the spring lines and prepare to cast off all but those at the bow and stern. Then came the final order from the bridge, the bow line was slackened to be cast off on the pier, and we hove it in on the thundering windlass and coiled it in its locker beneath the fo'c's'le head. While her deep-throated whistle boomed a prolonged blast and she slowly backed into the sunlit harbor, I saw Jim Mc-

Dermott running down the quay. I waved at him and he yelled back, "Good luck, Emery! From what I hear this is a real good ship."

And so it proved to be. From beginning to end of the long voyage it was a home away from home and a joyous adventure at every turn.

19. Blue Water Again

UNLIKE *Amphitrite,* whose sailors stood two watches in each twenty-four hours, *Winona*'s sailors stood three and a half watches during a full day and two and a half watches the following day. This was accomplished by using the old sailing ship system of "watch for watch" — four hours on duty and then four hours off. To vary the order, the watch from four to eight o'clock in the afternoon was "dogged," or split into two short watches of two hours each. Thus, a man on deck stood the graveyard watch from midnight to four in the morning only every other night. This made it possible for a man to get two watches below, with consequently more sleep every other night also. The system required one less watch detail, or two less men "on deck" than in the three-watch system; it was used only for the deck crews — the engineers employed the full three-watch system, that is, three full engine room crews for each twenty-four hours. After working four hours a man had eight hours off.

When I went to stand my trick at the wheel in the early part of the dogwatch at five o'clock in the afternoon when we sailed, we were already clear of the harbor, had dropped the pilot, and laid a course toward the east that would clear Cape Ténès in Algeria by about twenty miles. It was fortunate for me that I would have a chance to learn "the feel of the ship" and how she steered when I had plenty of sea room instead of the confined area in a harbor.

A man always mounted to the wheelhouse on the port side of the bridge (the starboard was reserved for the exclusive use of the captain except in exceptional circumstances, such as severe storm), and he always wore clean clothes and had washed his face and hands. Time was provided for these amenities before he went on watch. In *Winona* there were two men in each watch and at night when one was at the wheel the other stood watch on the fo'c's'le head, in the bow, unless the weather was so bad there might be danger of his being washed overboard. In such a case, the man on lookout duty would stand his watch in the port wing of the upper, or navigating, bridge.

I entered the wheelhouse to take the wheel from my watchmate.

"Course is eighty-five degrees," he said, "and she carries a little starboard helm."

Unlike sailing vessels, for greater accuracy steamships are steered by compass degrees instead of by "points" of the compass, such as east by north half east.

I repeated, "Eighty-five degrees," and grasped the wheel spokes.

Then my watchmate repeated the course to the mate on duty, according to custom, "Course is eighty-five degrees, sir."

"Very well," the mate replied.

The ship was actually headed at eighty-three degrees when he handed her over and I watched the compass card in the binnacle to see which way it was swinging. Sure enough, represented by the lubber line, the ship's head soon began to swing to the right, so I checked it with a quarter turn of the wheel toward the left. Not enough; she continued to swing. I turned the wheel a few spokes more toward the left; the swing slowed, then stopped at course eighty-five degrees, and I eased the wheel lest the ship start swinging again in the other direction and move too far to port next time.

The mate stood directly in front of me, pretending not to notice, but I knew his practiced eye was checking the swing of the ship's foremast against the horizon. Presently, when he moved out into the starboard wing of the bridge, I knew he was satisfied with my steering.

At four bells I was relieved and walked aft to eat my supper. Since I would be called to go on the night watch at eight o'clock it didn't seem worthwhile to turn in, so I started for the number five hatch to get acquainted with my new shipmates. Just before I stepped over the high sill at the door, the carpenter called me from his room.

Chips was in his sixties, a stocky, rotund man with a shock of gray hair and watery blue eyes that were supplemented by steel-rimmed glasses. His name happened to be Crocker and he was a cousin of the mate, he told me later. He had been a sailor nearly fifty years, almost all of it in sail, and had been mate of large schooners. With that background he made an unusually competent ship's carpenter.

"Come in, boy," he called as I stood outside his door. "I hear tell you're from Maine."

"Well, the family is, but I grew up mostly in Massachusetts," I replied as I entered the compact little room and extended my hand.

He was perched on the edge of his berth, filling a pipe.

"I hear you sailed in the *Kenwood* with old Grant?"

"Yes, I spent one summer with him coastwise."

"Crusty old cuss — but a good man. Them ships is mostly laid up now, ain't they? Hard to get a job in 'em. I been sailin' as carpenter with Bill the last six months. 'T ain't bad. And it's a sight better livin' than the old days."

While he continued talking, my attention was suddenly caught by what might be called artwork on the white wooden bulkhead behind him. It covered nearly the whole side of the room and consisted almost entirely of postcard-size photographs of nude women, all colors, races, sizes, and shapes. They were artistically arranged like the rays of a rising sun, extending out in neat rows from a central photograph that might have represented the center of the universe. It was an amazing display. Chips noticed my preoccupation and moved to one side in order to facilitate my view. I fear I stood wide-eyed and agape. He seemed disappointed in my reaction and soon laid his finger on the central photograph. It showed a deadly serious man gazing soberly out from behind a pair of spectacles, sitting fully clothed even to a vest and heavy gold watch chain slung across his belly and holding on each knee a completely naked large fat woman, each with an arm around the man's neck and grinning broadly from under a large hair ribbon tied into a high coiffure.

"Well," called Chips with a trace of disappointment as well as eagerness in his voice, "do you see that old gentleman? You do, don't you? Don't you recognize him?"

"Good Lord, Chips," I cried, "it's you!"

"You're damn right it's me!" he shouted. "Ain't them fine-lookin' ladies!"

"Where was that taken?" I asked.

"Right in Boston," he replied. "Ain't nothin' in this world finer than a Yankee girl. They know all the tricks and then some, and they got class. Gives me great pleasure to lay here in m' bunk and look 'em over."

In the waning light of early evening out on number five hatch, just outside the fo'c's'les, most of the crew except those actually on watch were "passing the time of day," as the saying is. Engine room and deck forces in this ship fraternized together, probably because they ate together, and the fo'c's'les were almost contiguous. They were certainly congenial. Some lay or sat about talking or smoking. One or two were reading books or old magazines, and one or two more washing clothes. In short, the living habits of seafaring men in a fo'c's'le are just about the same as they would be were they living at home. A fo'c's'le is not a "hellhole" as so frequently described in fiction by writers who have never been to sea. It is as civilized and agreeable a place as would be found in the native habitats of the occupants. The living quarters of crews from countries of origin where sanitation is inculcated from early childhood are scrupulously clean and sweet-smelling.

Filth is not tolerated for an instant, and any violator of the code is immediately indoctrinated into acceptable standards of conduct by his shipmates. The spoken conversation is also a bit of a surprise to the uninitiated. Although in every group there are usually one or two foul-mouthed individuals, the normal customary speech is the same that would be found in the homes of the men, and that is invariably very decent.

Winona's deck crew were all foreign-born except myself. My watch mate was called Harry Boneyard because the others couldn't pronounce his Danish name. He was a powerfully built, large young man in his midtwenties who had achieved his United States citizenship by enlisting and serving in the American army in the World War, and he was very proud of it.

The other wheel watch consisted of Nick, a large Greek-born sailor who had been an American citizen for many years and served as bosun in the former transports *George Washington* and *Susquehanna*, both one-time German passenger ships. Nick's watch mate was of Italian ancestry from an island in the Greek archipelago so he spoke better Greek and English than Italian. His name was Mike Simeon and he shared the quartermaster's room with me and Harry. Nick preferred to live in the fo'c's'le.

The four sailors assigned to daytime deck duty were John, a roly-poly, very jolly Greek; another Nick from Salonika, a former soldier in the Turkish army in 1912, who was greatly intrigued by my recent visit to Salonika and frequently asked me questions about the status of this or that in the city; Louie, who was Rumanian-born; and Lascery, rated as "ordinary seaman," an elderly Lebanese, a former coal-burning fireman who had been on the beach in New York so long looking for a ship that he was glad to ship out as an "ordinary" at forty-five dollars a month.

This was Winona's deck crew, plus the carpenter and a bosun. The Greek-born bosun was a huge, dour man who looked like a pirate, but since he had sailed with Mr. Crocker, the mate, for several years I knew he would be all right. These men accepted me into their company at once, possibly a little shyly and with reservations until I should prove myself one way or another by my behavior and performance.

When I was called at seven bells near the end of the graveyard watch on the morning of the second day, Winona was laboring in cascading mountainous seas with a full gale blowing very hard from the east. It was more like a North Atlantic storm than what one might look for in the usually placid blue Mediterranean, but this was mid-October and one could expect a little "weather." The decks were awash fore and aft, and the ship buried her entire fo'c's'le head every once in a while, the water thundering aft to crash against the bulkhead of the shelter deck under the forward house. Whenever this happened the ship lost headway and shuddered.

"You report to the bridge for lookout," said Mike when he called Harry Boneyard and me. "She's shippin' 'em green. You'll need your oilskins."

When we reached the bridge, Harry relieved the wheel and I took up my station in the port wing. The port door to the wheelhouse was closed tight against the spray driving high from the port bow on the fury of the screaming gale. Frequently a black rain squall rattled against the ship. Through the window in the wheelhouse and by the dim light of the binnacle I could see the captain standing inside with the mate. Then, over the howl of the storm, I could hear and feel a heavy thumping and banging from the direction of the bow. I wondered, with some apprehension, what could be wrong. Presently, the engine room telegraph bells jangled and the ship was slowed to a speed of five knots, in effect heaving her to on her established course. The wheelhouse door slid open and the mate stepped out and headed for the ladder.

"Come with me, mister," he said.

We made our way up the heaving deck forward on the lee side and entered the bosun's locker under the fo'c's'le head. Whatever was amiss was directly under us in a compartment just above the forepeak tank. The mate closed the steel door, and together we undogged the large hatch that opened down into the lower compartment. An awesome sight lay below us. Six or seven fifty-gallon steel drums filled with paint or oil had broken their lashings and were rolling from one side of the vessel to the other and fore and aft. Each weighed close to two hundred pounds and could easily crush a man. It was a wonder that none of them had yet ruptured and made the deck an impossible slippery mess. As we stared down the hatch ladder I was reminded of Victor Hugo's story in *Quatre-Vingt-Treize* of the gunner in the French navy whose cannon broke its lashings and threatened to smash out the sides of the vessel in a storm. The gunner managed to capture the rampaging cannon, and for this he was first decorated by his commanding officer for heroism and then ordered put to death for criminal neglect of duty.

The mate and I slowly climbed down the steel ladder and made the end of a line fast to it. Then, watching our chance, when a drum momentarily lay still near us, we would step out, tip it up on end, and quickly pass a couple of turns of the line around it and make it fast to the ladder. When a roll or plunge of the bow would send the others crashing into a bulkhead or the ship's side we would nimbly leap behind the ladder for protection or climb up a few rungs and hang there awaiting another lull. Then we would dash out again to upend another drum. Since we were both clad in oilskins and the compartment was poorly ventilated, by the end of thirty minutes we were soaked in sweat and breathing hard. But we had tied up all the loose drums and secured the others with extra lashings so we could climb out into the cold driving rain with a sense of satisfaction that there would be no more danger from the forepeak stores.

"Thanks," the mate said to me as we staggered aft toward the bridge.

He was a laconic man and I knew this was real praise. The unexpected and supreme accolade was delivered a few weeks later one morning down in the Indian Ocean when I was at the wheel and the captain and the mate were standing in the wing of the bridge discussing the crew, unaware that the wind carried their voices within my hearing. When my name was mentioned I heard the mate say, "Well, if I could keep him with me for about a year I think I could make a real sailor out of him."

20. The Tourist

ON THE SIXTH MORNING after leaving Barcelona, the low sandy shores of lower Egypt and the flat roofs of the great city of Alexandria abruptly rose on our starboard bow out of what was then called the Bay of Tripoli. Shortly after noon we were riding serenely at anchor in the inner harbor. We were scheduled to lie there three days unloading automobiles and case oil into lighters alongside. I looked longingly at this new strange city and wondered how I could contrive to get ashore for sightseeing during daylight hours. I sought out my friend Chips as the most likely source of reliable information, especially since he drew some water with the mate.

"Well yes," he said, "the mate might let ye go but ye'd hafta hire a substitute to work for ye durin' the day. I guess the goin' rate here is a dollar a day."

The mate was agreeable when I told him I wanted to go up to Cairo to see the pyramids. He laughed, "Now what are ye, mister, a sailor or a tourist? Fix it up with the bosun."

When I explained to the bosun that the mate had told me to arrange with him to hire a man to do my day work for two days so I could go to Cairo, he was quite dubious at first. But the mate's blessing on the enterprise finally led him to agree to make arrangements with the longshoreman boss, but I would have to hire two men, he said, because one man did only half as much work as I would do. I readily agreed to this at one dollar a day apiece, and I always suspected that the longshoreman boss simply detached two men from his regular gang and pocketed the money himself. The Egyptian laborers wouldn't object because chipping paint off a bulkhead was much easier work than unloading a ship.

Next morning I paid the bosun in advance and went ashore in a bumboat. At the landing I was besieged by a yelling swarm of men who represented themselves to be tourist guides. One of the noisiest was a large fellow in European clothes who said his name was "Liverpool Yank" and that he would show me the sights of the city on the way to the railroad station in time to catch the ten o'clock local express for Cairo for ten piasters, then worth fifty cents. Moreover, we would walk. Since I would save the price of a carriage, it seemed like a fair arrangement.

Mindful that Alexandria also had connections with Alexander the Great even more direct than Salonika, I was disappointed that there were even less mementos of him to be seen. Although he had founded the city in 332 B.C. after conquering the Egyptian armies, the place had been subjected to a long Roman occupation in subsequent centuries. This is attested by the more prominent tourist attractions such as the Roman Museum, the catacombs, and the ancient public gardens.

Liverpool Yank guided me almost at a trot, barely permitting me time to take pictures of such things as the statue of Mohammed Ali, who was viceroy of Egypt during most of the first half of the nineteenth century, in the great square that bears his name. When my films were developed later I discovered that Liverpool Yank had inserted himself prominently in the foreground of every one of them. He rushed me through well-paved tarvia streets shaded by palm and locust trees, all freshly washed down and clean smelling. But he got me to the railroad station in time to purchase a third-class ticket for forty-four piasters (a piaster was then worth five cents) and board the train with five minutes to spare. When I paid him he was so profuse in expressions of gratitude that I'm sure we were both satisfied.

The third-class coach in which I had elected to ride in order to see something of the common people was open on all sides under a wooden canopy with canvas curtains for use in case of rain. The hard benches allowed ample room for one to surround himself with baggage; nearly everybody carried a vast amount of it, ranging from personal equipment to farm produce. It was a noisy, cheerful crowd of people who talked continuously all at once and were obviously enjoying themselves immensely. They were most friendly to me, and the few who spoke English helped me buy such things as chunks of bread and cheese, a shoot of sugar cane, and a glass of cold lemonade all for half a piaster per unit. That was my lunch.

The countryside between the picturesque small cities along the route was like a vast flower garden, green and luxuriant with maize, sugar cane, cotton, cabbage, tobacco and garden truck. Canals and irrigation ditches ran everywhere. It seemed strange to see lateen-rigged cargo dhows piled high with farm crops apparently sailing across green fields. The mud-walled buildings of the towns frequently supported a beehive-shaped structure on their flat-topped roofs for drying dung to be used for fuel. On the outskirts of a place called Damanhur I was especially impressed by the stark beauty of a white mosque surrounded by tall fields of grass shimmering in the windy sunlight.

After a seven-hour ride, every minute of which was an exotic delight, at about five o'clock in the mellowing day, the train pulled in to Cairo. I bid farewell to my neighbors and walked up toward the second-class coaches where the ubiquitous crowd of tourist guides were noisily soliciting clients. On the outskirts of the group I accosted one who was looking over the situation quietly rather than attempting to develop business by the power of his lungs alone. He said his name was Ali Kalifa and showed me his credentials licensing him as an official guide for patrons of Shepheard's Hotel. He was a tall, rather handsome middle-aged man with a broad black mustache, and he was clothed in his native burnoose with sandals and a red fez. Ali told me his fee was forty piasters a day.

"Look," I said, "I've got two hundred piasters. I want a light supper, a good clean hotel room and bath, and two meals tomorrow. I want you to take me out to the pyramids and show me what I should see in Cairo, and you can have all the money left over."

Ali's eyes lighted with pleasure. First he told me that although he was a Shepheard guide, he would not take me there because the room alone would cost me from one hundred forty to one hundred sixty piasters a night (seven to eight dollars) and he considered that a foolish waste of money. Then, since it was my regular seafaring suppertime and I was getting hungry, he took me into a small clean restaurant where we each had a bowl of cabbage soup, a large omelet and bread, and a piece of pastry for eight piasters each, plus a bottle of beer for three piasters each. He winked at me and said, "You may call this an alcoholic drink but I call it a cereal beverage. Now will you please buy me some cigarettes."

After our supper he walked me to a place called Hotel Central, near the square of Atab el Khadrah, a very decent place where the clerk, after bargaining a bit with Ali, finally quoted a price of twenty-five piasters for room and bath but with no provision for breakfast. Although this was apparently the rock-bottom price, Ali refused to listen and marched me out. Next, he led to a comparable hostelry called Hotel Tewfik in a pleasant street named Shari Maghraby, and here he found an excellently furnished room with bath and breakfast for thirty piasters ($1.50). We inspected the room, on the second floor, which opened out on to a balcony overlooking a garden restaurant where a stringed orchestra was playing chamber music. With this Ali expressed his satisfaction, "I will leave you now and arrive after breakfast in the morning. Will you please to give me an advance on my fee now so that I may take something home to my wife?"

"Will twenty piasters be all right?" I asked.

It would and he took himself off in a flutter of his robes down the staircase.

I soon followed him out and walked a few blocks in the warm evening before returning to my hotel.

By this time it was dark, so I luxuriated in a bathtub and then smoked a cigar as I sat in an armchair in the shadows of my balcony and listened to the orchestra playing in the garden below. I felt that Mark Antony and Julius Caesar never enjoyed their visits in Egypt more than I.

At seven-fifteen in the morning, after nearly eleven hours of sound sleep, the waiter awakened me and brought in my breakfast — three boiled eggs, bread, butter, and two cups of tea in a pot, together with milk and sugar. At seven forty-five Ali arrived just as I had finished shaving; he was full of business and in a hurry to get under way. We repacked my shaving and tooth brushing equipment in a paper sack, this, plus my camera, being my entire baggage. Then we walked a few blocks to board an electric train that would take us eleven miles outside the city to the pyramids at Giza. The round-trip fare was five piasters each way. The route followed the river, crossed it, and after a beautiful ride among fragrant gardens and fields we reached the great desert plateau.

Ali would not let me buy any of the artifacts hawked at the base of the great pyramid.

"All fakes," he said, "all made in Italy for tourists. Waste of money. Please pass me a cigarette."

Nor would he let me ride on a camel where a horde of tourists were clumsily trying to make themselves comfortable on those awkward and uncomfortable animals. These camels must have been recently washed because they didn't smell bad like those I saw in Cyprus.

"Much too expensive," Ali decided. "Sinful waste of money."

Since I really didn't want to waste my time on this sort of thing I was content to explore the four pyramids and have Ali take my photograph standing at the edge of a sandpit in front of the Sphinx. Then we boarded the train for Cairo and for the Egyptian quarter, which I really wanted to see. We wandered slowly along a particularly picturesque street called Shari Taht-el-Babah. Under the overhanging balconies, blacksmith shops, bazaars for dry goods, tailor shops, bakeries, meat, and food markets all bulged into the street. At almost every turn in that crooked, crooked lane a slender, blue-tipped minaret arose from a cluster of stuccoed stone buildings. The people moved between the shadows cast by the balconies and awnings in a carnival-like babble of cries and voices. To my surprise I noticed that the women's faces were ill-concealed by transparent white veils over the white low-necked undergarment beneath their black robes. Ali Kalifa seemed to have many friends here, for he frequently greeted and spoke to merchants and passersby as we dodged among the donkeys and porters carrying bundles on their heads.

Knowing my interest in native food he took me into a restaurant so small that we literally sat at the edge of the street, there being no sidewalk. The shish kebab (lamb roasted on a skewer) and the wheat pilaf with their sauces were delicious. For this Ali asked me to pay the proprietor ten piasters each. He terminated almost every request with his oft-repeated phrase, "Please give me a cigarette." For some reason he would not carry the box himself, nor would he accept its depleted contents when we parted.

By the time we finished our noon meal, although earlier than usual for both of us, it was time to return to the railway station to board the noon express for Alexandria. Ali would not countenance my riding in third-class accommodations. Absolutely no! All gentlemen traveled second-class; fools and thieves traveled first-class, and third class was strictly for thieves and peasants. Since I was no peasant I could only be taken for a thief or worse if I were seen there, he explained. So I paid eighty-eight piasters ($4.40) for passage in a second-class coach that had leather-upholstered benches in the compartments and was comfortable. Moreover, this train traveled much faster than the one on which I arrived. Without deducting the ticket money, which was not part of our bargain, I gave Ali fifty-four piasters as the residue of my two hundred piasters. Including his advance of the previous evening, this made his compensation total seventy-four piasters. I felt that I had received more than good value because without his intercessions I would have spent much more money and enjoyed it less, while Ali was so pleased that he excused himself for a moment and returned with a present for me of a large paper bag of ripe dates of the Shaman-Hat crop just coming into the market from Upper Egypt. I was really pleased, and he also said that the next time I visited Cairo he would put me up in his own home so that I could sample Egyptian middle-class life.

The whistle tooted, and the train moved out of the noisy station, leaving Ali Kalifa waving at me as long as he could be seen.

When I finally climbed the *Winona*'s gangway ladder, Harry Boneyard was abusing the sailors' messboy, an ex-chorus man from Broadway. Gareth Hill had done nothing to offend Boneyard; his appearance and presence were enough to irritate the rough sailor. Hill was a dark-complexioned, sallow, and very thin young man of about thirty years. He pretended to be better educated than he was, depending upon affectation and an artificial manner of speech for the effect he created.

"I'm gawna t'row ya right overboard — right here and now," Boneyard shouted, having just returned aboard somewhat intoxicated, and he prepared to seize the sad-looking actor.

"Oh, take your filthy hands off of me, you insufferable creature," Hill lisped, at the same time cringing and turning to me for protection.

"Aw, let him alone, Harry," I interceded. Not choosing my words too carefully, I added, "It isn't worth getting yourself in trouble for."

Harry relinquished his grip on Hill's shirt and to my amazement Hill turned his vituperation on me.

"You're just as bad as he is," he hissed in his effeminate way. "It's on account of privileged characters like you that the steward wouldn't let me engage a substitute so I could become a tourist, too. So I demanded to be paid off and I'm going to leave the ship in the morning."

"Nuts," shouted Boneyard, "yer bein' paid off because you was trying to corrupt d' crew."

"No, Harry, that's not the reason," said the third mate who had been observing the altercation. "The captain's paying him off because he doesn't think the guy's got the stamina to live through a trip like this."

Boneyard began to laugh and forgot his threats. He moved aft to our room where he lectured me for half an hour in terms of outraged morality on the general uselessness of actors, and chorus men in particular.

In the morning Hill apologized to me for his outburst and

gave me a khaki woolen army shirt that he didn't want to take with him. The boat that took him to the quay returned with his replacement, a young fireman of Norwegian ancestry who had missed his ship and came aboard with only the clothes on his back and his identification card. Thorwald was a quiet-spoken, hardworking man of about thirty years, half of which had been spent at sea. He fitted into *Winona*'s crowd from the first and was a good addition to the crew.

When we sailed at eleven that same morning I was secretly worried that Hill's accusation of me as a "tourist" might adversely affect my status as a seaman. But the captain inadvertently put my mind at rest. I was at the wheel when we took her out, and after we had dropped the pilot he came into the wheelhouse and began pacing back and forth. He laughed and said, "Well, sonny, in a way I was sorry for old 'Good Mornin' Dearie' and I didn't know quite how to get rid of him. But he got mad because the steward told him it was all right for sailors and engineers to act like tourists but cooks and stewards had to work. So when I heard he wanted to quit the ship I sent for him. He's going to be put on an American ship bound for Savannah and he'll be happy."

I felt better. After all, perhaps I could arrange some more future working days ashore if I didn't do it too often.

21. An Excursion into the Countryside

THE VOYAGE up to Beirut only took thirty hours, the last five of which were in sight of the high mountainous coast of Lebanon.

Eight days after our arrival *Winona* was a few thousand tons lighter in case oil and steamed up the coast for Alexandretta, now called Iskenderun, 185 miles to the north. At that time Alexandretta was what may best be described as a quaint Syrian town of about ten thousand Syrian, Greek, and Turkish inhabitants. Today it is seven times larger. It lay at the upper end of a calm and beautiful deepwater bay at the foot of a rich green valley where oranges, melons, grapes, and garden vegetables were grown. There was much sheep-raising and a considerable export of live mutton as well as wool and native wine. This picture-book setting in late October color was hemmed

in by high, rough, and jagged mountains, rocky and brown
with sparse vegetation on the upper slopes. Lovely and picturesque as the town was, it was marshy and unhealthy. Sewerage lay stagnant in open cesspools and in the gutters of un-
paved back streets; some vacant areas were covered with
swamp water.

Alexandretta was founded by Alexander the Great just after
his great victory over the Persians in 333 B.C. at Issus about
forty miles inland, in order to establish a base for continued
operations against the Persian maritime power. It was said
that when Alexander attempted to recruit men in the neigh-
borhood, they refused to go out and fight. The women rallied
to him, however, so after his decisive victory he decreed that
henceforth men in that part of the world should wear dresses
and the women should wear trousers as a symbol of reversed
courage and sex. It was eight o'clock of a bright Sunday morning when *Winona* anchored just off the single modern, large
dock. She was the only large freighter in port. This dock was
covered with a large amount of ammunition guarded by
French Senegalese troops and said, by local gossip, to be destined for use by the Turkish army against the Greeks in Ana-
tolia. In spite of its rumored importance there was little attempt at security. The bumboats serving *Winona* used this
dock as their landing.

After our Sunday dinner just about everybody either went
swimming off the ship in the clear water of the harbor or went
ashore. I found myself in the company of eight or nine shipmates, some from the deck force and some from the engine
room. We wore clean dungarees and blue shirts because Alexandretta looked so provincial that there didn't seem much

point in sweating out a warm fall afternoon in our heavy American wool suits. Once ashore, there wasn't much to see of local historical interest. I suggested that we hire a couple of carriages and take a ride out into the country. While there wasn't any opposition to the proposal, there wasn't any enthusiasm either. In short, it was too early to do anything except sit down in a beer garden or sidewalk café. The trouble with this idea was that we couldn't find any. Not many people were walking about; the shops were either shuttered or empty.

"What do people do here on Sunday afternoon anyhow?" inquired Shorty Smith, one of the wipers.

"Well, if you ask me," I replied, "they're all at home in their back yards taking a siesta, and that's just where I'd be, too, if I had a back yard. How about hiring a hack and taking a ride?" I asked again.

"What's wrong wid dis place?" asked Boneyard, stopping in front of a café.

In we went, to the joy of the proprietor, and each ordered a bottle of French wine he recommended, called "Old Bordeaux." Although the place was completely open to the street, it was hot and stuffy and the flies swarmed as thickly as they might have been expected to do at a local abattoir. By the time half our wine was consumed, with the proprietor's permission we picked up our oblong tables and moved them bodily out into the street. There we could sit in the dust of the road and the shade of the building at our tables, which were placed end to end, and enjoy the better air. The flies were no worse, but we were soon surrounded by a crowd of children, adults, and dogs. A local gendarme thought something should be done about cluttering up the street, but the proprietor remonstrated so violently that the officer shrugged his shoulders and sat down with us. Business was good.

By the time the first bottles of wine were gone, my shipmates were receptive to the idea of taking a ride. We invited the proprietor and the policeman to go with us, and although the proprietor felt unable to leave his shop, the policeman decided to come. Soon three carriages, each drawn by a span of small horses, arrived from somewhere, summoned by someone, and we distributed ourselves and climbed in, each of us taking along an extra bottle for refreshment en route. We also told the café owner that we'd be back for supper.

The carriages, probably the only ones in the place for hire, trotted out of town along a very dusty road that climbed slowly up into the foothills among fruit groves and vineyards. The crops had been harvested so there was no point in disembarking, but after about an hour we reached a spot that gave a grand view of the town and bay below. Here we got out and sat down on the rocks of a sheep pasture, allowing the horses to rest while we continued to guzzle our wine. Mike Simeon had a fair tenor voice and an impulse to use it. Harry Boneyard began to describe his adventures in the war, and one of the oilers kept a circle of men doubled up with a series of funny stories, a gift that no one could previously have suspected he possessed.

About five o'clock we all became hungry and decided it was time to return to town. Mike and the policeman had exchanged hats. Two of the firemen had stripped to their dungarees to absorb the therapeutic rays of the sun. I decided to ride on one of the horses attached to my carriage, so Shorty had to do the same on the other. Boneyard thought this a good idea to demonstrate his previous experience in the artillery, but in climbing on he fell off the horse and lost most of the wine remaining in his last bottle. Thereafter he was content to sit up beside the driver and hold on to the seat.

Our return to town was accomplished in better time than our leaving of it. For one thing it was all gently downhill; for another the horses sensed they were headed for the stable and their own evening meal. They needed little urging to gallop. The immediate result of this equine motivation was that the two rear carriages were bunched close behind the first in a smothering cloud of dust, an intolerable situation to their passengers. Riding on the off horse on the first carriage out in the clear air I could faintly hear the outraged and profane protests of those hidden in the dust. The carriages behind were trying to pass mine.

Faster and faster we galloped along, the drivers trying to calm down the horses, their efforts nullified by the exhortations of myself and Shorty. Suddenly there loomed up ahead a large tree with a stout limb overhanging the road. On the way up we had avoided this limb by driving around it on the edge of a shallow ditch. But on the way down there was no avoiding it.

"Duck," I yelled, and bent forward on the horse's neck.

With a crash and tearing of wooden supports and canvas, the limb barely caught the carriage top, which shaded the back seat like a buggy top, and tore it from the vehicle. Fortunately, the limb was not low enough to strike anyone in the head or the results could have been very serious. A moment later the branch tore off the top of the second carriage. Our horses kept on galloping down the road. The third vehicle, in swerving to avoid the wreckage hanging on the branch, slipped off the road into the ditch, where it overturned. The shaft and harness broke, the driver lost his reins, and the horses kept right on cantering for their stable. They passed us about a quarter of a mile away from the scene of the accident when we finally reined down our panting and excited animals.

Looking back up the road as the dust began to settle we beheld a strange sight. Slowly there became visible the two black buggylike tops hanging in the tree, then the carriage in the ditch, which seemed to be intact except for the shaft and whiffletrees, and finally a strung-out procession of limping sailors whooping, laughing loudly, and waving bottles. I decided we had better settle for the damages right then and there before inflated values could develop. In terms of dollars, the drivers were satisfied with a sum which cost us about five dollars each in addition to the previously agreed fare, which was probably excessive at two dollars each. The policeman witnessed the transaction, we invited the drivers to supper (and they showed up, too), and we all climbed back into the two remaining carriages and proceeded into town at a walk, with the carriage beds bumping the axles.

There was considerable excitement in Alexandretta when our disorderly caravan arrived. A large crowd of people milled about in the street in front of our rendezvous. The arrival of the runaway horses from the third carriage had precipitated all kinds of rumors, the only one of which that was not exaggerated was the evidence that there had been an accident. A story was even being circulated that the driver had been robbed and murdered. And so forth. But our ultimate safe though hilarious arrival, including the policeman wearing the distinctive round white American sailor hat, dispelled the fake rumors and instigated new ones. For example, the policeman was said to have taken us all into custody and only his own garrulous befuddlement and obvious identity with the group soon demonstrated the falsity of that idea.

Nick and Mike Simeon negotiated with the restaurant owner for a satisfactory price to cover a supper for fifteen, including our guests. It amounted to about seventy-five cents each in our money, which was reasonable for a well-cooked meal of vegetable soup, skewered lamb, wheat and rice pilaf, fried eggplant, and pastry for dessert. All of this was flushed down by many bottles of wine for which we paid an equivalent of thirty cents per bottle. We ate this meal in the dusk of the street to the accompaniment of a talented accordionist whom we all suitably rewarded.

By the time we had concluded our supper we were slyly accosted by several pimps, aided by the connivance of the policeman, who assured the seamen that the prostitutes were all licensed and medically inspected and they would not be robbed during the night. I decided to return to the ship, having the horror of my recent escape from the "Abode of the Holy Innocents" in Barcelona still fresh in my mind. Shorty Smith and I left the others and proceeded to the central dock where the Senegalese sentries were sleeping soundly on cases of arms and ammunition. There was no bumboat in sight, not even one to be appropriated and rowed out by ourselves. So we logically decided to swim. This was not a great feat because the ship lay only about two hundred yards off the dock and the water was warm and absolutely calm. We stripped to our shorts, tied our clothes and shoes into a tight bundle, lowered ourselves off the landing, and leisurely swam. We were the only ones of those ashore who returned to the ship that night. But by seven o'clock the following morning all the others had arrived, too.

Four days sufficed to discharge that part of our cargo destined for Alexandretta and then we steamed down overnight to the Lebanese city of Tripoli. Like so many sailors we could only look at Tripoli from the deck of the ship, for we completed unloading in a single day and sailed at twilight for Port Said to begin our long voyage to the fabled Far East.

22. East of Suez

ALMOST EXACTLY TWO DAYS to the hour after leaving astern the mountains towering behind Tripoli in the golden reflection of a low afternoon sun, a wide jumble of steamship masts and funnels arose above and spread across the horizon dead ahead. Gradually a few domes and minarets appeared among the masts, and then the hulls of many anchored steamships and the low flat roofs of a fairly small city showed. This was Port Said. A long procession of ships of all types and sizes from large passenger vessels to small freighters steamed rapidly away toward the west; these were some of the ships that had made a northern transit of the canal during daylight hours.

At first *Winona* anchored in the roads off the eastern shore of the canal and outside the breakwater bearing the statue of

de Lesseps pointing to his canal. Later we moved in to the
Anglo-Persian oil docks to take aboard nine hundred tons of
fuel oil and several hundred more of fresh water for ballast, for
we carried only a thousand tons of paying freight for Batavia
and rode high in the water. As we moved into the dock we
passed a strange-looking craft, half the length of *Winona* and
painted gray but showing a good deal of rust. She was light in
the water and swung at two anchor cables as if she had been
there a long time; she had two straight and rather skinny funnels and a lot of hamper at the crosstrees on her two masts.

"What in the world is that?" I asked the mate who stood on
the fo'c's'le head with several of us waiting to handle the bow
lines when we should come alongside the loading pier.

He laughed. "Why that's Jock Ferguson's battleship! Ever
hear of it?"

I shook my head.

"She's an old British light cruiser — older'n the hills. They
stripped off her guns and sold her at auction after the war was
over. She was even almost too old during the war but they
used her for convoy work. A Scotch engineer named Jock Ferguson bought her and lives aboard of her. I hear tell he plans
to sell her to some crowd of fire-eatin' natives for use in some
revolt somewhere against somebody or other."

Nick chimed in, "He better hurry or she won't stay afloat
waitin' for 'em. She's been there more'n a year already."

"Yes," said Mr. Crocker, "my guess is he'll wind up sellin'
her to an Italian shipbreaker in Genoa. Hear he got her for a
song."

Since we didn't know just when we would be ordered to
enter the canal, there was no shore leave nor did we break

watches, but we were content to dicker with the bumboatmen who had spread out their merchandise on number three hatch amidships. Some things were cheap. For example, Dimitrino cigarettes in tin boxes of one hundred sold for twenty-five piasters or $1.25 each.

Orders to proceed into the canal arrived with a British pilot during the graveyard watch and we actually cast off our lines in inky darkness at three o'clock in the morning. Then we started down the eighty-seven-mile run to Suez. I was lucky enough to be at the wheel when we cast off, and I steered a few miles down the canal until we were ordered to tie up on our starboard hand to a set of bollards embedded in the high sandy bank for the purpose. Contrary to the general impression, the canal was so crooked and narrow at that time that ships could not pass unless one tied up to the bank. While a six-ship convoy coming from the south steamed by at a speed of about seven knots we lay there and then were joined by four other ships that fell into line astern of us and began to follow *Winona* down the canal. By that time the morning watch came on duty and I went below to sleep until seven-thirty.

During the first part of the eight to twelve watch on a bright sunny morning my job kept me on the fo'c's'le head chipping rust and paint from the windlass and handling mooring lines whenever we tied up to the bank, which was about once every two hours. We tied up only on alternate northbound convoys and used only two lines, one each on the bow and stern. The lines were received ashore by Egyptian seamen who sailed aboard *Winona* and were put ashore over the inboard side in a flat-bottomed work boat that was lowered or hoisted by our own cargo booms aft.

The ships we passed were interesting, just as a passing vessel always fascinates a sailor. One was a sleek and shining Dutch passenger ship, the *Volend*, hailing from Amsterdam, her rails crowded with well-dressed civilians going home from the East Indies. Another was a British & India Line passenger ship, *Manela*, hailing from Glasgow. A large Japanese freighter, *Matsumato Maru*, was followed by a huge English tanker, at that time about as large, fully loaded, as the canal could accommodate. Then we were impressed with a brand-new and very large German freighter, *Ludendorff*, of the old Stinnes Line, and reflected that it might have been a mistake to take all the German ships as reparations after the war because it enabled them to build more efficient and more competitive vessels.

About an hour's sailing time north of Ismailia both banks were piled with huge amounts of tangled and rusted barbed wire. This marked the place where a Turkish army had been repulsed in its effort to cross the canal and seize Egypt early in the war. But for the most part the canal wound through a barren waste of sandy desert, relieved only by occasional villages or Canal Company observation stations. Dredging and widening went on constantly, performed by huge dredges anchored securely in the edge of the canal and pumping the dredged sand over beyond the bank.

Just before eleven o'clock in the morning, when I was fortunate enough to be at the wheel again, we reached the Great Bitter Lake and headed for a buoy about a mile south of the northern part of the canal. It was the custom for ships in a convoy to race at full speed from this buoy to another twelve miles away just north of the entrance to the southern part of the dredged canal. Usually it was a race between the first two ships because the others had too much of a handicap unless one was a fast passenger ship. As we approached the buoy, the captain rang up "full speed ahead" on the engine room telegraph. I watched my steering as if my life depended on it. Then the pilot stood behind me and pointed out the tall buoy twelve miles away for which we were headed, and I fixed the jack staff on the fo'c's'le head on it and disregarded the compass until we reached it.

Meanwhile, the captain, the pilot, and the third mate, who was on watch, frequently walked out to the starboard wing of the bridge to cast an anxious eye on an Australian freighter and to measure with a stadimeter the interval of distance between us. Our wake was straight as an arrow but the Australian was slowly gaining. The captain entered the pilothouse and rang up the engine room. "Chief," he called, "can't you get a few more turns out of her? Good!"

Then he returned to the bridge. The *Winona* shook from the increased speed of the propeller, and presently the officers began to smile. Slowly we increased our distance and about halfway across the lake the Australian gave up the effort and slightly reduced his speed. But we retained ours and passed the entrance buoy comfortably ahead. As I was relieved by Mike at eight bells (noon) the pilot wished to compliment us, and he remarked to the captain so that we could hear, "You have good helmsmen, Captain."

"Yes," replied the captain, "thank you. We do have a good crew aboard this trip."

At four o'clock in the afternoon we emerged from the canal and anchored in the roads off the small, palm-shaded town of

Suez. Somehow, it seemed like the loneliest place in the world, for it was shut in from the western side of the Gulf of Suez by incredibly jagged, rough, parched-brown mountains. But we were not left to lugubrious reflections very long. In half an hour we began to grind our way south down the gulf between those high, inhospitable, and savage-looking coasts.

"In the old days of coal burners," the thickset, swarthy bosun told me, "most ships used to take aboard gangs of Arab firemen and coal passers to spell off the regular crew because it was so hot the Europeans got sick. But it ain't so worse in oil burners so they don't do it no more."

The Red Sea wasn't as hot as we had expected, ranging from eighty-five to ninety-five degrees Fahrenheit, and our comfort was partly helped by a strong head wind. But during the summer months a merciless sun on a windless day frequently produces heat up to one hundred and thirty degrees on deck. One thing that did surprise me, however, was the great distance covered by the length of the Red Sea. Steaming just under three hundred miles a day, *Winona* spent a full day in the Gulf of Suez and five full days in the Red Sea.

In the sixth afternoon of clear, hot, windy days we rounded Perim, a stone and mud village that was dominated by a radio station and signal tower on the Arabian shore of the Strait of Bab el Mandeb. Only seventeen miles wide, the straits were like a gateway between two mountain barriers of especially jagged peaks. Then we entered the Gulf of Aden, running east and west in direction, and spent two more days butting into a heavy head wind and a strong current set up by the northeast monsoon, which was blowing at this time, in the middle of November.

Two days later we passed the end of Cape Guardafui and its curious little group of islands known as the "twelve apostles" and were now in the Indian Ocean headed for Java Head and the Strait of Sunda. For twelve more lonely but bright and cheerful days *Winona* pitched steadily into the monsoon-driven sea, meeting only one vessel in all that time, a South African passenger ship bound for Colombo.

In the last half of the dogwatch a few of the crew were sitting one evening in the late twilight on number five hatch in the lee of the afterhouse, which sheltered us from the relentless wind. We were smoking and spinning yarns, that is, talking about ourselves and our exploits as sailors love to do. Presently, the chief cook climbed down the starboard ladder and joined us. He was more than welcome and a very popular person with all hands because this man was a real cook.

He was slightly built, with graying sandy hair and a heavily wrinkled face. American-born, he had the improbable name of Erastus Phoenix. He had been recruited for *Winona* by the chief steward one cold, rainy September afternoon in Brooklyn, together with his baker, Johnny MacDonald, for a good team of cooks frequently sail together for years. The steward had known them several years before. He bought a few rounds of drinks, all the while urging them to join him and spend the winter in the warm weather of the Far East, which would certainly be preferable to slamming around in the icy North Atlantic. Moreover, he repeated frequently, a crew of thirty-two made much less work for the cooks than a passenger ship like the one from which they had recently been paid off. Whether they had begun to weary of the two weeks of vacation they had already enjoyed, or whether the idea of blue tropic seas and exotic islands appealed to them, or whether it was because they knew the steward's quality of old, or whether it was a combination of these ideas, at any rate they decided to sign on the *Winona*.

All three arrived at the Staten Island pier in a taxicab in a violent downpour of cold rain about four o'clock in the afternoon with sea bags, suitcases, and several bottles of whiskey. *Winona* cast off and sailed three hours later. The steward told his new cooks to go on with their party and he and the pantryman got supper for the crew. The following afternoon Erastus and Johnny emerged from their quarters bathed, shaved, and combed, and pitched in to prepare a passenger-ship quality supper for a skeptical crew.

From my first meal aboard *Winona* when we were leaving Barcelona I knew I was in luck. I knew at once that I was at last in a taut and happy ship, so different from *Amphitrite*, which was a sloppy and decidedly unhappy ship. The quality of the food made most of the difference; basically it was the same, but in one case it was ruined in the cooking while in *Winona* it tasted delicious. The greater efficiency of one crew was a logical result.

I moved over a bit on the hatch combing and Erastus perched beside me and took a few contemplative puffs on his pipe. "Well," he finally said, "I wonder if we'll get into the Philippines this trip."

"I hear we're going to pick up some rubber in Sarawak," I replied, "and that isn't far from the southernmost Philippine islands in the Sulu Archipelago."

"Ah, the Sulu Islands," he sighed. "I was there once, in Jolo. They're all Mohammedans–Moro–great fighting men."

He was silent a moment and we all waited for what he might say next because we sensed that a story was about to be unfolded.

"I can't swear to the truth o' this," Erastus began, "and I never seen it myself, but I have no doubt of it, considerin' the people who told me. But they swear, in one of them islands is a perfect walled city, sort of a fort built on the shore of a sheltered natural harbor that used to be a waterin' place for ships at one time.

"About a hundred-odd years ago, a Spanish revenue ship put in there for water one day and the ship's boat with a mate and six men hadn't hardly got on the beach when a whole tribe o' Moros swooped down on 'em and killed or wounded every one. They dragged the bodies back up in the jungle and the ship's captain, seein' he was badly outnumbered, decided to get out o' there and go on up to Manila without no more water.

"Well, it seems one man, the mate, wasn't killed. He come to that night while the natives was boozin' it up with whatever they drink and they didn't notice him crawlin' off. He was hurt pretty bad but he walked along trails for some miles when he stumbled into the campfire of another band of foragin' Moros, enemies of the first tribe.

"They was surprised all right, but bein' a little short of warriors, they decided to fix him up and take him back to their village and get him to help them out. So they got him a wife to nurse him along and out o' gratitude, when he got well, he taught 'em a lot about warfare. He showed 'em how to build a stockade around their main village, and build catapults and to fight in formation instead of single-handed combat.

"After a while, his band attacked a large tribe that had been raisin' Ned with his own people. They hit 'em all at once on four sides, killed a good many, and took the rest captive. Then he was made a chief.

"Once, when they was away on the warpath, another tribe sacked their own village. When the women and children finally come out o' the jungle where they was hidin', he decided to move the village and build a new one at the place where he had first come ashore. But the thing about this was that he built a Spanish walled town with heavy basalt walls with gates and towers and a central square with streets leadin' out of it, and he built a reservoir up in the hills behind his town and piped fresh water down over an aqueduct like the one in Spain where he'd been brought up as a boy.

"Somehow this guy had given up hope o' goin' home some time. He was sittin' pretty as the head chief, his tribe was the strongest in the islands, and he'd raised quite a family by this time. I guess I'd have felt like stayin' there myself. But one day an enemy tribe poisoned his reservoir and a good many people died before they found out about it. So do you know what he done next?

"Well, his army went out and captured most of the men in the tribes they suspected of bein' most likely to do a thing like that. And then they located some springs in the hills and built a pipeline o' hollowed-out ebony logs buried in a trench and covered up the springs. And do y' know, them springs and pipeline still give the town its whole water supply, and nobody has ever found out where it comes from. Do y' know why? Because nobody ever knew except the Spaniard and the captives. And after the job was finished he had every single one of 'em murdered!"

Then seven bells sounded and Harry Boneyard and I went

up to the petty officers' messroom to draw off some coffee
from the nickel-plated steam urn before we went on watch.

A few days later, just after midnight when I had taken up
my post as lookout on the fo'c's'le head in a luminous, starry
night, I sighted the glow of a flashing light off our port bow in
the northeast. It was Croce Light on southern Sumatra. At
almost the same time I became aware of an indescribably delicate scent borne by a light breeze on the damp night air. It
was the odor of a hothouse filled with the moist scent of pungent blossoms like frangipani, hibiscus, swamp plants, jungle
flowers, and every sweet-smelling flower I could imagine. I
breathed deeply until I began to feel lightheaded. It may have
been due to the contrast of such a long period of breathing
heavy salt air, but I had never enjoyed such an experience before. What a prelude to watching the dark mass of the old
volcano called Java Head climb over the horizon at break of
day! What an introduction to the beauty of the Strait of
Sunda, the old sailing ship route of our ancestors! No wonder
the East Indies (now called Indonesia) were then known as
"The Garden of the Golden East."

23. The Garden of the Golden East

At DAYBREAK we were near Java Head and entering a wide passage formed by volcanic islands, green under their thick foliage of jungle trees. With wide channels between them, many were symmetrical volcanic cones frequently crested with a wisp of steam. *Winona* steamed quietly in fairly calm water among these fabulously beautiful islands all day, only the grumble of her propeller and the high-pitched whine of her turbine intruding upon the silence. In the middle of the dog-watch we came in sight of the tall white lighthouse standing out to sea a dozen miles from Tandjungpriok, a city that serves the port of Batavia (now called Djakarta), which was the capital of the Dutch East Indies and a great city of nearly three million people. Reaching the lighthouse in the darkness, we anchored in shoal water a few miles toward the port to await a pilot in the morning.

Morning dawned bright and warm, and soon the Dutch pilot, a tall, brown-haired, square-jawed sailor clad in a freshly pressed white suit, climbed over the side from his launch. At once we raised the anchor and started to steam between two breakwaters into the protected inner harbor. There we swung into position between two huge mooring buoys and made fast with double cables fore and aft. Then we looked around at the other ships. A gleaming new German freighter, the *Hagen* of the German-Australia Line, lay closest to us on the other side of the main channel, and another American ship, slightly smaller than *Winona*, the *West Chopaka* operated out of San Francisco, entered just as we were making fast to the buoys. Almost at once several lighters arrived alongside and we started unloading some machinery for Batavia and loading fifteen hundred tons of rubber and tapioca flour for Boston and New York.

Tandjungpriok consisted of several large piers and ship repair facilities, a railroad yard with huge storage sheds, a main business street largely given over to the automobile business, and a Malay village that seemed to spread out with no organized plan at all. There were many Chinese shops and clay-covered houses occupied by Malay laborers and their families, all looking cool and uncrowded under the shade of a great number of huge, wide-spreading tropical trees like the banyan.

By comparison with European stock the Malays were small, brown, slender, and decidedly good-looking people. They had straight black hair, brown eyes, straight noses, small features, and their teeth and lips were stained deep red from the

universal custom of chewing betel nuts. At this time they
were also afflicted, in the seaports, with an alarmingly high
incidence of syphilis.

The next day being Sunday, I was able to take the train for a
journey of nine miles inland to Batavia. The route led
through swampy jungle thick with climbing vines and lush
plants, smelling like a hothouse filled with fresh blossoms.
Wild monkeys chattered ceaselessly in the trees, green parrots
and golden-crested white cockatoos squawked and shrieked,
and red-and-green songbirds swooped and sang melodious
notes to each other as the rush of the little train disturbed
them.

Batavia looked in part like a piece of Holland transplanted
to a tropical landscape. It lay in hilly country slightly above
sea level and was hot and damp, as expected. Many of the
buildings in the core of the city were of Dutch architecture
and filled with Dutch, Germans, English, and a few Americans. The stores were like those in any European or North
American city, with large plate-glass windows; they were filled
with Christmas merchandise and decorations. The leading
hotels looked luxurious and expensive, but comparatively they
were not; they merely seemed expensive to a man earning
forty-five dollars a month. Beyond the European center, the
city spread out endlessly into commercial and residential areas
with a noticeably large number of Chinese shops and stores.
Electric car lines radiated in all directions and were heavily
patronized. Although the day was Sunday, business as usual
seemed to be carried on in the native quarters.

I ate a good dinner in one of the more modest hotel dining gardens, ordering only local dishes of rice and chicken

so deliciously flavored with cinnamon and coconut that I never forgot that exotic delight. In the afternoon I took a long ride on a sightseeing bus that was loading with tourists in front of a hotel. That was a sensible thing to do and I took as many snapshots with my camera as anyone. But I did feel out of place. For I was dressed in a gray wool suit, much too heavy for the climate, and I was the only person everywhere I went who was not clad in a white suit or native costume.

I wanted to travel on to Bandung, Java's third largest city, of nearly a million people, which lies about eighty miles to the southeast of Batavia several thousand feet higher in the mountains. Being much cooler, it was thought of as a health resort and contained many resort hotels and clubs. It could be reached in six hours by train or about two hours by automobile, but I had insufficient time for either, so back I went on the train to Tandjungpriok and *Winona*.

The following afternoon we cast off from the mooring buoys and steamed east in the Java Sea along the north coast of Java, a coast of towering mountains covered with luxuriant jungle vegetation. It was a memorable sight. That night we sailed continuously (and dangerously for them) among many prahus (fishing boats) anchored several miles from shore directly in the coastal steamship route. To alert us of his presence, if the fisherman thought we were steering directly toward him he would light a lantern or a flare. It seemed as if the bow lookout reported a new light every few minutes. Even so, some of the fishermen did not show a light, and in one case we missed running over one by only a few feet. We were on top of him before we saw him and could only hold our course; our bow wash pushed him away from the hull and he did not capsize but he must have nearly swamped. The second mate decided the fisherman must have been asleep.

In midmorning we arrived off Semarang and anchored several miles offshore at a mooring place where several other ships were lying. The rather sizable city of about one quarter of a million people lay on a jungle hillside under the shelter of a tremendous volcanic cone just west of it. Another great volcano lay to the east on a long reach of land that shut the city away from the Java Sea. We were told that crews seldom got ashore there because it was considered to be a "fever hole," but we couldn't have got ashore anyhow due to lack of time. We loaded about one thousand tons of smoked sheet rubber, packaged in bundles measuring nearly a yard on each dimension, and tapioca flour, hides, and sisal.

We also loaded several hundred tons of a choice blending tea that was packed in the usual square wooden chests used in the export trade. While it was being stowed in a section of the 'tween decks under number five hatch, a sling of chests being hoisted aboard fell apart and crashed on the steel deck. Fortunately, only one chest was irreparably smashed, and this was moved to one side and left on deck. Almost at once the steward and Erastus Phoenix, the chief cook, arrived with several dishpans and empty tin boxes.

"Mister, we're in luck," cried the steward. "This is Mayling tea, one of the most expensive. It's used only for blending and there's none finer in the world."

I dropped the scraper with which I was preparing a section of the well deck for painting and helped them transfer tea from the lead-foil-lined broken chest into pans and boxes, and thence into a storeroom.

"Do you think I could cadge a little of this to take home?" I asked.

For answer, the steward handed me an empty Huntley & Palmer biscuit tin.

"Is this big enough, Emery?" he asked. "We've got more than enough for the ship."

Observing what I had acquired, several of *Winona*'s crew soon appeared with assorted containers, and in only a few minutes, more than a hundred pounds of choice tea had been scraped up off the deck and sequestered in the fo'c's'le and various cabins. During the rest of the voyage we drank one of the world's finest rare teas.

We finished loading about four o'clock in the afternoon and left at once for Surabaya.

The next day was Thanksgiving and daylight arrived in a drenching rain squall. About nine o'clock we steamed into the Strait of Madura, which separates the island of Madura from the great Javanese city of Surabaya by about seventeen miles. The city is the second largest in Indonesia, having at the time of our visit about two million people. Continuing easterly down the strait we anchored off Surabaya late in the morning and looked at the port from the ship through curtains of rain. We were given a holiday, which meant no day work, the same as a Sunday, but the rain discouraged shoreward ventures. Moreover, we knew we would have an excellent dinner, which would take time to digest. The dinner was as good as we expected and after eating, everybody except the standby watches turned in for a nap. This dinner was worth remembering, especially to anyone who had sailed in ships where the food really was poor. We had cream of celery soup, roast chicken and dressing with various vegetables, wine jelly, mince pie, and the usual coffee and tea.

About the middle of the afternoon, the rain having stopped, Shorty Smith, the little wiper, and Brown, one of the oilers, induced me to go ashore with them. At the bumboat landing we hired a two-wheeled pony cart and driver for the four-mile ride up to Surabaya itself. The dusty road ran between a tree-shaded canal on one side and a railroad track on the other. And the thick brown water of the canal or river ran sluggishly between its banks down to the harbor and was used by an almost solid line of women and children along each bank both as a laundry and a bathtub. The women pounded the washing with sticks against the muddy bank and then rinsed it in the stream. Some of them had soap, but most used the traditional method of pounding and rinsing, all the while chattering gaily with each other and keeping an eye on the naked children.

Since our driver understood enough English to serve as a fair tourist guide, we continued his services to drive us around the city, which had become very hot in the full afternoon sunshine. It was a surprise to find one section of the city as Chinese as we imagined Shanghai might be, with pagodas, crowded streets swarming with people under fluttering paper streamers overhead, and distinctive Chinese architecture in the buildings. Another section was Indian, with the men wearing turbans and the women in graceful saris, and a good many elaborately carved façades on Hindu temples.

At suppertime (as we called it in those days in accordance with rural American custom) we went to the Oranje Hotel for an East Indian meal. This was, of course, quite different from the Thanksgiving dinner we had savored at noon, but it was a rare experience for us to eat such delicately flavored food as we were served.

The ride back to the port in another pony cart, one riding up front with the driver and the other two facing aft, was another joggling experience in which those riding behind felt that they might be suddenly pitched out on their faces in the road.

Next morning at breakfast, some of the seamen in the messroom were still just as drunk as when they had returned to the ship a few hours earlier, having decided to celebrate Thanksgiving night ashore in a thoroughly seagoing way. There was much bantering and trading of insults. Nick, the older quartermaster, was feeling especially belligerent. At one point he slammed his fist down on the wooden table so hard that all the plates bounced. "I can lick any son-of-a-bitch in de ship!" he roared.

Harry Boneyard began to laugh, and I sputtered with a mouth full of scrambled eggs, "Oh, why don't you go off and take two sticks and fight a hen turd."

Without looking at Nick, I reached for a doughnut and was about to take a bite when crash! My head was almost knocked down into my plate of eggs. Slowly, it dawned on me that Nick had picked up the enameled milk pitcher and hit me very hard on my forehead. I tenderly touched my left temple and could feel the blood starting to run. With deliberation I turned toward Nick who sat two removed from me, on the other side of Mike, who was scrambling to get out of the way. As Nick and I glared at each other, I suddenly swung my left fist, putting my entire hundred and ninety pounds behind the force of the blow, and struck him squarely in the mouth so hard that it lifted him from the bench. In falling, he upset the coffee and tea cans, with his rear end resting in a flood of scalding liquid while I clamped my right hand on his throat and held him there raining blows on his face with my left.

The uproar in the messroom was tremendous. Seeing Nick was getting the worst of it, some of his friends started to pull me off. Then Boneyard became excited. He climbed up on the table with his knees literally in the dishes and pushed Nick's friends away, all the time roaring, "This is a gentlemen's messroom! Out on deck you sons-o'-bitches! Don't fight in here!"

I released my grip on Nick's throat and we both scrambled to our feet. He ran out onto the deck and I followed close behind, but just as I reached the high threshold of the steel door, I automatically jerked back. Just in time. As I expected, he swung from behind the door expecting to catch me in the face. Instead, his fist crashed into the steel door jamb. It must have hurt him badly because he backed away and seemed to be in a daze with his guard down when I stepped out and nearly lifted him off his feet with a long right-hand blow to the tip of his chin.

The fight was really over then, but I was now too fired up to be aware of it. I rained blow after blow on Nick, driving him backward up the deck until we were abeam of the mainmast. At that point, he grabbed my fists in front of his chest, but as we collided our momentum caused us to fall. His bald head struck a line of rivets heavily and he lapsed into a coma. Lying on top of him, I alternately smashed him one way and then the other, while yelling, "Had enough?"

Meanwhile, somebody had interrupted the officers' breakfast in the saloon by shouting, "Big fight down aft! Big fight down aft!"

Just about everybody not on watch came racing down the ladders. I felt the captain and the mate lifting me firmly to my feet. Two other officers hoisted up Nick, who was a sorry sight, covered with his own blood and mine where I had bled down on him. I guess I was as bloody as he because, although he had never touched me with a fist, the cut on my temple flushed down the side of my head. I also noticed that everybody was wreathed in smiles. It seemed that Nick had a mean reputation for being a bully and they were delighted to see him beaten.

As we stood there we were both far from finished. Nick seemed to be struggling to get at me again, so I yelled, "Now you dirty son-of-a-bitch, apologize!" He didn't reply, possibly because he was too groggy to comprehend anything. So, in a flash, I wrenched myself from the loose grasp of the captain and the mate, hauled back, and knocked him flying backward out of the arms of the chief engineer and the third mate. He lay quiet, stretched out on his back. "Haw, haw!" everybody guffawed.

I looked around, feeling a little foolish. "Well," I said, "now I'd like to finish my breakfast," and started aft.

"I'll come down and fix that cut," the mate said.

The messroom was deserted except for Harry Boneyard, who sat in the ruins of the breakfast. He had been too disturbed to go out on deck with the others, and he now stared at me with horror in his eyes, but said nothing. I methodically finished my scrambled eggs. My doughnut was lost and my mug of tea had overturned and there was no more. A drop of blood falling on my plate reminded me that I had better get myself washed up, and I couldn't help thinking that in all my worst moments in the *Amphitrite,* I had never seen a shambles that remotely resembled this messroom.

The mate entered our quartermaster's room as I was washing my face in the small sink.

"Here," he said, "we better put some salve and a dressin' on that cut and it ought to be all right."

After he had ministered to me in silence, he asked, "Where did you learn to fight like that?"

"In college," I replied.

His eyes widened.

"Well, I never knew they taught anythin' as useful as that in college."

He looked at me closely, and added, "You take the mornin' off and turn to after dinner."

After he left, Harry Boneyard entered the room and observed me in clean clothes and looking quite pert except for the gauze covering my left temple. The big Dane sat down and regarded me solemnly with narrowed gray eyes. "Who come out on top?" he asked at length.

"I did," I announced quietly. "Didn't they tell you?"

Harry slapped his knee with a resounding clap. "You did?" he said. "You did! Well, that's good. That's great! That puts the big bastard in his place. Now you're the king of the fo'c's'le."

"Oh, no, none of that," I said, "I only want peace and civility."

About an hour later I was sitting quietly under the awning we had rigged over the fantail to keep the sun from heating up the deck too much over our heads below, when Nick came up. He had been given the morning off also. He looked at me tentatively and sat down beside me on the small hatch. At last the words came that would approximate the nearest thing to an apology I could expect.

"Was you ever in the ring?" he asked.

"Oh, no, just for fun," I replied.

"Well, you fight like a bastard. Next time we go ashore I want to go with you."

24. Tourism and Typhoons

On the Sunday afternoon after Thanksgiving Day, the second mate and the third engineer invited me to go up to Surabaya with them. Our tastes in recreation and entertainment were similar. We enjoyed the jolting pony cart ride, and at suppertime we found an impressive-looking hotel, the Simpang, where we ate a large East Indian meal on a broad veranda. While eating we listened to a stringed orchestra and enjoyed a few vaudeville acts and singers, none of which we could understand because the speech was all in Dutch. It was like attending an old-fashioned silent movie without benefit of script.

After lingering over our meal as long as we could without feeling too self-conscious, we found a park near the opera house where we listened to an old-fashioned band concert.

Although the evening air was warm and moist, the bright, star-spattered sky showed through the palm tops, and a languid feeling overcame us as we absorbed a lot of sentimental pieces. The concert concluded a little after nine o'clock and we sought another pony cart in which to joggle back to the harbor.

Near the sampan landing, in a sandy spot under a streetlight adjacent to the road and the railroad tracks, I noticed a strange thing. A Malay girl was squatting on her knees in the sand drawing lines and sweeping a palm frond across them, all the time with her face uplifted toward a bright full moon and droning a weird chant. She was young, slender, and rather attractive in her plain brown sarong with her black hair knotted tightly behind. We stopped a few feet away to watch and listen to her, but she seemed oblivious to our presence. Before long a tall, white-suited Dutch naval officer strolled by on his way to the landing.

"What is she saying?" I asked him.

He spoke a few words in native dialect and she answered him softly in a singsong voice without ceasing to brush away the sand configurations with her palm frond.

"Oh, she's a local crazy girl," he said. "She says she's cleaning up the earth."

This sentiment startled me. "Cleaning up the earth!" I assumed she meant the moral and spiritual aspects of the world, but upon more mature reflection I decided her limitations and empty existence would confine her ambitions to those of simple sanitary and orderly housekeeping.

"Is she safe out here?" I asked. "Shouldn't someone take her somewhere?"

"Oh, I daresay her people are keeping an eye on her. They'll come and take her home before long. It's not far away. People like you and I must never interfere in matters like this."

Then he added, "It's too early. Come with me to Chinee Joe's bar across the tracks and let me buy you a beer before you go back aboard."

The second mate and I decided to go with him, but the third engineer had a repair job to do in the morning and thought he should return to the ship. We left the poor girl in her sand hole and accompanied our new naval friend into a Chinese bar that consisted of a high thatched-roof building with one closed side; the rest was wide-open to whatever breezes might blow. We sat at a table near the center. Evidently the Dutchman had either just left or was well-known there, judging from the familiarity of the reception given him by the proprietor, a short plump Chinese in a white suit.

"Now we'll all have a glass of schnapps," he declared.

Strong liquor was the last thing the second mate or I wanted. We were feeling mellow and peacefully weary and looked forward to a good night's sleep. Our Dutch friend suggested whiskey and then rum, both of which we turned down; by the time he had got to beer we didn't want that either and began to regret we hadn't returned to the *Winona*. Suddenly the Hollander's face lighted up with inspiration. "Ah," he exclaimed, "you will have some of our local mineral water?"

That was a good idea, we thought, and we nodded enthusiastically. The Hollander gave the order in Dutch and the proprietor remonstrated volubly, but our friend was adamant and waved aside all objections. Soon we were served a small bottle with a slightly sulphurous smell and our friend drank a large tumbler of schnapps. With a little distaste we swallowed our mineral water and offered to buy our benefactor another schnapps, but by that time he wanted no more.

About three hours after I had turned in, I was awakened with very violent cramps in the stomach. I rushed for the head. Thereafter, I repeated the performance about once an hour but finally slept away the end of the night. After breakfast, when I was about to perform some work amidships, I met the second mate sitting disconsolately hunched over on number three hatch. He appeared to be in a condition of extreme misery.

"You look as if you'd been up all night," he said to me.

"You look worse," I replied.

"Do you know what that guy did to us?" he asked.

"I suspect he gave us the local equivalent of Pluto Water," I reasoned. "Hereafter you and I better not be such strong supporters of temperance and I think, also, we better beware of the Dutch when they come bearing gifts."

Two days later, with our holds about three-quarters full of rubber, tea, tin, tapioca flour, and other similar East Indian products, we cast off from the mooring buoys, noisily hauled up our anchor, and steamed down the Strait of Madura, out into the Java Sea again, and finally into the South China Sea. We were headed for Kuching, the capital and principal port of Sarawak in British North Borneo, which we reached on the second morning. From the ship the city looked like a clean, prosperous rubber town with the usual preponderance of Malay and Chinese population. The central area looked new, the buildings clearly showing English influence, but strung along the shore on the fringes of the town there were many palm-thatched and peaked-roof houses raised on pilings above the surface of the bay and reached only by sampan. We never got ashore, of course, because we quickly loaded our thousand tons of smoked sheet rubber and sailed for Singapore shortly after dinner.

Early in the morning of the next day we ran into a typhoon. During the previous evening black clouds swept up from the northeast and quickly blotted out the stars. At the same time the wind began to pipe up, literally pipe up with a musical sounding wail in the rigging, for although we had covered and firmly battened down the hatches and had lashed the cargo booms in place, we had left the guy ropes and rigging attached to the masts, king posts, and booms. That evening the captain and the mates frequently entered the chart room, behind the wheelhouse, and looked apprehensively at the barometer.

"Those storm warnin's Sparks picked up this afternoon gave me some hope we might only get the fringes of this," the captain observed, "but I've a notion we're hittin' it right on the nose."

"Looks like it to me," said the mate. "And I'm sort o' glad for once to be in steam instead o' sail. We're only about a hundred miles offshore and that don't leave much room for a sailin' vessel to maneuver in if she has to run for it."

"Yeah," the captain agreed, "but if we hold our course I've a notion we ain't goin' any place for a while."

When Mike called Harry Boneyard and me at seven bells to go on the morning watch at four o'clock, he said,

"Lookout's on the bridge. She ain't takin' nothin' aboard but the wind is likely to blow ye overboard. Be careful now. Ye'll have to leave here through the hatch on the fantail."

Coming from dead ahead, the gale was the heaviest I had yet known. Harry and I actually had to crawl on our hands and knees against wind, rain, and spray that knocked us down unless we hung on to a line that had been rigged between the afterhouse and the fantail. In climbing up the ladders to the navigating bridge we literally pulled ourselves up by the strength of our hands and arms. Because the South China Sea is so shallow, being only thirty fathoms deep in some places, the sea was not rough in the sense that the gale piled up seas like large hills. Instead of contending with giant waves, we were thrashed with opaque sheets of flying salt-water and jets of solid foam and rain. The surface of the sea was literally blown flat. We couldn't tell whether the hurricane force winds were laden with rain or seawater.

All day this enormous wind blew with a great roaring sound like a train in a tunnel. We held our course but would have had no idea of progress or position had we not navigated by frequent depth soundings, like the fishing schooners on the Grand Banks of Newfoundland. Comparing our line of soundings with those on the chart gave a really accurate position, and in one watch we made absolutely no progress at all, even though the propeller was turning at cruising speed — eighty-eight revolutions a minute.

That night we began to run out of the typhoon, and two days later when we approached Singapore island the weather was sunny and tranquil. We entered the lower Strait of Singapore early in an evening, passing the rusted wreck of an old French passenger ship that had long ago become the victim of an earlier typhoon. In the evening watch we anchored off quarantine to await daylight and the port officials, after which we should move in near the breakwater.

The day of arrival was a Saturday and we painted more than half the ship in the morning, working on stages slung over the side. The mate was so pleased that he gave the sailors the afternoon off, the first Saturday afternoon of liberty on the voyage. But it began to rain hard after dinner, before we could change our clothes, so we all stayed aboard and loafed and looked at a sodden white city through the rain squalls. Then it cleared right after supper as suddenly as it had begun to rain, so I quickly arrayed myself in my only suit of clothes, a good, gray-checked one, however, took my toilet articles in a paper bag, and had myself rowed ashore alone in a sampan.

Upon arriving at the general landing I engaged a jinriksha drawn by a Chinese coolie who spoke enough English to understand where I wanted to go and soon arrived at the English Seamen's Home, a white, impressive-looking club building intended for officers of merchant ships.

"I'm from the American ship *Winona*, just arrived today," I announced to the very official-looking clerk, "and I'd like to stay overnight if you have any accommodations."

"Certainly," he replied, "if you don't mind sleeping in a semiprivate dormitory."

"That will be entirely satisfactory," I said, wondering what a semiprivate dormitory was.

It proved to be a high-ceilinged ward with roofless cubicles, quite private, and the whole area cooled by large overhead, slowly turning electric fans. There was an armchair, a wash-stand and mirror, a clothes locker, desk, and a cloth-screened, cane-seated Chinese bed that was quite comfortable. The door locked on the inside and I felt private and luxurious. For this I paid in advance two Singapore dollars, equivalent to about seventy United States cents. Then, leaving my toilet articles on the desk of my airy cell, I rejoined my jinriksha boy who had waited to take me on more of an excursion until theater time.

In the gathering dusk I couldn't appreciate the emptying streets of the bank and commercial districts near the Singapore River, which was filled with lighters and sampans, but the large park with the very Victorian-looking St. Andrews Cathedral could very well have been a bit of English countryside. After a while we arrived at a large movie palace, the Alhambra Theatre. This was high-posted with open spaces at the top under the roof for ventilation, and it also hummed with electric fans depending from the ceiling. Large oil paintings of landscapes and British colonial officers of the past hung on two walls; the third was occupied by the movie screen, and the fourth side opened into a refreshment garden where food and cold drinks were sold during a long intermission.

The single show didn't begin until nine o'clock when I was beginning to feel sleepy from the effects of breaking my long routine of seagoing watch for watch. I found myself sitting next to two congenial young soldiers from a Sussex regiment; our seats were good although the auditorium was not pitched, and the movies were American-made. The first was a bumptious and boring affair, about what one should expect from a production called *Go Get 'em Hutch*, and the second was what was then called a "tear-jerker," *East Lynne*, but it was so well done that the evening was quite successful. I treated the soldier boys to a lemonade and picked up much interesting lore about Singapore and British army life, and since *East Lynne* made me weep I had a very good evening indeed. Unfortunately, when the show was over I couldn't seem to find a ricksha boy who understood enough English to take me to the English Seamen's Home, so I finally arrived in a state of assuaged frustration rather than the sentimental euphoria with which I had left the theater.

Having left no call, I slept eight solid hours and awakened at eight o'clock when it was again raining. About ten o'clock the rain ceased, so I got up and inquired about breakfast. No meals were served at the Home since it adjoined the Hotel Marlborough, which was reached by walking across a lawn and through a hedge. Here I was served ripe mangoes with a carroty taste, three boiled guinea hen eggs, toast, and coffee for eighty Singapore cents, about twenty-five United States cents.

In a very humid but not excessively hot sunny day I carried out more sightseeing in a rather primitive taxicab — an open-side English touring car — driving across the island to the edge of the huge naval dockyard and finally to the top of a fairly high hill on the west side of the city from which one could look across a wide expanse of city and harbor. My excursion wound up at the Hotel Raffles, near the Hotel Marlborough, and here I ate a large dinner of curried beef so highly spiced that it subsequently caused me acute distress, similar to that of Pat Mahoney after he allegedly ate the goat stew.

Late in the afternoon I walked back to the landing and returned to the *Winona* feeling smug and quite satisfied with
my latest experience with tourism.

25. Mr. Briggs

"This is a good ship," said Mr. Briggs, "except for one thing. It needs some animals aboard. Animals are a civilizin' influence. Now, consider our situation. Here we are in a practically brand-new ship, well designed and well built, with the best equipment in the world — she'll never be turned back into the boneyard. And what's more, we've got as good a crew, in all departments, as I ever sailed with. Especially the cooks. Why, we're a floatin' resort hotel — a regular Poland Springs or a Homestead. We're almost a home — but not quite."

Captain Braun nodded agreement.

"Yes, Chief," he replied, "what you say is true. If you want a dog or a cat, why don't you get one?"

Captain Roger Braun and Mr. Leander Briggs, the chief engineer, were waiting at the gangway about one o'clock on this bright December afternoon for a sampan to approach and convey them to the general small craft landing in Singapore. Although they were friends and respected each other's competence they usually did not spend time with each other ashore. They were not planning to spend this afternoon together either. The words of William McFee, at that time an aspiring candidate for the distinction of being the poet laureate of seafaring men while chief engineer in a vessel operated by the United Fruit Company in the banana trade between Boston and Central American ports, could not be said to apply to Captain Braun and Mr. Briggs.

Since I was standing the gangway watch near number three hatch amidships I couldn't help hearing the conversation, and the McFee verse naturally came to my mind:

> *"The Skipper and Chief have gone ashore*
> *And each is a married man,*
> *So I'll tell you a tale of Singapore*
> *Of the ladies of old Japan —*

> *Chorus:*

> *O drink to the men who have Gone Ashore*
> *(I 'spect they're drinkin' some)*
> *Half a dozen men on the Mess Room floor,*
> *Six good men with their throats all sore*
> *Drinkin' to the men who have Gone Ashore*
> *(Both of 'em married — O dear, O Lor!)*
> *Yo ho for a bottle o' rum!"*

Captain Braun and Mr. Briggs offered no similarity to Mr. McFee's literary characters, but they could easily be recognized for ship's officers. Each wore a stiff-brimmed straw hat and each nervously fingered the brim of his hat lest it be swept away by the pert breeze that was blowing. Captain Braun wore a white suit and white shoes with a broad blue necktie and a soft, collar-attached shirt. He carried a brief-case, since he was headed for the offices of the ship's agent.

Whereas Captain Braun was a smooth-shaven, stocky man of middle height, with a good growth of brown hair as befitted his age of about thirty-seven, Mr. Briggs was a large and powerful man with huge hands and shoulders and was in his middle forties. The brown hair that once adorned Mr. Briggs's bald head was now concentrated in a wide, bushy handlebar mustache. Unlike the captain, he wore a heavy-weight, navy-blue suit with vest and large gold watch chain, a high, starched batwing collar with a bright red bow tie, and his black shoes were highly polished. Moreover, he carried a huge cane whenever he went ashore.

"I find it a solid comfort," he frequently explained about the cane. "Even a thug would think twice before he attacked me."

Mr. Briggs was a native of Boston and an engineering graduate just before the turn of the century of the Massachusetts Nautical Training School. He was a "family" man, sincerely devoted to his wife and his four sons, all four of whom he had managed to educate, the youngest being an undergraduate at the Massachusetts Institute of Technology. With his usually severe, mirthless countenance, he could well be described as formidable. Like the captain he had a strong voice; they customarily conversed in shouts and sonorous sentences with much gaiety.

Presently a sampan rounded up alongside the *Winona*, doused her lateen sail, and made fast to the foot of the gangway. "Your boat has arrived, gentlemen," I announced. "Happy sailing."

Mr. Briggs regarded me with amusement. "Captain," he said, "since you've no cane like I have, hadn't you better take our heavyweight boxin' champion along with you as a bodyguard?"

"No, I think he can be more useful here to help you back aboard with the dog you've been talkin' about," bantered the captain.

"But I'm not bringin' any dogs aboard," the chief remonstrated. "I've twenty dollars to buy my wife some silk piece goods she's wantin' me to bring home."

As they boarded the sampan I could still hear them joking about the absence of animals aboard. And the last remark within my hearing was the captain's. "Well, Leander, if you buy a cat you'll have to be sure it don't eat up Boneyard's silly cockatoo."

"Oh, that —" and Mr. Briggs's voice was drowned out by the slatting of the sampan's sail.

The captain returned to the ship just before supper. Mr. Briggs, on the other hand, was unexpectedly late. It was a rare thing for him to fail to return for a meal. Especially in *Winona*. He considered the cookery of Erastus Phoenix and Johnny MacDonald superior to anything except the efforts of Mrs. Briggs. Coupled with his culinary preferences, his New England frugality had not allowed him to waste his money on a meal ashore thus far during this entire voyage. Consequently, there was considerable speculation about his absence at suppertime in the dining saloon.

"I can't imagine what's happened to the chief," the captain observed anxiously.

"It ain't good," said Mr. Kelly, the first assistant engineer, "he said he'd be back for supper."

"Somethin' has befell him," chimed in the pantryman, quite out of turn, in his concern for his friend.

It was nearly dark when a sampan rattled against the gangway and Mr. Briggs began to climb the steps. His progress seemed slow, not because he was "impaired," as the phrase is used today, nor was he burdened with excessive bundles, but he seemed to be towing a bulky object up the ladder behind him. As he stepped on deck, the nature of the bulky object became apparent. It was a small brown bear tethered unwillingly to the end of a length of stout two-inch manila line.

"Well, how d'ye like the new mascot?" inquired Mr. Briggs thickly.

"I thought you was goin' to buy some silk for your wife," accused Mr. Kelly.

"Ah, Brian, m'boy," replied Mr. Briggs, "I did. And I have it here!" he added, waving a large cylindrical package. "And the mascot is an added starter. It's for myself!"

The little bear was about the size of a collie dog and it looked lean but powerful. It was frightened and cowered up against the hatch coaming with its tongue hanging out of its long snout and dripping saliva.

"He's thirsty and he's hungry," explained Mr. Briggs. "Steward, can y' spare a little lunch for him? Maybe some hamburger? We got to quiet him down, make him feel to home."

All the excitement had attracted the captain and he now

appeared in white trousers and skivvy shirt. "For goodness sake, Leander," he said, "I thought you were going to buy a dog or a cat! How come you raided a zoo?"

"Well, it was like this, Roger," Mr. Briggs began, "after I finished my piece goods transactions I headed back for the landin' and on my way I stepped in to the Raffles' men's bar. And who was in there but my old friend Angus Cameron who I sailed with in the old schoolship *Nantucket*.

" 'Lee, old boy, have a drink,' he says.

" 'What are you doin' out here?' I says.

" 'I'm chief o' the *West Isleta*,' he says.

"So we had a couple and I said I was goin' to buy a dog to take back to the ship. 'What kind of a dog?' says he.

" 'Oh, I don't know. Nothin' special. A good-sized dog for protection, I guess!'

" 'Well, I'll help y' pick one out,' he says, 'I know a lot about dogs.'

"Well, we had a couple more and then we ate some rice an' curry an' had a couple more to wash down the pesky hot curry. Then Angus took me to a animal store. 'Now, Lee,' he says, 'what d' you want a dog for. Why don'tcha get a real distinctive dog, like that appealin' little bear over there?'

"The bear only cost a hundred Singapore dollars but I got him for sixty, which comes down to about twenty in our money, as I figger it. So I made him fast to this stout line and the Chinaman gave me a pocket full of crackers to sort of quiet him with in the boat. But he's ate 'em all up, and he's still hungry."

The steward soon appeared with about two pounds of chopped meat and the cook bore a large pan of water, all of which the bear consumed in an astonishingly short time. The food and water did reassure the little bear, and he lay down on the deck and allowed himself to be patted and stroked.

"By the way, Chief," asked the steward, "what's his name?"

Mr. Briggs chuckled, "The animal man said his name was Wo Fat, but I've decided to call him Marmaduke. That's an unusual name and he's an unusual animal." Then he added, "Come on Marmaduke — bedtime." And he led the bear back to the afterhouse and installed him in the office adjoining his own sleeping quarters.

Next morning, Marmaduke, not being housebroken, was evicted from the chief engineer's office and tethered outside the fiddley, where he slept and cavorted in the shade, with pans of food and water hard by, an old mattress to lie on, and an area of tarpaulin that was supposed to serve as his restroom. We all made jokes concerned with the vicissitudes and amenities of a bear's life.

Marmaduke seemed to enjoy life aboard ship. He ate well and suffered himself to be petted. But one had to be careful. He was inclined to be playful but he was also irritable, especially when he was disturbed in his sleep. And his claws were sharp as knives and inflicted several bad scratches before people learned to approach him slowly and watch him with respect.

Then there came a night about five days after Mr. Briggs had brought Marmaduke aboard when the little bear disappeared. *Winona* was steaming up the Strait of Malacca bound for a port in northeastern Sumatra called Belawan. It was a river port, some three miles up the deep Deli River, and the port city for Medan, an important trading city of a quarter of a million people.

The last person to see Marmaduke was the ship's carpenter, who said he had somehow become untied and was ambling around on number three hatch. If he had decided to jump overboard and swim for it, he could have been successful, for the ship passed only a couple of miles off the seaward points of the Sumatran coast that night and bears are supposed to be good swimmers. He was as well nourished and healthy as he ever had been and he probably reached shore and freedom. At least we all hoped so. A clarifying circumstance concerned with the bear's departure was the concomitant appearance of several deep lacerations on the carpenter's forearms. He tried to conceal them by wearing his shirt-sleeves buttoned down to his wrists, but this only attracted more attention to the singular coincidence of the bear's absence and Chips's fresh wounds.

Mr. Briggs was as much impressed with circumstantial evidence as anyone.

"I know that miserable old man threw my bear overboard," he went about confiding to everyone who stopped to express his sympathy. And to Chips himself, he stormed, "You're a filthy old, connivin' bastard, you are, to throw my bear overboard. And I just want to warn ye of one thing — stay out of my engine room! Don't ye dare step foot in it! I mean that, too."

"Now, Chief, I didn't throw your bear overboard," Chips retorted. "I found him untied and runnin' round loose when I went up to the p.o. mess to get a mug-up of coffee 'bout four bells last evenin'. I tried to tie him up but he lashed out at me and run off, an' that's the last I see of him. That's the God's truth, Chief."

"Well, I don't believe ye!" Mr. Briggs shouted and stomped off.

Three days later Mr. Briggs got his fancied revenge on the carpenter. We had left Belawan and were at the upper end of the Strait of Malacca about to enter the Indian Ocean, steaming for Colombo. It was a sunny bright December morning and I was working with big Nick up on the boat deck, applying a coat of red lead to the skylights looking down into the engine room. Shorty Smith and the other wiper were down there washing down some white work, preparatory to painting it; the third assistant engineer was watching his gauges and adjusting a valve occasionally. Presently, at a door from the main deck leading to a grating and a series of ladders down into the engine room we saw the grizzled gray head of old Chips appear. He looked all about with great caution. Satisfied that only the third assistant was on duty, he stepped out on the grating and proceeded to climb down the ladders, carrying a bucket in which he needed to obtain a supply of waste lubricating oil to apply to the cargo winches on deck, their lubrication being one of his duties.

I saw something Chips did not see and I nudged Nick while placing a finger on my lips. Down on the lowest engine room deck Mr. Briggs was working at a bench hidden from the sight of the carpenter. Suddenly, and quite adventitiously, he glanced up and observed the carpenter's legs coming slowly into view down the ladder. He moved quickly behind a stanchion, seizing a broom in his right hand. Slowly, step by step, Chips lowered himself into the forbidden engine room. Nick and I held our breaths.

Suddenly, just as Chips was halfway down the last of four

ladders, Mr. Briggs let out a whoop and a yell and rushed out toward the ladder. The startled carpenter dropped his bucket with a clattering crash, turned, and started to climb back as fast as he could. But he was no match in a climbing contest with the younger man.

Thwack! Thwack!

Mr. Briggs lashed out with his broom handle across the carpenter's hindquarters, all the while yelling with demonic fury. Chips yowled and yelled with enormous vigor for a man his age.

Thwack! Thwack!

All the way up all four ladders Mr. Briggs pummeled the carpenter's backsides. The shouting and cursing could clearly be heard above the whine of the great turbine and its gears. Nick and I and the engine room crew on duty sat or stood open-mouthed. The flight and pursuit were soon terminated. When Chips stumbled over the coaming of the engine room door at the main deck he kept right on running and didn't stop until he reached his own room in the fantail. Mr. Briggs called off the chase at the top of the last ladder. There he happened to glance up and caught sight of me and big Nick peering down through the skylight. He paused, looked up a second time, and gave us a big wink while looking as pleased with himself as a bright-eyed woodchuck peering over the top of his huge mustache. "Thar, that'll larn him!" he shouted half to himself and started back down the ladder.

Chips was angry enough to murder Mr. Briggs. "That bald-headed old porkypine! I'll kill him!" he announced. Hearing of Chips's disaffection, his cousin, the mate, came aft to counsel moderation and assuage the carpenter's injured dignity.

By the time I caught up with Chips after dinner his violence was comparatively tempered. "Many a man has been killed in an engine room by havin' a bucket dropped on his head," he rumbled.

"Oh, Chips," I said, "he really thinks you threw his bear overboard."

"I guess he does," Chips ruminated. "Well, boy, I swear on a stack of Bibles that I didn't. Here, look at this!"

With that he rolled up the right leg of his dungarees, revealing a particularly nasty scratch from his knee to his ankle. It had scabbed over and was not infected, but it must have been sore.

"Ripped my dungarees almost in two! I still got to sew 'em up. But I didn't even cuff the little rascal. I backed off and give up trying to tie him and I guess he really did jump overboard and swim ashore after I'd went aft to fix up my scratches."

"I'll tell the chief, if you want me to," I offered.

"No, I don't want you to say nothin'. But you know," he added, "in one way the chief is right. We oughta have more animals in this ship. Make it seem more like home. When we get to Colombo I've a mind to get me a pussycat."

Next day I met Mr. Briggs amidships when I was returning to the boat deck to continue my painting job on the ventilator cowls. He eyed me with a severe face and asked, "Well, boy, what did you think of the engine room battle you saw yesterday morning?"

"My, but you're a violent man, Mr. Briggs!" I offered.

He laughed, but without humor. Perhaps I could be forgiven an impertinence because I was a fellow New Englander.

So I decided to intrude where angels might hesitate. "Mr. Briggs," I ventured, "I don't believe he threw your bear overboard at all. He likes animals. In fact he'd like to get himself a cat but he's afraid you might throw it overboard."

Mr. Briggs scowled so fiercely that I feared I had offended him.

"Did he tell you to speak to me?" he demanded.

"No, sir. He told me to mind my own business."

Mr. Briggs continued to scowl and I began to quake inwardly. Then he growled, "What does he think I am anyway! Throwin' little animals overboard! My foot! You tell him to go get his cat and I'll see that no harm comes to it. We need more animals aboard here — not less."

Then I knew that the feud would soon end and they would become friends again.

26. Home Was Never Like This

IN THE BRIGHT MORNING SUNLIGHT following the night when
Marmaduke had disappeared from *Winona*, we entered the
lower reaches of the Deli River in northeastern Sumatra.
This body of water was more like an arm of the sea than a
river. It was broad, perhaps a quarter of a mile wide for the
first three miles up to the port of Belawan, and deep enough
for ships drawing forty feet to steam safely at half speed between the low banks, which were covered with dense tropical
foliage. After steaming quietly for about half an hour in dead
calm water along this dark green avenue through the rain
forests we rounded a broad bend and came in sight of Belawan, the port of the large city of Medan. So deep was the
water along the shore that a long bulkhead had been built as
a dock parallel to the bank and to this we moored alongside.

On the southern bank of white-plastered buildings, the town was largely hidden under dense foliage; great banyan trees grew in profusion and bright tropical flowers glowed under the green canopy of the trees. For all its beauty, the port facilities were thoroughly modern, with traveling cranes, tanks, pumps, and derricks. We were to load several hundred tons of liquid latex rubber in our forepeak tank as an experiment to determine whether or not in this way it would be practical to transport rubber long distances by sea. We were also to load a few hundred tons of smoked sheet rubber in bales, so we knew we would complete loading in a few hours and sail about sunset.

As soon as we had made fast our mooring lines, Captain Braun was met on the dock by the ship's agent in a Model T Ford automobile and carried away to Medan for the rest of the day. Mr. Briggs departed soon after the arrival of a representative of a machine shop that was to undertake a welding job for a piece of the ship's machinery. And after dinner Mr. Kelly, the first assistant engineer, departed on business of his own. Mr. Crocker, the mate, decided I was intelligent enough to deny access to the ship of unauthorized persons who might be intent on stowing away for purposes of emigration, so I was installed at the gangway as ship's watchman. This was a fortuitous circumstance for me because I became a firsthand witness to subsequent interesting events.

The first visitors to appear at the gangway were two or three traders, each of whom carried a large sack of goods for sale. Knowing these people would not attempt to stow themselves away the mate permitted them to spread out their wares on the number three hatch amidships. About three o'clock there was a hubbub down the street from the dock. Presently, I discerned a lanky, tall, ruddy-faced man in blue shirt and dungarees running toward the ship. His speed was determined by the large amount of distance he covered in each step rather than the frequency of the plop, plop of his heavy, oversized work shoes. He was hatless and carried under one arm a huge white goose that was flapping one wing and honking loudly, although the man maintained a firm grip of the bird's neck. Half a dozen Malay men were running after him, all yelling. As he approached the ship's ladder leading down to the dock I recognized Mr. Kelly, who presently struggled up the steps, nearly out of breath and puffing fiercely. I thought of the old nursery rhyme, "Tom, Tom, the piper's son, stole a goose and away he run —"

"Don't let 'em aboard," Mr. Kelly gasped and rushed toward the companionway in the afterhouse.

I blocked the gangway and the natives all began shouting at once. None of them could speak English. "Hey, Harry," I called over my shoulder to Boneyard, "go get the longshoreman boss to talk to these guys."

The man in charge of loading rubber into number two hatch on the forward well-deck soon stood beside me. After a few sentences with the aggrieved people who had pursued Mr. Kelly, he said, "Dese mans, he say engine man no pay plenty for geese."

"How much did he pay?" I asked. "Wasn't it enough?"

After a prolonged conversation in which the crowd argued among themselves alternately with the interpreter, he finally turned to me, "Engine man pay plenty. Dey want more. I tell dese mans go away." The shouting of those who had pursued Mr. Kelly gradually diminished in volume, and they descended to the dock, where the altercation continued for some time.

Meanwhile, Mr. Kelly, with the assistance of one of the oilers, had acquired a fire ax and confined himself and Erastus Phoenix, the chief cook, in the engineer's bathroom, a porthole of which looked out on the number three hatch amidships. The cook had agreed to prepare and cook the goose if Mr. Kelly would behead it and pluck the feathers. A sound of stamping, scuffling, honking and loud swearing issued from the engineer's bath. It seemed that Mr. Kelly was having difficulty in dispatching the goose. I approached the open port and peered in through the screen. The cook was cowering in a corner by the washbasin attempting to fend off attacks of the huge goose, which was pecking at him and flapping its wings furiously. Mr. Kelly had been knocked down and now sprawled on the tiles wedged in between the toilet and the bathtub. Both Mr. Kelly and Mr. Phoenix were shouting and the goose made a great racket, too. It was an appalling scene.

Presently Mr. Kelly scrambled to his feet, seized the goose by its neck with his left hand, and attempted to lay it across the edge of the bathtub. The cook crawled out from under the washstand, grabbed the bird's feet, and held them firmly, but the great wings continued to thrash and keep the would-be executioners off balance. Finally, Mr. Kelly raised the fire ax high and brought it crashing down on the enamel of the tub's edge and the goose's neck. In this maneuver the goose's head was completely severed, but the great bird continued to flutter, spattering blood literally all over the place. Mr. Kelly then glanced at his hand and uttered a great yell. It looked as if he had cut off his thumb. At this point I hurried to the mate's cabin.

"Mr. Crocker," I called, "you better come with your medicine chest. There's been an accident in the engineer's bathroom."

He groaned. "I knew those monkeys would hurt themselves," he said.

By the time the mate reached the gory place, the goose had flapped its last and Mr. Kelly had discovered that he had not amputated his thumb, but had merely cut it rather deeply.

"Well, I guess I'll have to defeather it myself," the cook soliloquized. "Brian," he said to Mr. Kelly, "I can't get it cooked in time for supper but we can get it ready for dinner tomorrow."

For an hour after the affair of the goose, things were quite dull at the gangway. Then Mr. Briggs arrived. He showed evidence of having been entertained fulsomely by the engineering company. Convoying the truck that carried his repaired machinery, which he had refused to let out of his sight, he had been transported in a chauffeur-driven touring car accompanied by the Hollander who owned the machine shop. Mr. Briggs stepped out of the car, stiff straw hat, red bow tie, batwing collar and all, carrying his ponderous cane in one hand and a delicate wooden cage containing two green, red, and yellow parakeets or lovebirds in the other. He personified stiff dignity. In all respects his deportment and appearance were impeccable, and with great pomposity he strode across the dock and mounted the gangway. At the deck he nodded to me, "Emery, will you kindly open the screen door to my bedroom? My hands are full. Ain't these birds beautiful! I decided they would make my quarters more homelike."

I opened the screen door to his room and stood aside to allow him to enter. Then I don't know just what happened. As he stepped over the high coaming he either caught his foot or got tangled up in his cane, but he lost his balance and pitched forward over the lintel flat on his chest, crushing the fragile birdcage. Fortunately, he did not fall directly on it, for the birds presently crawled from under and began to flutter wildly about the room. I let the screen door slam shut, closed the door to the office, and grabbed up a pillow to stuff against the open port above his berth. Mr. Briggs rolled around on the deck so that he could get on his knees and rise. Then this usually dour and mirthless man revealed a new characteristic that one would never have suspected: he could laugh at himself. He began to laugh loudly, never forgetting the realities of the situation. He retrieved the porthole screen from a shelf, sprawled across his berth while fitting it into the port, and then sat in his armchair, all the time laughing loudly and watching the birds swoop around the room. At last he stopped and said to me, "Thanks, boy! Now we're caged in with the birds. They'll make it home like all right. But home was never like this! Hee, hee! Haw, haw! We got to get another bird cage. Haw, haw!" I slipped out through his office to search for the third assistant engineer, who was about to discover that he was going ashore at once to buy a new and bigger cage for Mr. Briggs's lovebirds.

Next to arrive was Captain Braun, who led on a leash a frisky, very young black cocker spaniel who kept tumbling over himself. "This is a present from the ship's agent to the chief," he announced upon gaining the deck. "His family had a whole litter of pups and is givin' 'em away wherever they can find a good home. Will you see if you can find the chief, sonny?" the captain addressed me.

Mr. Briggs was still sitting in his armchair watching the parakeets, which were now scratching happily in a small pile of birdseed strewn on a newspaper on the berth. Before I could knock on the screen door he looked up, "This is workin' out all right, boy," he said. "Just as soon as we get a new cage they'll feel right to home. I aim to hang it over my file cabinet. They'll act real cute when I let them out to walk around, but I'll have to keep my door locked."

"Mr. Briggs," I said, "the captain asked if you will kindly come to the gangway to see him."

"What's that!" he snorted. "If he thinks he's going to interfere with my birds he's outa his mind."

"Oh, no, sir! It's nothing like that," I hastened to explain. "He's got a present for you."

Mr. Briggs growled. "Present for me? Now, what's he up to!"

But he carefully let himself out on deck through his office and approached the gangway in his vest and shirt-sleeves with their red arm elastics. At sight of the puppy he stopped short and opened his mouth, but was speechless.

The captain chuckled. "Well, Leander, since you've lost your bear the agent and I thought you'd like a real dog. You don't have to think up a classic name for him, either. He's got a Sumatran name — Marapi, which is the name of a volcano here."

Mr. Briggs shifted his eyes from the puppy to the captain's

face and back again. He was visibly moved, wagging his bald head while his lips worked soundlessly. Then he stopped, picked up the quivering black pup, and held him up to his mustache. Holding the little dog with one great hand, he laid the other on the captain's shoulder and said, "Roger, I don't know how to thank you. Between the two of us we'll make a home outa this ship yet."

As he turned toward his cabin he spied the old tarpaulin that had served Marmaduke as a restroom. "Jim," he said to one of the off-duty oilers who was standing near, "will you do me a favor and get that tarpaulin scrubbed up? We got to get Marapi housebroke in a hurry."

In another hour we cast off *Winona's* lines and started down through the late afternoon shadows of the mirrorlike Deli River. I was on the fo'c's'le head with the mate on the anchor detail and would remain there until we left the river when it might no longer be necessary to anchor in an emergency, such as failure of the steering mechanism. Only the reduced whine of the turbine and the distant wash of the ship's wake against the shore disturbed the comparative quiet of the jungle with its birdsongs and chattering monkeys and little animal sounds. A few gulls and very large birds wheeled overhead as if to convoy the ship downstream. Presently, one of them lighted on the very top of the foremast and stood there with its wings folded like a sinister black sentinel. It had a reddish, scaly head and neck, huge curved beak, scaly legs and feet, and looked like a turkey, but we knew it was a vulture.

"Well, now, what kind of a omen is that?" asked Chips, who stood by the windlass with Marmaduke's scratches on his arms quite visible.

"Guess it smells the dog," suggested the mate.

"Perhaps it's only tired and wants to stow away to Ceylon," I suggested.

"We'll have some fun with the chief," the mate rejoined. "He won't feel safe about his new dog so long as that fella's up on the masthead. Bet he'll want to shoot it."

It was later reported that Mr. Briggs had considered doing just that. But the captain suggested that he wait until the ship was out of Dutch jurisdiction and well at sea, and the pilot thought there might be complications also. So the chief fretted and marched around on the forward well-deck, shouting to frighten off the buzzard. All to no avail. Meanwhile, he had locked up Marapi, the puppy, in his office with the lovebirds, which had been recaged in a splendid new bamboo pagodalike cage where they trilled and squawked continuously.

But he didn't have to borrow the ship's rifle to dispose of the vulture. It departed with the pilot as if it had been a sort of mascot to him all along. Mr. Briggs was relieved; he didn't want to shoot anything. Moreover, he was supremely contented. He had a fine puppy that would sail with him many years, and his quarters rang with the chirping and cooing of his lovebirds.

"Well, sir," he announced at supper in the officers' saloon, "home was never like this!"

27. The Crown Prince

On my way back to *Winona* late on a Sunday afternoon, I walked out on the long pier in Colombo where the ship was berthed. About midway on the pier I passed a Singhalese man clad in a long white garment that resembled a dirty nightgown. He had apparently just left *Winona*. I might not have noticed him had he not been carrying in one hand a large, white, sulphur-crested cockatoo loosely fastened to a perch, while on the other arm the jacket and vest of a brown suit of clothes were draped. The bird was observing his passage up the pier in comparative silence, which it occasionally interrupted with a very loud squawk. As the Singhalese passed me I turned to look, and, strangely enough, the big cockatoo turned to look at me and trilled some incomprehensible bird language as if to say, "Goodbye, old boy, and good luck. I'm bound for fresh fields and pastures new."

"By Jove," I said to myself, "I'll bet that's the Crown Prince."

While the man and his cockatoo continued to move up the pier toward the waterfront, I remained rooted to the spot where I had turned in the first place and thought back over recent weeks to my first acquaintance with the Crown Prince.

We were lying off Surabaya at the time and Harry Boneyard was sunning himself on number six hatch while digesting his dinner of beef stew and rice pudding. Harry was feeling pensive, and he was also quite depressed because he had spent the last of his money the previous evening in a Chinese barroom and had had a throbbing headache ever since he turned to more than six hours earlier. He was also quite lonely. The only romance he had ever had in his life seemed to have gone sour.

Harry had joined the crew of the *Winona* after paying off from a Black Diamond Line freighter running between New York and European channel ports. For two years he had sailed in a particular ship of that American line, serving as bosun the last year. And during this period he had regularly patronized a plump, blue-eyed blond prostitute who lived in a little house on the Schiedamse Dike in Rotterdam, finally falling in love with her. On his last visit he had invited the girl to marry him and emigrate to New York. To her credit, she was skeptical of the idea, not being accustomed to honest affection, and she insisted that he stay away for a few months. After that time, when he returned, if he still wanted to marry her she would think about it.

When I first met Harry, the large, fair-haired Dane was struggling with a suspicion of disillusionment. About a week before *Winona* touched at Barcelona, where I had come

aboard to replace a man who was far advanced in tuberculo-
sis, Harry exhibited symptoms of venereal disease. When he
went ashore to the hospital for an examination it was con-
firmed that he had contracted syphilis. It could only have
originated in Rotterdam. So overwhelmed was he by this disaster that he became excessively moody, remaining silent
for long periods. Then his anger began to smolder and he
would sit up on the edge of his pipe berth, legs hanging down
into the air space of Mike Simeon's berth, muttering in his
shock and grief.

"Ach, that miserable cow! How could she have done
this to me? She musta knowed she had the old siff!"

"No," I would reply, "I don't think she knew any more than
you did. It probably was a surprise to her. You know, in her
business these things are more likely to happen than not."

"Ach, there's going to be a sorry cow in Rotterdam when I
get back there!" he would repeat again and again through the
fumes of iodoform powder with which our quartermaster's
room as well as the fo'c's'le reeked.

By the time we had reached Alexandria, Harry had the situation in better perspective. I had tried to drum into his
mind the idea that the disease was not going to be fatal to
him, since he was taking remedial medication, and since she
was probably doing the same thing, it might put some sense
into her head and she'd be glad to marry him and move to
New York and start out on a different tack.

"Ach, that damn cow!" was about as affectionate as he
could sound.

But his mind kept right on dwelling on the subject and,
surprisingly, he took action consistent with his heart. He
drew every cent in allowance to which he was entitled in

Alexandria and cabled it to her in Rotterdam, to be redeemed by him later if it lay unclaimed. He also wrote her a letter, which he read to me for approval, and mailed it.

"Dear Meike," it read, "I come down with siff which I got from you. You can't work so I sending you fifty dollar U.S. You write me S. S. Winona, care American Consul, Singapore. I come Rotterdam late spring. We marry then. I send more money when I hear from you Singapore. Love, Harry."

"Ach, that damn cow!" Mike and I heard several times a day.

The grief caused by all his uncertainty was eating the man's heart out. He seldom went ashore and he drew very little spending money against his meager wages. But he remained a very lonely young man with a lot of potential honest affection and nothing but a tarnished dream at which to direct it. Thus he was filled with unrequited symptoms of love, remorse for his previous evening's excessive consumption of gin, and genuine loneliness.

While Harry sat with his large tanned head in his hands, taking a little solace from the hot rays of the November sun on this particular day off Surabaya, he was approached by a Javanese trader bearing a mature sulphur-crested cockatoo. The trader held out the bird, chained by one leg to a wooden perch-stand. Harry looked at the white bird, cooing and preening its feathers; he looked at the Javanese and he looked at me, but he said nothing. At last, he held out a finger to the bird, which clamped down on the finger but not hard enough to hurt.

"Ach, look at that!" he exclaimed. "He don't hurt. He must like me."

The trader said, "You buy. Good bird. Much talk."

"How much?" asked Harry innocently.

The trader replied in a jargon partly English, partly Dutch, and goodness knows partly what else, but the message came through, "Ten gilders."

"That ain't much," Harry said to me. "But I ain't got no money at all."

Then he abruptly got up, said "wait," and disappeared into the fantail. The Javanese, thinking Harry had lost interest, began to try to sell the big cockatoo to me. Presently Harry returned carrying the brown pants of his second-best suit of clothes.

"Here," he thrust the pants at the trader and grasped the perch.

For a moment the Javanese looked uncertain and held on to both the pants and the perch, but gradually it became clear to him that he had a fair bargain and he relinquished his hold on the cockatoo's perch and examined the pants to make certain they were in good condition. Then he reached into his robe to extract a bag of birdseed that he placed on the hatch beside Harry, bowed, and walked away.

"I forgot to find out his name," Harry grumbled.

"He looks like the German crown prince," I suggested, "big nose and fine bunch of yellow feathers on his helmet."

Harry grinned. "Ah! That's what I call him. The Crown Prince! Hey, Prince, old boy, you're goin' to be a sailor."

In that way the white cockatoo became known as the Crown Prince. The bird had a good effect on Harry; it took his mind off himself. The first thing he did was to seek out Chips and get the carpenter to build an elaborate arrangement that embodied a perch extended from a bracket that could be lashed to the steel upright stanchion of Harry's berth, the whole elevated above a platform about eighteen inches square under the perch for sanitary measures.

It was a good arrangement, aside from the fact that the Crown Prince was a bit messy in his feeding and kicked so much of his seeds and bread crumbs onto Harry's sheets and pillowcase that he had to remake his berth every time he wanted to turn in. Much of Harry's spare time was spent sitting up on the edge of his pipe berth conversing with his bird.

"Pretty polly," Harry would address the cockatoo.

"Squawk," the bird would reply.

Then Harry would laugh gleefully. "See, he understands me," he would exclaim.

Sometimes the bird would trill melodiously.

"I dunno what he's singin' about," Harry invariably said, "but y' can see he likes me."

This went on for days. The fact that the Crown Prince couldn't seem to master the English language didn't perturb his master one bit. Harry tried Dutch and Danish on his bird, too, but with the same result. In time, both Mike and I began to become annoyed. I determined to say nothing, no matter how disaffected I might become, because I knew how important it was for Harry to have some sort of live object on which to expend his affection.

"Aw, Harry, that bird ain't gonna talk," Mike would complain, "he's too old to learn."

Or it would be, "Why don'tcha get rid of it! It ain't the kind of parrot that talks. It makes a mess all over the place. And it stinks."

But Harry turned a deaf ear to Mike, and Mike sulked.

"Why don'tcha get him to get rid of it?" Mike would complain to me when Harry wasn't in our presence. "He'd take it from you."

"Well," I replied, "it means so much to him I haven't got the heart to say anything. Besides, the Crown Prince's droppings don't fall on my pillow."

"Well, they do on mine," Mike burst out with his brown eyes flashing above the unshaven stubble of his heavy beard. "I have to shovel out my bunk every watch."

We almost had a crisis when we reached Singapore. There was no letter for Harry from Rotterdam. He couldn't believe she had taken his money and not even thanked him. He moped about his work, and he hung over the rail on the fantail when he was off duty, a solitary figure silhouetted against the sky. He lost interest in the Crown Prince. "I think I heave the damn thing overboard," he said, nodding toward the cockatoo, which sat silent with ruffled feathers.

"That won't do any good, boy," I replied. "Give the poor thing a chance. If you don't want it, at least take it ashore and sell it or turn it loose."

Then he relented, untied the cockatoo from his perch, tied on a piece of twine about twenty feet long to the bird's leg, and took it out on the hatch, where the cockatoo would walk about on deck, flutter up on the rail, and shake its wings, all the time trilling and squawking in the sunshine and the open air.

"See," I said, "the Crown Prince loves you anyhow."

Harry chuckled and felt much better.

When the *Winona* arrived off Colombo just a few days be-

fore Christmas a series of events ensued that gave promise of
good luck and a happy passage on the long voyage home to
the American Atlantic coast. In the first place we almost, but
not quite, had an accident when we entered the harbor between the breakwaters. Winona's steering telemotor system
suddenly lost pressure and the rudder failed to respond to the
wheel. I was at the wheel at the time, early in the morning
with the sun just rising above the ragged edge of misty palm
trees on the fringing hills beyond the city. The pilot gave an
order, "Port a little."

I turned a half revolution to port, and nothing happened.
The pilot and the captain both turned to look at me. Breaking out in a sweat, I kept turning more to port and Winona's
bow moved a few degrees to port, but we were headed squarely
for a small stone lighthouse on the port edge of the starboard
jetty. Reaching the limit of a hard-a-port position and feeling
little resistance, I let the wheel spin back to center and then
turned it rapidly back to port. The bow responded several
degrees, and it became clear, considering the speed and distance, that we would have no trouble in passing down the
center of the channel. "That's right, sonny," said Captain
Braun, "keep her right down the middle. You're handling
the wheel just right."

Then the pilot said, "You know, one of Alfred Holt's Blue
Funnel liners had an accident here a year ago and knocked
that light beacon right off the jetty. I thought for a moment
we'd have to anchor to avoid doing it again."

The rudder responded normally to a starboard wheel, and
in half an hour Winona lay alongside a pier to load about two
thousand linear tons of tea in chests. After this came aboard

she couldn't have stowed another ton of anything, but because most of her cargo was light she still rode fairly high in the water. When I left the wheelhouse I felt as if I had already done a day's work, and I also felt the satisfaction of having turned in an acceptable performance.

The second event of good portent was the early arrival of mail. A consular messenger arrived with it just as we went in to breakfast, and the third mate wasted no time in bringing the crew's mail aft to the messroom, contrary to the practice in most ships at that time. It usually took longer. Harry Boneyard had a letter from Rotterdam, forwarded from Singapore, but it was in a strange hand so he stuffed it in his shirt and finished his breakfast. Then he climbed up on the fantail to read the contents with hope and apprehension.

After a while he burst into our room where Mike and I were smoking our pipes because neither of us had received any mail nor had anything else to do. Harry was so excited and radiant that we knew he must have good news. "Y'know, she hired sombody to write it for her because she don't write so good," he said. "Here, you can read it," and he handed it to me.

It was in Dutch, in a fancy flowing hand, and although I could read German script this was altogether beyond my abilities. I looked up hopelessly. Harry laughed. "Well, she says she's well now but she can't get no license for her business and don't want it nohow, so she got a job as a waitress and when I come back she wants to marry me and move to New York. Hot damn! Wha'd'ye think of that!"

The next day being Sunday, I took my camera and went ashore for sightseeing. This great seaport of half a million people and capital of Ceylon had so many buildings and parks to photograph that I soon exhausted all my films. I ate an elaborate Sunday noon dinner at the huge red sandstone Galle Face hotel, so imposing that it resembled a parliament building on the edge of a seaside park. Then I decided to return to the ship in time for supper and turn in early to make up for lost sleep. This was the occasion when on the dock I saw the Crown Prince for the last time.

Apparently, Harry Boneyard felt that the cockatoo, having served him well when he needed a friend, should be spared the misery and coldness of the North Atlantic in winter. So I inferred that he had "sold" him so that the Crown Prince could get a fresh start in a warm country in a bird and animal store. The terms of "sale" were indeed interesting. Having failed to attract a monetary offer for the bird, even being unable to give it away, he had obviously given somebody the vest and coat that belonged to the pair of pants with which the Crown Prince was originally purchased, merely to take the bird. I decided it might be embarrassing to Harry if he suspected I had an idea of the cockatoo's ransom price, so I determined not to mention the subject. After all, in emotional value alone Harry had obtained much satisfaction from a secondhand suit of clothes.

28. So Ends

OUR TWO THOUSAND TONS of tea were loaded all in one day, on a Monday, and we sailed from Colombo about nine o'clock in the evening. We were homeward bound, without a stop, direct to Boston where much of our tea was consigned. I was on the fo'c's'le head with the mate's anchor detail, but by the time we had stowed the last of the bow lines in their locker we were off soundings and the lights on the jetties blinked far astern. A new moon was setting in the sea off the port bow, the sea wind of the northeast monsoon began to pipe up over the starboard quarter, and we all tingled with the joyful anticipation of a long period at sea.

Next day the dry monsoon blew with increasing weight. It piled up huge long swells and pushed against *Winona's* superstructure, adding more than a knot an hour to her speed.

There was not a cloud in the sky; the sun burned down warm and bright. Ideal sailing weather it would have been for the old-time sailing vessels bearing in such a wind off toward the southwest, and it was ideal for us, too, heading back northwest toward the Red Sea. When the sun set ahead of us as we rolled down its sparkling path we came into a Christmas Eve that was unlike any I had known before in the usually cold and snowy streets of a New England town. It was my first Christmas Eve at sea, the first of many that would come later, so it had its own special aspect of pensiveness and beauty.

I went on lookout at eight bells at the end of the dogwatch. Under a cloudless sky the entire heavens shone so brightly that *Winona* seemed to be plunging along in a half-light. Since one's eyes soon became accustomed to it, one had no need of artificial light. When the night world glowed with starlight and the phosphorescent glitter of the waves, the fo'c's'le head became an exciting and poetic place on which to be. The ship traveled a little faster than the waves, contantly overtaking them, sometimes racing down a long slope with a vast hiss and swish of speed and then mounting up and up over the crest of the mountain of water ahead, breaking through with a vibrating roar like the sound of breaking surf on a beach. *Winona* would thrust her bow through the wave's crest with fifty or sixty feet of red underbody suspended in the air before the moving wave would gather its force to hurl her downhill and forward into the next wave. Sailing or steaming downwind in the open sea is as delightful an experience as smashing into a heavy head wind and sea is horrendous. Whereas slamming into head seas day after day is usually a physically exhausting exercise, when a high wind and sea blows from astern the ship moves in delightful motion — rolling slowly, heaving easily, and planing down the long gentle slopes of water hills as if she were coasting.

Possibly even more noticeable is the difference in sounds. In a heavy head sea the sounds of the sea and the ship are all violent; they sound threatening and frequently are, because sea damage to a vessel is almost always caused by water rather than by wind. In a following sea the sounds are not only gentle, like a slow, hollow-sounding surf or a gurgling river, but they are musical. On this Christmas Eve during my two hours of lookout on the fo'c's'le head I was particularly enthralled by the music of the bow wash and the murmuring chorus of the near waves even more than I had ever been before. It didn't require much imagination to hear the sonorous strains of a great symphony orchestra playing the chords and melodies one would hear if listening to any of the great composers in a hall or an opera house. My duty on watch under these conditions was one of sheer delight. I would sing or hum with full throat any one of the great symphonies the sea might be playing, and so deep and loud was the orchestration that my voice never carried back against the wind to the pilothouse.

Then there came to my mind Masefield's beautiful poem called "Christmas Eve at Sea." Although his verse was written of the wooden sailing ship era, it is equally appropriate for the mechanized steel vessels of the present:

> *Unquiet ripples lisp and purr,*
> *A block there pipes and chirps i' the sheave,*

The wheel-ropes jar, the reef-points stir
Faintly — and it is Christmas Eve.

To-night beneath the dripping bows
Where flashing bubbles burst and throng,
The bow-wash murmurs and sighs and soughs
A message from the angel's song.

The drowsy helmsman strikes the bell;
The moon goes nodding down the west,
Rex Judaeorum natus est,
I charge you, brothers, sing Nowell, Nowell
Rex Judaeorum natus est.

Four bells came too soon to suit me for once, and when I had rung them up and repeated "All lights are burning bright, sir" I reluctantly left my fancied box seat over the orchestra pit and climbed up to the bridge to relieve my watchmate.

Christmas Day was a holiday, of course. Our dinner at noon was a repetition of the Thanksgiving Day dinner except that instead of mince pie we had "plum duff with down-haul" — a dark plum pudding filled with fruit and nuts and an egg and sugar sauce called "down-haul" to haul the pudding down into your belly, Chips explained to me, because sometimes a poor cook would produce an almost indigestible pudding that couldn't otherwise be swallowed.

Glorious day succeeded glorious day, the moon set later each night so that we were soon sailing part of the night watches down a sparkling pathway of moonbeams, and we lost count of the days and dates. New Year's Day came while we were still in the Indian Ocean, and we celebrated another holiday with a notable ship's dinner and extra rest. We were living in some sort of fantastic seagoing Elysium and most of us knew it. The eternal sea was showing us the face that cause men to fall in love with it. But there are always some who seek to improve their well-being at the expense of others and that was when tragedy struck some of *Winona's* crew.

On the morning when we entered the Gulf of Aden, still hustled along by the great winds of the dry northeast monsoon, now blowing in its full fury, two of the crew didn't turn to for breakfast — a fireman and one of the wipers. Soon the tall, first assistant engineer, Brian Kelly, arrived in the crew's messroom just as we had finished eating.

"Anybody seen Krause and Rocco?" he asked. "Shorty Smith is alone in the engine room with the third, and the fireman on the four to eight hasn't been relieved."

"That's right," the third fireman agreed. "Their bunks are empty and I supposed they had gone on duty."

The search led into the fireman's fo'c's'le and revealed nothing except that the bunks of the missing men were indeed empty. Then the search entered other parts of the ship. Almost at once a shout came down the ladder from the topside of the fantail. It was the bosun. "Hey, you guys," he called, "come up here."

Up the ladder we rushed to find the bosun pointing to a piece of line made fast to a section of port rail and trailing down under the stern. It reached nearly to the water and passed directly in front of the open porthole of a spare room in which the steward had stored some fancy canned food. Mr. Kelly took a long look and departed to call the captain, the chief, and the steward.

The steward unlocked the door to the room, not knowing what might be revealed inside, but the room was empty except for the stores and apparently had not been disturbed. Outside the porthole the rope swayed in the wind.

"Well," the captain reasoned, "it looks like they tried to enter here through the port to steal some grub. We'll never know what happened. The port's too small for either one to have crawled through, so one must have tried to reach through while the other held him up and the knot slipped and they both fell overboard."

"It must have happened in the graveyard watch," Mr. Briggs, the chief engineer, thought, "because they both stood their watch from eight to twelve. And nobody sits up in a fo'c's'le during the twelve to four unless he's sick."

"Well," said Mr. Kelly, "we got to do something about a new fireman."

"I'll get the mate and let you and him put your heads together," the captain replied.

Mr. Kelly and Mr. Crocker soon had a solution.

"The ship's all painted on the outside and there's nothin' much to do on the inside, either, so I can spare a couple of men," the mate said. "Why don't you take Lascery — he's an old-time fireman anyhow and he's only an ordinary aboard here — he'll be so happy to get back in a firin' room he'll probably stay with ye 'til kingdom come."

"That's white of ye," Mr. Kelly answered. "I'd be glad to have him. And I understand there's another good oiler in Thorwald, the crew's messboy, the one who was on the beach in Alexandria. He'd probably like a man's job again."

"It's all right with me," said the mate. "If the steward goes along with us, you and me can find someone to double up as messboy and he can collect the extry pay for both jobs."

So it was decided that Lascery would move into the fire-men's fo'c's'le, Thorwald would become a wiper and would bring the food aft at mealtimes. The day workers among the sailors would clean their fo'c's'le and the messroom, and the wipers would clean the engine room quarters on the port side.

We didn't hold any funeral or commemorative services and continued to steam along as happy and efficient a ship as ever sailed. The Red Sea was comfortable, not hot, swept white by the heavy wind that had assailed us on the outbound voyage. The Suez Canal was distinctly cool in mid-January; even the traders and bumboatmen were muffled up in woolen garments and scarfs when they spread out their wares on number three hatch after dark when we had completed our passage through the canal and were again made fast to the dock of the Anglo-Persian Oil Company to fill our fuel tanks.

The Mediterranean in January was comfortable and calm for the most part, but I was so thoroughly in the rhythm of four hours of work and four hours of rest that each day suc-ceeded another with little novelty except the sight of pas-sing ships, and time meant almost nothing. When we passed Gibraltar during the first night watch about six bells, I had lost so much romantic feeling that I was content to remain asleep in my bunk.

In the Atlantic we sailed the great circle southern route for Boston, so we had warm sunny weather for eight days before the weather turned distinctly cold near the end of January. The distinguishing feature of this passage was a tremendous gale that blew fair from the east from the day after we passed Gibraltar. *Winona* had been a most fortunate ship, weather-wise, ever since she had sailed from Colombo. In the Indian Ocean we had the heavy northeast monsoon to push us along, in the Mediterranean the seas were calm, and in the Atlantic for eight consecutive days we were blown westward by this great wind of full gale force under clear skies and bright sunshine. We were sorry for the eastbound ships we passed, butting into the huge seas, taking it green over the bows, and seemingly making little or no progress during all that beating while *Winona* rolled and slid along, decks as dry as if she were riding a maritime roller coaster homeward.

We did have one situation aboard that worried us. Chips was very ill. In Singapore he had come down with a high fever. The staff at the marine hospital could only diagnose it as some obscure tropical disease and gave him prescriptions for palliatives and suggested that he stay with his ship and try to get home. He lost weight rapidly and seriously. Then he began to break out with festering sores that broke and suppurated. His appetite declined and his strength ebbed. He lived largely by will power. When we stood for health inspection at Port Said, the mate and the bosun helped him dress, carried him up the ladder to the shelter deck amidships, and propped him up against a winch while the port doctor walked along our line and counted heads. Then the bosun and I got him back to his berth and fed him some hot beef broth that the steward had prepared. He seemed as much dead as alive that night.

Now back in the Atlantic and the cooler weather he began to hold his own; at least, we now felt that he would live because he had passed some sort of crisis in the Mediterranean after which his appetite improved and he seemed to gain strength. Whatever the malady might be, it was not venereal and it was not infectious. But the festering sores all over his body caused him great pain and suffering until they ruptured.

"Guess I'll have to retire into Sailor's Snug Harbor if I ever live through this," he would say.

"Oh, no, Chips," I would reply, "you're not through yet. You'll be shipping out again in the spring when you get well. Just wait and see!"

"Well, in all my misspent years I never had nothin' like this," he would reply. And this conversation repeated almost every day seemed to cheer him a lot.

One morning there was considerable ice on the forward deck when daybreak came. It was cold, too, and few of us had any warm clothing other than sweaters. The old army shirt that Gareth Hill had given me in Alexandria the morning he left the ship became a boon to me. We were approaching Boston with mixed feelings because the weather reports received by radio described subzero temperatures there. It was much warmer at sea because of the more constant temperature of the ocean, but we couldn't take that in to the harbor with us.

We steamed in past Boston Light on a very cold bright January morning and tied up at Commonwealth Pier. When the port medical examiner came aboard to release us from quarantine, we went through the same performance with Chips, except that he was now strong enough to get up the ladder with a little help. It was so cold on deck that we returned to our fo'c's'le as soon as we could, and then I was somewhat shocked at Chips's decision to remain aboard until the ship reached New York.

"Why Chips," I protested, "one of the best marine hospitals in the whole world is right here in Chelsea."

"Yep, I know, but me and the mate's got a nephew on the staff of the hospital in Staten Island and we'll feel better to have him hard by," he replied.

Then the mate sent for me. "What do you aim to do, Cleaves?" he asked. "Do you want to pay off here or are you going on to New York with us?"

"Why, I want to go on to New York," I replied.

"All right. That's good. We're kinda short-handed and we'd like to keep you."

Then he added, "Once you told me you was thinkin' of followin' the sea or goin' into the shippin' business?"

"Yes, I was," I said shaking my head, "but I don't think the American people are seriously interested in keeping American ships on the seas. Oh, the politicians make a big fuss about it and they're spending millions on the Shipping Board and they'll keep or sell the lines they establish, but the economics are wrong and foreign governments discriminate against us and the only overseas lines that make sense to me are those owned by companies whose own products they carry.

Mr. Crocker nodded in agreement and I continued. "Even then, you could probably do better in an industrial company or a profession, but as far as our shipping business is concerned, I guess I was born about sixty years too late or forty years too early."

This was quite a speech, but he agreed with me.

"Yes," he said. "You're right. Look for something ashore. That's what I'd like to do. But bein' on deck, what can I do ashore as good as I got afloat — while it lasts? Aside from stevedorin' and stowin' cargo, what can a deck man do? Oh, the engineers — sure, they got a engineerin' profession. They can do anything from shipyard repair jobs to being engineer of an apartment house. Anybody goin' to sea today should go in the engine room.

"By the way," he added, "why don't you take the day off and go ashore and get yourself a coat and go over to Cambridge and visit with your friends? It's too cold to work on deck today so I'm letting anybody take the day off who wants to."

Thus it happened that I took the subway and streetcar to my grandmother's house in Dorchester to pick up my overcoat. I also took the Huntley & Palmer biscuit tin full of Mayling tea that I had scooped up off the deck of the ship in Semarang. It was tied up with a piece of rope yarn and certainly didn't look elegant, but my English-born grandmother took one sniff and said, "Oh, my, this is real good tea. You couldn't have brought me anything nicer. We'll have some with our lunch."

In the afternoon I went to Cambridge and took two of my classmates, who were then in their last year, back to the *Winona* for supper. The day must have been a Thursday because we had boiled saffron rice and curried veal for supper, as we did every Thursday evening. According to my Thursday custom, I heaped my white enamelware plate high with rice and ate it with butter and salt. Then I filled it again and covered the rice with an oversized mound of curried veal. When this was gone I ate a quarter of an apple pie and drank a large dipper of tea. My friends watched me with amazement and provided themselves with what I considered minuscule portions of rice and curried veal. Their birdlike appetites also impressed Shorty Smith, the wiper, and Harry Boneyard, my watchmate, who alone remained aboard and ate with us in the messroom.

"Go ahead, eat it," called Shorty, "it won't kill you!"

"You guys ain't feelin' well?" Harry observed.

"Oh, yes," one of my friends replied. "We just like to sample it first. Say, it is good! I'll take some more. No wonder you got fat, Emery."

"He ain't fat," Harry rejoined. "He's all muscle. Look at him. He can lick anyone in the fo'c's'le."

"Oh, no, nothing like that," I hastened to say to my friends, "but remember I told you we fed better in this ship than you do in Cambridge."

On our way out of the fantail, Chips hollered from his room, "Emery, bring your friends in here. I want to show 'em somethin'."

"Be prepared for a shock," I warned. "He's not well."

We stepped inside the open door where Chips lay in his berth. At first my friends had eyes only for the pictorial display of naked women above the berth, but Chips soon terminated that.

"Now, boys," he quavered, "I want to show you an object lesson. I'm an old man. I done as I pleased all my life and I done plenty of things that warn't right. But the good Lord caught up with me at last, and I don't know what I done to deserve this nor what it is I got. But let me be an example to you to prove that there's no fool like an old fool and the same thing can happen to you if you think you're as all-fired smart as I did."

With that he threw back the bedcovers, revealing his emaciated naked body almost entirely covered with the brown festering sores that leaked orange-colored pus. Both of my friends blanched and bolted through the door and out on to the cold dark deck in the frozen air.

"Guess this was a mite too rough for them, Chips," I said. "You got your point across all right."

Boston was really the end of the voyage. The rest seemed anticlimactic. *Winona* sailed on the second afternoon just at dusk. She took the route outside Cape Cod and Nantucket and Long Island because it was easier to enter New York Harbor through Ambrose Channel and dock at a Staten Island pier than to dodge the traffic in the East River and the upper harbor. Having cast off in Boston just before a pallid January sunset we docked in New York at about noon next morning. Then Harry Boneyard, Shorty Smith, and I, who were the only ones going to pay off, dressed in our best clothes, packed our gear, and sat around until we would be summoned to the officers' dining saloon to receive the residue of our wages.

My emotions were mixed. Returning home from the last eight months of seafaring in steam vessels I felt entirely different than I did when I had entered so blithely into my sentimental adventures. In the softness of my well-protected youth I imagined that I had suffered harshly during the first four months. But I had certainly loved the last four. Possibly I had grown more mature. I had been accepted on equal terms by better men than I knew myself to be. Perhaps I had even developed a little common sense, because I now recognized that I would never be able to realize my storybook ambition of making a career of ships and shipping at this time in the manner of which I had dreamed. My career would have to be sought in a modern and different world.

But I also knew that I had become bound to the sea and love of a seafaring life irrevocably and permanently. I would never again be able to catch a glimpse of the sea without feeling a quickening of the heartbeat and a lump of longing in my throat. Henceforth, there would be many ventures along the coast in small craft and occasional trips to the Grand Banks in Gloucestermen until they disappeared. And there would be nearly four years at sea in navy ships during a great war in the Pacific so perversely filled with contentment that what might have been the flat dead level of middle life became instead a shining horizon of glorious memories.

All this grew out of the rough months of bone-weary hard work, of illness, fear, and discouragement, expecially in *Amphitrite*, which had forever put an end to impractical, romantic, and childish ideas. The good sea had been a stern and thorough teacher.

In the days of the old sailing ships the captain always closed out each day's record of events in his log with the phrase — So Ends. Because it was not the ultimate end, it seems appropriate to close out this account of my first long voyage with the same words — So Ends.